D0094906

A·D·

Also by Kate Millett

Sexual Politics

The Prostitution Papers

Flying

Sita

The Basement

Going to Iran

The Loony Bin Trip

The Politics of Cruelty

KATE MILLETT

a memoir

W. W. NORTON & COMPANY

NEW YORK ✦ LONDON

Printed in the United States of America
First Edition

The text of this book is composed in Bembo
with the display set in Felix Titling
Composition and manufacturing by Maple-Vail Book
Manufacturing Group.

Book design by Beth Tondreau Design / Robin Bentz

LIBRARY OF CONGRESS CATALOGING-IN-PUBLICATION DATA
Millett, Kate.
A.D., a memoir / by Kate Millett.
p. cm.
ISBN 0-393-03524-7
1. Millett, Kate—Family. 2. Feminists—United States—Family relationships. 3. Lesbians—United States—Family relationships. 4. Aunts—United States—Case Studies. 5. Nieces—United States—Case studies. I. Title.
HQ1413.M54M55 1995
306.87—dc20 95-1727

ISBN 0-393-03524-7

W·W· Norton & Company, Inc., 500 Fifth Avenue, New York, N.Y. 10110
W·W· Norton & Company Ltd., 10 Coptic Street, London WC1A 1PU

1 2 3 4 5 6 7 8 9 0

PART ONE

The white walls, the white floor, the cool dusk of the coming evening. I have a visitor and it's just quitting time; in a moment a glass of white wine and then out to the meeting at my gallery. How fresh and clean this studio is, my own again after years of sublets and other people invading the space because I was too hard up or too depressed to possess it myself and work here full-time. But this year I have a show coming up in April; so here all through December I made my stand by repainting the place. Then built a great wonderful workbench—I'll be sculpting now. A rack for pictures too so that everything will be tidy,out of the way, systematic. The thousands of drawings, the hundreds of portfolios. My visitor admires the bench, solid as a rock. I built it right into the brick wall with lead anchors—have you ever used them? She nods, and goes on to tell me about her anti-nuclear work, the guerilla theater pieces she staged in Grand Central over the holidays. Barbara George is someone who helped me build the lavender barn at the farm with a tireless, selfless generosity; I am much in her debt. This evening I am returning her sleeping bag and a sack full of clothes she left behind, sorry that we can't talk longer.

But there's the meeting; hell or high water mustn't keep me away: "I'm the prodigal member of our co-op; tonight I really have to show my face there." Barbara lifts her head—"Isn't that your phone?" Since Mother's illness I have come to dread telephones; for a second it is reassuring to hear that it is her voice on the line—then she's all right, breathe easy. Only last week I was out there for Christmas with my sister Sally and her sons. A good Christmas, peaceful, nearly perfect, a reunion without quarrels or sore spots or rivalries—home. "I'll be home for Christmas" would croon out of the cowboy radio station as I painted the walls of the studio and I'd choke up against all better judgment. Because for once it would be that way: not only in my dreams but in fact I would be at one with my family, my tribe, the cast of spirits who still people my dreams and power my unconscious night after night. Mother was mending, had survived a double mastectomy at eighty-one, could laugh about her new shape and boast that she now had fewer cancer cells than anyone she knew. She was finer somehow, stronger, more serene, more "grown up", less fearful, bigger and wiser and easier. Going under the knife can do that, can make you want to live, and she had that direction now, that appetite and zest. So why this low awful tone in her voice?

"I have something to tell you. Sally's just called. Aunt Dorothy is dead." Sally—but my sister Sally and I looked each other in the eye one afternoon in St. Paul when Mother was out of the room—because there are the two, Mother and Aunt Dorothy, A.D. as we called her—and the rivalry between them: caste, class, and the fact that the one was my father Jim Millett's sister and the other his wife, whom the sister never quite approved of. A rivalry over us since childhood: Dorothy pulling for the Milletts, Mother for her own good simpler people against the Millett arrogance and money and hauteur. Pretension, she would have called it in Dorothy. And we said, Sally and I, that afternoon, turning to each other—conspirators in love with this aunt all our lives—do you suppose we should call A.D.? Smiling uneasily in our complicity. It was after all Christmas and we aren't home that often. I stir inside—yes. But if we got to go out there, it would mean leaving Mother alone for an afternoon or evening. "If we got to go"—meaning, if she invited us, if we were granted an audience. To her old age and infirmity and pique. The great house on the lake and her beauty dying within it.

And the last time I saw Aunt Dorothy—I wilt remembering it, the coldness, the hard unforgiving of my long-ago sin. With me still. Always, all the sins. Artist. Lesbian. Writer of those books she hates. I look up at Sally and she laughs: "She might hang up on us, you know," a nervous, self-conscious laugh. It's hard to believe; for years Sally has been the only one of us to be in touch. Suddenly we are both tense, embarrassed. My elder sister the lawyer, the pillar of the family. "You too?" "She's been awful lately. Do you know that two years ago she forbade me to ask her how she is. What do you say after hello? How are you?—of course. But you can't say it. 'Sally, I forbid you to use that phrase to me again.' " "Is she sick, is she that sick?" "She won't tell; there is no way in the whole damn world to find out anything about her." "There was the broken pelvis—but that was years ago." "So you know as much as I do. There's something else, circulatory or something, but I've no idea." And then Mother came back into the room and we returned to what had been the intention after all—that this was Mother's Christmas. Though she kept saying it was mine because I was home again at Christmas after so many years away. No, this was Mother's Christmas: Mother just back with us from the surgeon's knife, from cancer, from death. And splendid.

And all the while a dragon sat outside the gate. To strike now in Mother's simple phrase: Aunt Dorothy is dead. Oh God the folly the lunacy the hubris the sacrilege—"Mother, do you realize that we were there just a week ago; Sally and I talked about calling her and we didn't. We didn't do it. Good Jesus." Mother's voice going on in kindly platitudes: "Think of how ill she was; it wouldn't have helped. You probably couldn't have seen her." A violet left on the doorsill in the snow—hell, anything, any sign of respect or caring. "Mother, listen—we said what the hell, she might just hang up on us—do you hear me?" "She might very well have; she was like that. And remember, she was sick enough to die, just a few days later." No, you miss the point, I want to say. And dare not. Mother, you will never understand, perhaps never countenance or forgive the adoration I had for this aunt. It is like hearing of the end of the affair from one who saw it as an infidelity.

Somehow I must explain to the visitor in my studio, but how—the magnitude and horror of the telephone call that had taken me away from her, half a glass of white wine in each of our glasses. Suddenly I have to get away from her as well. "Was that the aunt you always talked about, the one you were so crazy about?" Barbara asks this, trying to be kind. I do not want to talk; this is too remote, a desecration. "Yes," the word is torn out of me, "Yes, I adored her. What will I do now? She died without forgiving me. We never were friends again. I thought there would be time." "I guess I see what you mean. You must feel terrible." "Barbara. I think I better go soon—I hardly need a boring meeting tonight. But I can't stay home."

Already I knew that on the phone: that I must go out into the streets, even sit through the tedium of a gallery meeting, any distraction. Mother's voice saying there will be no funeral: there is nothing to go home for, really nothing to be done. It is over. She can hardly believe it. "Mom, I've got to call you back. I need some time. I'll talk to you later." Not one more moment of this, not another sentence—necessity recoils from injury. Then the visitor to face, to explain my tears, to feel the temptation to tell her who has died. Squelch it: only you know. You couldn't tell your best cronies right now. Not even Sophie. The wound throbbing already: I feel it like a physical presence in the gut. And it has only just begun, is a few moments old.

I drive my old VW station wagon through Soho, making mistakes despite great efforts of attention. Each street and corner is a new stab—the futility of life itself—that these mean streets, so long familiar to me, my second neighborhood after the Bowery, should become so foreign now, now that I bring her with me. Whole lives are lived down here, artist's lives, their work, their desperate ambition. The world I left home for and how small it is, how insignificant. I had loved her first, most, always, still. That first great love of my life snuffed out over long distance while I was building a drawing rack and painting a studio to make my life new again, fresh again, preparing for a new show—the dates set, the stretch of time I have before me—thinking I knew where I was going . . . and then a word entered my side and it is all senseless. There is death. She died without ever forgiving me. I thought I would get to you in time, I say aloud. We never settled it. Soho tumbles. Error. All dirty brick nonsense. Death is real. Home was. She was. We are so far from St. Paul. In her eyes, which are mine now again too, the rag merchants, the remnant dealers are a last grotesque detail; this gallery its members pay a monumental rent to hold is silly, the sort of foolishness one would expect in New York.

Coming down the stairs, I bring A.D. with me and, we really liked the paintings in Stephanie Rauchenbush's show. For a moment simply eating a beautiful blue and white piece of canvas with the eyes, spontaneous, for a second forgetting grief, we consume the blue and white paint like whipped cream. The stripes of a painted tablecloth like Dutch chocolate. For a second that whiff of unalloyed pleasure. It was for this I have lived. For that delight. For that I left home. Yet I even learned it at home, from you, Aunt, teacher, mentor, my line to the fine arts. Which were absent in Mother's house. Books, yes, but not pictures. Pictures were at Aunt Dorothy's—all over the walls and in picture books: rows of illustrations and reproductions, rare volumes of Picasso, special editions, Matisse, Leger, Braque. All the masters in their volumes: da Vinci and Raphael or Titian and Velásquez. And the middle guys Rembrandt and Goya on up to Monet. You could spend days, even weeks, with them in the big boat in the library, a special and wonderful sofa shaped like a galley, the penultimate in leisure seating or sprawling, with its own vicuña rug in case you wanted to snuggle. It held two people easily so we could lie side by side together and look at pictures. Reverently or irreverently, since you could be silly with her, you could be whimsical. In her aura life itself was that: a party or fun or adventure, amusing—full of things.

Tonight I see the paintings through tears and grind my

teeth and take my chair. How to get through this ordeal, the ordeal of the meeting; the ordeal without it? That plate painted so delightfully and well upon a table, for these paintings are an essay on the still life: conscious, erudite, full of references and jokes and bits of this or that master. Appealing in the most sensuous way, lovely and light and magnificently painted, so that the decorated plate is the emblem and embodiment of every pretty thing, the art of decoration itself: sparkling artifacts that came from the East, the round sheen of china, the dollops of flowers blue and red. How at this moment, when its charm is heightened, how it hurts, actually hurts to absorb it; a lifetime of seeing, habitual in its pleasure, is intensified now to a crush of understanding. It was from her I learned it all, learned it first. Damn, not dead, not without goodbye, not without forgiveness.

Oh, the grand, the many, the sumptuous reconciliations there were to have been. Flickering lower in hope over the years. Not feasts together on the Bowery: raffish, my world. No, quieter, her house, that house—no, pay attention to the meeting. Screw the meeting. Something small and quiet: we would merely look at each other in the coming hush of a Minnesota evening. Perhaps snow and the dread that comes with its evenings, but still it would be there, the forgiveness at last, the final erasure of that long exile. Irma is talking to you, pay attention; tell her how nice the gallery looks in its new location. She and Leon worked so hard to find another space when the rent on the old place was raised past all possibility and we knew we would have to move. How clean it is, how well furbished; how professional we seem at last. Out of Noho into Soho, only a few blocks to the southern side of Houston Street, but really an enormous distance, another world; out of the no man's land of a freewheeling cooperative with wonderful light and space and into much smaller quarters a few steps below the street but with the magical address right in the art market.

Libby and Margo Robinson come in, old-timers in our gallery, founding members like myself. "We lost our mother in November—did you hear?" I am more understanding tonight than I would usually be, the pain in my gut so sharp I can hardly keep my seat. It was a mistake to have come here; I may not last out the meeting. "We miss her so much. She was like a friend, like someone our own age—you know we were all in vaudeville together? You knew that we were in vaudeville when we were kids—up till our twenties even." The assurance in all that, the enviable—"like friends, like someone our own age"—it comes in a whirl over me. The guilt and shame again. No, we were not like friends the same age—an impossible idea. I had never hoped for anything that outrageous.

Ah, but of course I had. Of course that was just my fantasy all the years apart, that we would come together as adults, all behind us, forgiven. But I was never forgiven. Even two years ago when last I saw her, crazy I suppose I was—bringing myself out there with manuscripts, photographs, a general review. Being backed out the door after half an hour because it was now time for her to rest—or did she have someone else there and was just getting rid of me? After all I'd gotten lost and arrived forty-five minutes late; you don't do that sort of thing with her. Backed out the door still trying to interest her in the *Elegy for Sita,* "It's a pretty book; we only made three hundred and fifty copies; you'll like the paper." "I hated *Sita.*" She says it just like that. Everything is possible to her; she has simply said what she felt all her life. She is rich and spoiled and a great lady and can be like ice, the very tones of her voice when annoyed turn me white. Or mute. And backed further to the doorway, I make one last attempt: "I have a copy of my new book with me, *Going to Iran.* It's not published yet; this is just manuscript, but it's a very good typescript." "Send it when it's published." "It has a bit about you and about Mother in passing; I thought you'd be interested." "Send it." "Aunt Dorothy?" "What?" "I just wanted to say how much I love you." "Yes. Goodbye."

It's hopeless, forget it; concentrate on the viewing. There's a viewing tonight of new work. I don't like anything in the viewing. For the first time, I who vote for everyone, especially struggling young women artists, I who imagine everyone who submits will get better, will show promise eventually—I am voting everybody down. Even though Stephanie had said that our hopefuls tonight are presenting especially good work, I give all five a zero and only reconsider one, a guy who paints flowers, and put him up to a two. Five is tops. The rest of the members seem to have felt the same; when the ballots are counted no new artist is asked to join. Leon says we are enough now anyway. He proceeds to business: elections, a new banner for the front, etc., and I float away. Listening to one of her operas in my mind, holding on to the chair with the muscles of my thighs—we never even called her, we were there at Christmas for Mother and we never even telephoned—Jesus, we could have at least done that. If she'd hung up on us maybe we could have called the number at the cottage and gotten the butler on the phone and heard she was ill, driven there, flown through the night and the snow if only to leave a note, a message to be conveyed through the still of the house up to her pain. An African violet left on the doorstep; Christ, it's our fault, all our own fault. Mine. I wanted to call. Why did I listen to Sally, why did I bow before an elder sister's decision, guided, passive? Older than I, a lawyer. Sally's always been in touch with Dorothy, all the years I hadn't been: why would she think we'd be hung up on—because I was on the line too? I had been afraid to insist that afternoon. And so I missed my chance.

I listened to Sally when she said it was pointless to go to our father's funeral; I almost believed her. "What's the use, you stand there with people you don't even know—no one in his family is coming—you look at a hole in the ground in Arizona—Really, what is served by that, I ask you?" And as I teetered, wondering how to get money for a ticket after banking hours, a dress—I called her back and her husband said she had already caught a plane. So I should know by now. But I didn't. It seemed so plausible when she who still had favor said the great aunt was utterly unsociable. It's possible she was only protecting my feelings lest I be hung up on. Or she believed Dorothy would see no one, not even herself. But what if the truth were otherwise—it was Christmas after all. And now I know the woman was dying, an old woman, deeply ill and dying alone in that house by the lake. Maybe she would have welcomed us, been glad. I would have the sound of her voice being kind and loving or curmudgeonly and funny. I would have that love to go out on. Losing her was inevitable; she was old, she would die, we all die and so forth. I sit on a folding chair telling myself this. But it is all in how we die. Or how the dead leave us. Vote, it's time to vote. I vote the slate.

When the meeting breaks up Irma stands next to me, a kindly presence, but as I look over the new space, trying to plan a show here, I feel ungracious about the place. It is rather small for sculpture. I was thinking to show sculpture here in April. The old gallery was large and wonderful, a great expanse of floor and light, direct light from windows right on the street. Here we are below ground level in what is not quite a basement. And our gallery leads to two other galleries. So from the point of view of a sculptor it is merely a pathway; its floor space cannot be interrupted by big sculptures because these other tenants will be loud in protesting. The bitterness of real estate in New York: this guy is renting a basement to several different tenants and making over six thousand dollars a month on it. Irma understands the problem: "You see, when the old landlord's son wanted eight times what we'd been paying, we spent the whole summer looking and this is all we could find." "I know. I know how hard you worked, Irma." Suddenly I feel irascible with how things are, even with our compromise: "It's a great place for pictures and it's wonderful to hear that we are selling so much here." "Stephanie and Olga sold a great deal." "But for sculptors—it seems that we weren't taken into account." "I'm sure you'll come up with something; you always build to suit"—she smiles, laughs actually into my rising anger. Which is an undirected force, coming from another hurt, yet suddenly compounded by noticing that the floor isn't even flat; part of it is elevated a few inches. Like a stage. A detail like that could direct the course of an entire exhibition—go with it then—perhaps a cage there, chairs. I had been thinking along the line of a large cage with figures on chairs. And other chairs as if for spectators set outside the cage, the same kind of figures surveying their opposites in captivity. Could I do that here? Look at the size of the platform—probably big enough. But the fact that the rest of the flooring leads to the galleries behind—like a path. "So, they complain—the hell with them," Irma says, "We'll deal with it. You'll be all right." Again her smile. Her face wide in this grin which is not a grin: she is really afraid, not amused. I struggle towards not correct but at least reasonable behavior—it is not her fault. My disappointment a grudge not even formed: I have not yet measured the space nor sat down to deal with it. I am still refurbishing my studio as I usually do before a show, tooling up. And now like a blight into the joy of preparation, into the clean new-painted walls, the brick so white and fresh, the floor an immaculate white enamel to enhance the light—into this happiness, this brand new playroom, death comes to fly about the walls with the brushing wing of an evil bird. The show is months away and though the floor plan is very important, there is time to deal with it all. Not tonight, not with all that has happened.

I GET BACK INTO MY OLD CAR. The bottom has fallen out of what I do and what I am. Stupid little show. As pointless as all the others. She never even saw one of them. Did not like my books. When I was home at Christmas I was astonished to discover in Mother's basement—but hung up on the wall—not only one of those first bad paintings I had insisted on giving her—but the poster from every show I had ever done. I nearly cried in gratitude and amazement when I looked around and realized she had saved these things over the years, my mother who doesn't know or pretend to "appreciate" art. But is my mother. Yet it was my aunt who made me an artist, or made that idea possible. A.D. In the twenty-five years since I was cursed by you I have produced, exhibited, published—and I would throw it all away tonight for one word from you. One sign or token. Everything reproaches me, recalls you. On the street around me, the gallery, all the galleries, the artists' hustle, our poor little hopes, Olga's gross and wonderful, nearly animal enthusiasm in describing a sale, a critic, a review—even the tour guides who bring in buses of suburban ladies and then want a cut if you sell something. I'd tell them to take a flying fuck, Olga, I had wanted to say but restrained myself.

How shoddy it all is in her eyes, now that I see again with the eyes of my aunt, the eyes I began with. One set of eyes. Another was Mother's, the sturdy peasant honesty of her stock complementing but more often contradicting the implacable aristocratic gaiety and distance, snobbery and playfulness of the Milletts. All so long ago. I have lived twenty-five years in refutation of my origins, both sides of them. And I will go back home alone tonight, Millett enough to drink a martini and have a fire before I eat that little piece of steak I thawed out this morning. And then I will be like my mother enough to call, to start burning up the long distance, just to hear anything, like a hand stretching out for company, blood, kindred.

First Sally; I will have to see what she knows, what she can tell me. The Milletts have to talk to her if not to me; she is the eldest and the head of the family. They think like that. Then Mother again, for comfort, if not information. So far it is only that a lawyer called Aunt Harriet who called Sally who called Mother. Keep tracking it down. How did she die? That means everything. Though it means nothing because she is forever dead. Permanent, it's so damn permanent.

Pacing the loft, trying to organize a drink—it takes a half hour. With A.D. once in her big car outside Great Uncle William O'Connell's house, the high man and head of the family for some reason that is still mysterious but has to do with the name O'Connell in Irish history, its power reaching us even in a car in the Minnesota night at Hastings, for this noble old man is dead like a chieftain and we must dare to go in and look, actually see the body in state. My eyes will see death. She will show it to me, patiently, kindly, tenderly. Unusually tender and forbearing because I am afraid. The big brown eyes of this quiet little niece, frightened, diffident. A.D. is asking a hard thing. She does all the time—you have to be a doggone encyclopedia to keep up with her. But this isn't like playground slides and horseback riding and stuff like that that scared you; this is different and I don't even know what it is. But if she wants me to know and she's so nice and being so serious about it too, it must be awful important. I'll ask her that, if it really is awful important. This is stalling for time while I get ready to be brave. "Awful, yes, it is awful—exactly the word." Even as I realize I should have said awfully, not awful. There are a bunch of words I say wrong like the kids at school. She calls it dialect or something. It isn't slang and it's not cursing anyway. She does that all the time, but of course I'm not supposed to. You have to be so careful with Aunt Dorothy not to do anything wrong and there are so many things you can do wrong. By mistake now I got the right word. Awful sounds like the power of the Holy Ghost or something when she says it. But she ain't religious, so watch out for that stuff too. She's Catholic but don't go to Mass at all. Like Daddy, she's critical, Mom says. Mom ain't critical. I'm getting a little bit critical though Mom says I don't know what I'm talking about. "Death is awful, Kate," putting her arm around my shoulder. "But you must learn what it is." "Will he look funny, I mean strange?" "No, he'll just look like he's asleep. But he isn't. He's dead because the spirit has left him. Completely. He will never be alive again." She waits a moment. "It's permanent, darling. That's the trouble with it; it's so damn permanent."

There were tears in her voice and I followed her meekly, staring at the lace bedspread under the figure. Permanent. Now she is old and dead who was that beautiful young woman, my aunt. Dying, she makes me know death so much harder this time than last. My own age and my own death coming. My own childhood gone now forever. In dying she has taken all hopes of its retrieval, even the knowing of it perhaps. I never finished the book on my father and my childhood; it came to have too much of her in it as well and took strange and outlandish turns when I had to examine my love for the two of them, brother and sister. For I not only loved them, I was also in love with them. Utterly and completely in love as children are and that never changed or diminished as I began to grow up and my father left us and became only the handsome stranger of his youth. Remaining this even after the one time I saw him in old age and was able—at least there—to make peace. Because he sought it and I was delighted. But it was still Dorothy I adored. Chastely, in fact. Yet not really, not in my mind, my wishes and imaginings in childhood. And all the years since have been incestuous. Also blankly innocent. But my desire was for both of them; never satisfied, it persisted.

For my father was not that old man who arrived in New York who merely resembled him. And Dorothy never faded: even old she was herself still to me, still beautiful if ravaged. That she did not let people see her in her last years made no difference to me; both the old and the young woman were my hope and joy, my pride, my ambition, my goal in thousands of amorous dreams I woke from without astonishment. I was in love. Even with the idea of a cup of tea, a drink, and a fire: a whole lifetime spent in her company, an old age, hers or mine. Cohabitation. Or only a chat. The touch of her hand on an object was a fetish, the golden down on her cheek.

"Your aunt is only an old woman with hair on her face," Percy Carroll said to me one night at his house in St. Paul, now that he was on the Arts Board and went to meetings with her. "Forget her; she's a cold old woman." "Sacrilege and blasphemy. I've been in love with her all my life." "You're an idiot then. She's an old bitch. And you're wasting your time." If you were not my own Uncle Harry's putative illegitimate son, I would punch you in the nose, I think, looking at him grown paunchy and bitter, looking every day more like Oscar Wilde for reasons his wife and two children may soon come to regret. How can you be bitter living in this house? Fifteen rooms and six bathrooms—our usual joke about it: the Persian rugs, the seat on the Arts Board—you stayed home and got it all. From being Percy Carroll from Carroll Avenue, a little boy who didn't seem to have a father and whose mother's best friend was my uncle. Then running in college with the fast set, the rich boys—our gang, though neither of us were to the manor born and you were even a music student to increase your risk—go into banking and money enough to be a patron of the arts. Like my aunt you're putting down. Does she squelch you with that basilisk glare of hers, did you try to be intimate, were you too friendly?

Percy, last year in your kitchen before dinner, getting wonderfully drunk with you and my old pal who is your wife—how satisfactory of the two of you to marry each other and acquire such a fine house—we drank to that. While Janey Washburn and I were still starving artists on the Bowery, doing that thing, the two of you were having kids and living high at home. We could admire each other—between us we had it all. One morning you even padded into my bedroom to announce that we ought to buy a house on the St. Croix jointly so that we'd each have a bit of the river together. I was all for it.

And I came to you for refuge when the family saw fit to lock me up at the university psychiatric "facility." After the trial that declared me sane, a wonderful exercise in law, it was your home I came to. To call my aunt. Because that was the next move: when in dutch with one side of the family, consult the other. If my mother wants to put me away, I will flee to my aunt. And when she was very charming but couldn't see me for several days—though I was welcome for dinner on Tuesday with a very remarkably educated Irish priest who was great company, but not till then—I gave up and said the hell with it; I live in the East and I have a farm to go to. Next time.

ALWAYS NEXT TIME. All those years of postponements, abortive attempts, edgy little interviews that came to nothing. For example: that time I was going to apologize. Just before I went to Iran. I told her ahead of time, laid it out, made it clear that I understood how I had been in the wrong. Not just admitting as I might have years before that the whole affair with Jaycee was a bust, a bad trip. Not in those words of course. An "error in judgement," more her line of phrase. But of course not actually saying that either—a mistake, a terrible mistake all around. The words hanging in the air. For of course that had been my sin—twenty years before my aunt had sent me to Oxford stipulating I was never to see a certain woman again. And thereby cease to be a lesbian. Or I would lose the chance to study there. I refused to be saved; wanting Oxford, I took the money and ran. With the lover who later betrayed me. In the process, I lost my aunt.

You do not say later that the woman you loved and betrayed your own blood for was in fact sleeping with someone else from the very moment you arrived home in America from Oxford. To pay tepid court to your beloved aunt who had sent you there. Tepid because you belonged to another, were committed there, had risked all for this connection. And were honor-bound with what little honor was left. It would be reserved for another lesbian, a member of my own generation, the woman I had lived wit already three years. And would endure a fourth year as the third party in a triangle, oafishly unaware of the goings-on behind my back while I was off teaching school and earning for all three of us—they didn't work; they were artists. One a writer, one a painter. I was their patroness, dreaming of setting up an art gallery. Merely a scholar, I could not participate in their wonders; I was a slug.

But in those days I had meant that I had made a mistake only in choosing wrongly, the wrong lover. They are not all that bad. Consider Fumio, the man I married, the soul of integrity. Of course going off to Oxford with Jaycee was a mistake, bad judgment. But there had still not been the admission that I had done wrong in lying to my aunt, in deceiving, in imagining my freedom would weigh equally with truthfulness itself. That time before Iran—and then it had to be canceled so I could get the last plane into Tehran in case they closed the airport. That time I was going to admit how wrong I had been. Wrong not for loving, but for lying, giving in and selling out for the one shining opportunity. Though I had admitted it to myself and to others for a decade. Despite their objections, their gay propaganda, their fervor and loyalty to the cause of love, their love, the persecuted and therefore indulged variety.

Jaycee was a nickname. Her background was alien: Eastern Brahmin. But she had an awkwardness and humor that made me love her: vulnerable, always about to make us discovered. A capacity for telling the truth. And for laughter. Adventure. She was recently and painfully separated from her husband, another graduate student, a Jew whom she had married against the wishes of her family, mainline Eastern Protestants. She said outrageous things to tease me, breathtaking East Coast assumptions such as that I was "very well brought up for someone Catholic and from St. Paul." She had been chief justice at some terrible court of student conduct in the Seven Sisters circuit and had thereafter arrived in Greenwich Village. She had an intriguing and glamorous past made prosaic by her new life in Minnesota where she was now frantically earnest about Eng. Lit., her rented room full of stacks of tiny cards with Anglo-Saxon vocabulary written out in her immaculate hand and which she went through rigorously several times a day to come up with straight A's. We could talk authors. I was still an undergraduate; she was my entire introduction to graduate school requirements, professional scholarship and graduate classes, a number of which we attended together.

Above all, Jaycee was my introduction to lesbianism. She had had an affair with a friend in Greenwich Village a few years before, in her heyday, before being dropped in God-forsaken Minneapolis through a marriage and a scholarship. Then she was one, the forbidden word, so forbidden one didn't even think it by its name, only by an emanation, a musk. Working in an office near hers and coming to like and then admire her I felt a subterranean pull. Hers. Mine. She was one. I knew it, felt it. Dared to admit this in myself and pursued. The marriage over, she reverted, the perfume of her eroticism breathing through her clothes: the get-up of a teaching assistant assigned to counsel students, the very skirt and blouse and nylons of correctitude. I hounded that secret. Was seduced by it—or rather followed it with intense looks and surprise visits even on Saturdays. To the place where I was a clerk for pocket money and she was a student counselor for survival. Always just short of indiscretion, always hungry, sniffing the scent of the forbidden, what I had to know. Find. Do.

Become. Be initiated into finally as a destiny already reserved for me by crushes, even the teenage antics of sleeping with Mary Quinn at the end of senior year in high school, finally experimenting with sex after four years of courtship. An experiment I cut short in terror of Catholic sin and the nuns' voices, the pope himself, the church fathers and the Inquisition yelling in my head that early June night. Mother's room. Mother out of town, before the geraniums blooming in Mother's balcony.

That was chicken, but now, in my senior year of college I was ready for afternoons of *Cosi fan Tutti* and embraces, apprehensive with daring but pointed like an arrow toward the snowy early evening, a holiday, Washington's Birthday (later when I met Fumio I was bewildered to learn it was his birthday as well, his very name a pun on the numerality of the twenty-second day of the second month) but it was my birthday too in a way, for that afternoon Jaycee brought me out, birthed me into sisterhood, the route through her knees my canal into another life. From that moment on, I was transformed. I had crossed the line into the taboo. Knew myself unalterably different from my chums, from Mother when I finally called her up in the middle of the night to report myself alive and her car still intact. For all my tacky lies about staying over at the Theta House, Thetas ready to back me up—she knew. Mother had a way of knowing. A.D. did too.

WHAT THEY DIDN'T KNOW was the ecstasy of this sensuality, the excitement of hearing Mozart opera under these conditions, the talk, the taste of gin in this bed, the way making love was neither boring nor dangerous as it had been heretofore. But a happiness almost to madness, to passing out. Orgasm. The mystery. I had invented and discovered it. The adventure of being in love. Secret, undiscovered, forbidden love. Of coming together into Allen Tate's poetry class the next morning to scandalize the whole room while listening to him analyze *The Rape of the Lock,* a lecture every word of which I still remember.

No, they didn't know. I had discovered another world, a heightened existence, a hidden reality. Not just love. Other, illicit love. Holding back sometimes in fear, in shame, brazen sometimes, blazing as we entered Tate's class in Folwell Hall that day. For all our careful discretion. Unmistakably lovers despite our serene deportment, we shouted eroticism to the blackboard and wooden desks, the graduate students' overshoes. Tate himself, doing his business with the cigarette holder. We might even have given it all energy, light—for the lecture that day was as wonderful as the poem it was about. The lock, as Tate made delightedly clear, was virginity; Belinda had lost it in losing a curl—it was much ado about nothing—the subject of truly civilized art. The poem as fluid, as clear and fine as music,as clever as thought, a series of equations. I listened knowing it was all about me and our secret Mozartean world of sentiment; yet at the same time as different from Pope as realism: bedsheets and lies to your Mother. I was now on the plains alone, beyond the pale.

Would it have been the same if I'd gone to Oxford with a young man against my aunt's wishes? Only that would never have happened. There is always this to take in—that it was not only illicit, but illegal; not merely without respectability but criminal, this liaison. It was with a woman and she was one and I was as well. So that it was another breach, a betrayal too dangerous to explore. But from the solid family point of view of the Milletts, her sisters, the aunts Lucy and Harriet, the uncles Bob and La Rue, the tribe could never abide my deviation and called a conclave against it. Never mind Harriet's ambiguous gesture in giving me *The Well of Loneliness* to read as I passed through Swarthmore en route to England. Was it a warning, or an acknowledgment? And Dorothy at lunch in the Minnesota Club over an interminable chicken salad, fumbling to tell me that she too had been embroiled in this sort of thing at my age. With a woman. Her eyes down to her plate—how terribly I love that face. How afraid of it I am, of the eyes as they rise to meet the challenge of my own. Being momentarily brave as she who is never flustered is nearly flustered. "And Lucy, your Aunt Lucy extricated me from it. I've never stopped being glad she got me out of that." Why? How many why's: her marriage to Louis Hill for one, a millionaire. Even if you're in love with him you are Cinderella. And when it is over you have one million dollars.

Or so she told me one day doing her nails on a curious little machine, the two of us lolling about one long happy afternoon in her bedroom. I am the page that can dare to ask such questions and moreover she humors me and permits me really to say anything to her: I am under twelve years old. "How much money do you have, Aunt Dorothy? I mean, are you a millionaire?" Of course I had heard that at home in tones of envy, contempt, admiration, grudging recognition of power, loathing for the selfish insensitivity of the rich, the ease of their lives. But not from my father. Jim Millett adored his sister Dorothy and might have struck anyone but his wife who ever spoke against her. And when the paper announced her divorce from Louis Hill who had the bad judgment to dismiss her in favor of a secretary he had maybe put in the family way and now felt obliged to marry, Daddy read it in a fury. That they would publish the divorce; divorce was private. Jim did not want to see her name in the paper, his despair and shame and protective anger refraining with ever so much effort from crushing the thing in his hand. How wonderfully long his arm with the black hair on it, the white of his shirt, his flannel trousers, his white shoes—it was Sunday in summer. "Well, her name is in the paper every day. In the society column," Mother says, not helping matters at all. His beautiful and vulnerable younger sister, whom he educated, protected until he could do so no more. The cruel ones got her, the rich and heartless, and now they will tear her apart. She who was their star, their instant wonder, the most clever and ingenious in revelry, in dancing all night, in giving parties you remember a lifetime and that define an age and a generation. And she will have to go on among them living that opprobrium.

Money is killing him, an engineer bounded on every side by the facts of material reality: time, bids, his long-dreamed-of company fading. The limited deadly little salary from the highway department blocking off his hopes like a picket fence. Other men so much less gifted are making millions now in the construction boom—are their own masters, do not have to obey lesser minds, can create and build. Not someone else's bridge or highway but their own. And now all those jackasses, those grown men who were still called Charley and Puff, those women with names out of their school days like Dody and Su-Su, would turn on her. She had trusted them, she was their Bonnie, Louie's name for her became everyone's; she made the parties, she made their lives fly. But now they could down her, humiliate her.

My father was the only member of his family who ever worked for a living. Harriet and Lucy married well. Dorothy had married such wealth and power as princes have. Harry, near to all this, did very little in the practical way, lived off Dorothy, prepared occasionally and unsuccessfully for the bar. And in other bars, like the Angus and the St. Regis and Fitzgerald's own Commodore bar, he dispensed advice, traded witticisms, and flourished as a raconteur. Huddling both with the drinking priests and the supposed representatives of the Irish Republican Army. This was a good arrangement all around. But now the house has tumbled and the duchess is dethroned. Harry's sister, even Jim's sister, was the queen of the town. And now the lady has fallen. What will they subject her to now, those cruel sillies in whom she placed her trust, gave her affection? My father's arm tightens along the kitchen table under the clock on a Sunday morning, the plaster wall behind him. He was once so annoyed with me that he slapped me in this room and I fell against that wall, thinking him a monster. But today I understand his fury—my God, what if they were mean to my aunt, these people? Divorce is a word I do not understand: what after all happens in it; do you fall somewhere? If the Church kicks you out where do people go?

It was near that time that I thought I'd just see how much money Aunt Dorothy had, having a communal feeling about money within a family and knowing that my dad made exactly three hundred and fifty dollars a month, had for years and would for many more under civil service regulations. So let's see if my Aunt Dorothy is a millionaire but let's find out first how much a million is. How many zeros? Write it out in your head: a hundred, a thousand, ten thousand, not so much maybe; a hundred thousand—that's a lot. The next step up is a million. Gee—her eyes looking at me square and fair—"yes, I am a millionaire, I guess. Louis left me a million at our divorce." "How many millions does he have?" "Seven or eight, I suppose." "The paper said that when Cordie Hill died he left eighty million. Mom read about it." "He well could have. I don't follow these things anymore." She shifts; this is deeper water than mere honesty to a child; this is the Hill dynasty. "He was the first generation, Jim Hill's own son." "Like Louis Senior was his son, right? And Louis Junior was Uncle Louis. Is he still my godfather?" "I really don't know"—she looks at me, this odd child.

I HAD LOVED my Uncle Louis very much; he was great fun. But when Daddy said he was an empty-headed cad, I quietly dropped him. As he has quietly dropped me; he is extraneous, no longer even an in-law. My aunt is the Millett, the real connection, the be-all and end-all, because she is everything I love and admire. Beautiful and knows everything and makes being rich very pretty. Carefree. And I am sick to death of the money talk at home, the bickering, the loathing, the envy, and the worry. The haven't got for the roof or the carpet. Mother's anxiety, Daddy's fury. It's nice with Aunt Dorothy playing lady while she does up her nails, sitting in the big cushions of the boat sofa. For the boat is in her bedroom in this house: Virginia Avenue, the first and grandest house of all, pure Georgian, perfect in proportion. And it even has a bedroom for me when I come to visit. Which is lots now. For all that, when she said did I want to try the machine to buff my nails, I gave it a polite trial and then passed it up. Something of Mother drew the line there.

Yet how good, for a grown-up, how really decent of A.D. to explain money to me. Everyone talks about it without actually explaining it: but it's there behind every thought they have. For lifetimes. And it has power and ruins people's happiness—what if Mother had plenty of money, wouldn't she be happy and frivolous too? If she exercised her father Patrick Henry's smarts and invested well. She is not an Irish immigrant millionaire's daughter for nothing: Patrick gambled a cow which was his wife's dowry and a four-thousand-dollar farm into a little empire in Farmington, Minnesota. Then he left his money to his six children—with one string: his eldest son Tom got half of the grain elevator as well as his own sixth. So there lies all the bitterness and debate in Mother's family: all the unchallenged smug patriarchal power of Tom and his heirs, all his sisters' concerted efforts to get anything voted their way. Tom has seven out of twelve votes and his brothers are in his pocket. One sister is widowed and no provision is made for her or little in all the years of hard country annual business meetings in the summer heat of the old house down in Farmington. I've seen a lot about money already. Daddy's anger, his disappointment. Mother's fear, her sense of being surrounded with money while having none. As Patrick's youngest and most petted daughter, she has come off with only a pittance. Teaching school was her independence before marriage, but it was only subsistence. Now as Jim Millett's wife she cannot earn a penny nor advance her cause or her family's cause at all. Only by stinting, worrying, nagging, holding back.

And yet, managing the placid sunny petty bourgeois household together with her maid, Celia, a Bohemian girl from the country, there is still a music to her life. Celia was to spend a season or two acquiring city manners and cooking skills, but she's stayed for a decade now and become our treasure. Under Celia and Mother, life is very golden indeed: the butter is delivered in stone crocks with the milk and cream. There is baking every day, contests about the best coffee. There's the fruit man who comes with a wagon; there's a butcher you go to visit. There are eggs and cream in everything; there are house specialties like French meringues with strawberries.

But it all lacks the *élan* of Virginia Avenue, Aunt Dorothy's fairy-tale house. As the life of the comfortable small burgher never approaches the grandeur of aristocracy. The great staircase as you come in, the black and white marble squares in the entranceway, the mellow glow of the table where calling cards are tossed on a silver dish, the sweep of drawing rooms and sitting rooms. The dining room and the wash of Haydn at dinner time, afternoons of Mozart or the drama of an opera. Always there was music on the Capehardt, an astonishing machine that actually turned over the records for you. There was a small floor-to-ceiling cupboard just for phonograph records, the golden spines of boxed editions. The old 78's. And when 33⅓'s came in, my aunt donated the 78's to Hamline College. I remember being offended they were not given to me. A possessive fool who didn't need a thousand out-of-date phonograph records, whatever the value of the old performances, I only wanted to absorb everything that had been hers. The way I would treasure a cast-off pair of loafers that didn't quite fit, wear them for the sake that they had been hers. They were red, they were special, they had been hers. "See if this will fit you," she'd say, lazily going through her closet. Perfectly and they were perfect.

Everything about her was intriguing. That she wore trousers, for example. When trousers were not yet worn. All those long-legged slender grays and blues and browns, slacks with a blouse or a sweater. Riding things and riding. The horses at her farm, East Bushka, where I first rode, trembling along behind Sally on a horse called Me Too. But especially what suited and characterized her most of all, were her Chinese clothes: the tunics, the silk trousers, the stiff embroidery, the traced and etched patterns in the willing silk, the sumptuous colors. Hong Kong. Exotic as the Chinese trunk she brought home for me, red with golden dragons, lacquered and strong and with a curious lock whose key I had already lost years before that Bowery night a thief made off with it at a moment when it contained only the love letters of a Marine I had made the family uneasy by going steady with and appearing to be about to marry. At the juncture when Jaycee arrived to make them still more uneasy.

By the night that trunk was stolen from the old loft on the Bowery it was all I had left of my Aunt Dorothy. I wept at the cruelty of the loss. What if I had called her right then and said so—or written and explained how much it meant? Never mind; you wrote often enough, letters with lines like "I love you, Aunt Dorothy, I have always loved you"—phrases she would mimic much later when I would be granted an interview. "I love you, I have always loved you"—her terrifying green eyes burning into me, accusing. "Yes, I meant it." "You haven't conducted yourself as if you did." And I would despair. Is it possible this is only a proud woman who wants to be told again and again? What of all the long years she waited for you to come back to her? What—it drives one mad to think that way.

Of course we took refuge in calling her a cold old woman, cut off from everyone. "For twenty-five years she has eaten dinner alone," Sally would say. Mother too: "She never calls me." But of course she wouldn't, Mother; you are not a Millett and she is a snob. That estrangement was built in, was caste. Whereas ours, we imagined, was offense. We were Milletts, her nieces once. And what is it like to dine alone for twenty-five years? A butler. A fire. Anguish of solitude in tedious splendor. Nonsense, she had a whole raft of cronies out there, the persons on hand for the memorial which is not a funeral, the figures gathering now at her house. Wayzeta society. She had grown past family, forsworn it as a disappointment. And there were still the O'Connells, Great Uncle William O'Connell's sons, one a priest: the Milletts have even produced a priest. There are her sisters Lucy and Harriet as well. It is only the nieces who are lost to her across the years. Misunderstandings, neglect. With me the trespass and the fear that kept me away for twenty-five years.

But when I lived on her chintz, and the embroidered star patterns were mine for a week, to share with my sisters Sally or Mallory or to have all to myself—as I had her all to myself often in that grand big house on Virginia Avenue, with the music floating up the staircase, as the big red whale that was my Christmas present one year floated from the balustrade above us, anchored with a transparent fishing line, a miracle occurring in my honor—then that was happiness. The greatest I have ever known; the rhapsody of being young and beloved, favored and treasured. I was "the French one" with my long brown hair, my brown eyes. Soft and quiet and a tomboy too; studious and a smart aleck when encouraged.

How loved I was and never realized—my hands grip the steering wheel at an intersection coming home to the Bowery. At the light on Second Avenue, just before turning into the filth and chaos of First Street, the wrecked and abandoned and cannibalized cars, nighttime and still the afterglow of Christmas in the red of a stoplight—you were home at Christmas—I realize she is dead. I do not even have a photograph. Not even a photograph, for chrissakes: you have lost her forever now and lack even a piece of paper with the image of her beauty to prove that she existed. The forbidding face of an old woman who frightened me into keeping my distance all these years—damn it, think of what she was in her youth and beauty. There are only those two silhouettes of her and of Harriet at twenty: not even photographs, cut profiles in black paper. Lovely, striking old-fashioned things always on my dresser. Friends over for dinner always ask about them: the pictures of my father, the rare wondrous beauty of Grandmother Millett in her oval frame with the convex glass which I cracked inadvertently last year. Fix it; have you no sense of what is important?

And get some pictures. It is possible they still exist, that she did not destroy the evidence of her youth. All those hundreds of photographs of her and of her sisters, the uncles too, the bunch of them like a club that traveled together, played together, partied in their own world, kin but contemporaries too, friends as well as blood to each other. The trip to Greece, for example. A voyage Dorothy took with her sisters and everyone's husbands and Uncle Louie's brother Jerome Hill thrown in for good measure and it was all photographed, Jerome's beautiful photographs: the wind in a sail, a figure far below the mast. Published in a wonderful large book bound in linen. A delight, an idyll. If you were very good you could look at this book. Sally even had the nerve to ask for a copy. The copies remaining would be in the library still. Forget about the library: you have lost all right to that long ago. But if there were a copy of this book. Or old photographs strewn about, stuffed in a drawer in that great cold house by the lake tonight; gray like the walls, gray like her hair, gray even as she must be now. And you have nothing to remember her by except your own folly, your foolish neglect. A lifetime denying or admitting her and what she is or was: you couldn't get much farther from the aristocratic principle than the Bowery and First Street where you park your car amidst broken whiskey bottles. Yes, and hate rich people: the phonies, the patrons, the bureaucrats that dribble a little cash down to the artists. And control and make all mediocre. What was it that she said once—when you became an artist—that artists were people one might know but did not invite home for dinner. Resist, refuse, the long career of it. But now what does it all matter, the long quarrel—I loved her and she is dead.

PART TWO

"Aunt Dorothy is dead." I have waited twenty-five years for these words, waited in terror, knowing they would come in your voice, Mother. Or in Sally's. If it were Sally, it would be the two of us, her nieces, knowing the final end of the aunt we had adored in childhood and loved so fruitlessly as adults. But in Mother's voice, it becomes the final claim of the nearer connection. Not triumph in her voice but sorrow. Yet she had outlived her competition and had us all to herself. As it should be. But the heart cries out for the other, the second mother, the influence so strong in childhood it could efface our own mother's. For what was she then compared to A.D., this grace, this beauty, the riches and gallantry, the adventure and mystery—the star. Fickle, mesmerized, we were drawn by an irresistible force of gravity, charm. Our adolescent pun, Anno Domina, for she was that to us. And before our town: the baroness, the duchess, even the queen of our enamored consciousness. And for all the alienation over the years, she remained that.

She is still that, in my voice, crying out in pain and fury. "Damn, Mother, damn it—I never got her back. We never made it up—don't you understand?" "Yes, but you mustn't think of that. Think of the good things. And she was so cold at the end: it would have been hopeless." Cold; we are big on her coldness. But how cold was I, being there and not even calling? How cold was Christmas to her alone out there in the house at Wayzeta, the pale gray and perfect house? That beautiful house. But how empty those rooms in their last days. Even goddamned Christmas, as she might have called it, and the temperature twenty below zero day after day. Fires and a butler to build them, a perfect couple to wait upon her—she has had a new pair for years and I don't even know them. The man seemed almost to sneer at me and gave me a bad martini on my last visit, a prodigal niece he must survey and protect her from. I thought he was brand-new and simply didn't know how to mix one. I suspected his youth and good looks and did not even know of his wife, for of course there must be a wife to cook; the two live together in the cottage. Which has a different number than the house—all those fumbling times I would call the cottage by mistake. Or because I was afraid of the house.

For it is she who answers the phone at the house, the round County Mayo wheel of her voice, so soft, so beautifully formed. So easy at sarcasm, so capable of cruelty and rejection, the art of telling you off. An art quite lost these days but preserved in that wonderful voice. Once, begging for a visit, frightened even of calling her I mumbled, "I wrote and you didn't answer." "Surely that was answer enough," she replied. I wished I could have laughed; it was so good, so adroit. Retort, repartee. That voice when it was tender warmed you right through, loved with a magical beneficence. County Mayo and high Irish, high as Irish ever got, yet musical and soft. Round and balanced, elegant and powerful like a steering wheel on some magnificent touring car: her own Buick years ago, later her Cadillac convertibles. But perhaps more like that gorgeous old Buick when I was a little girl. Such a relic that it was never sold outside but kept in the family. Her sister, my Aunt Lucy, has it now. If it still runs and is not ready for a museum. I am talking of a car forty years old.

That voice, the delicate and quartered circle, so mobile, so sensitive—the smooth wheel that would catch you mid-sentence, mid-fright, after four days of preparation for this call, the hangovers and gin that inspired this folly—of trying again, of apologizing one more time, of grasping after peace like a daisy upright before a mowing machine. The breath held, the friends who heard yards and yards of your Aunt Dorothy and how you love her: how great she was, how terrible, how cold and cruel and domineering. But how kind in childhood, how she was everything then. How much she taught you of art, the world, literature, the lives of your relatives, naughty stories, irreverent points of view, wit, uncharity, humor. Her own notions of goodness and honor.

And you transgressed them all, every code, going to Oxford with Jaycee after having promised your Aunt Dorothy that if she sent you there you would break with this woman, this "divorcée." Absurd phrase: wasn't Dorothy a divorcée herself? Her sister Lucy as well, my own mother; how old-fashioned and St. Paul to use that phrase. But even then I knew she inferred a good deal more. The divorcée was in her opinion a bad influence. "That woman dominates you," Dorothy announced to me in her library in Wayzeta, solemnly justifying the control she herself was now assuming over my life by forbidding me to see such a person. No, not that; she couldn't do that. She simply forbade you to go to Oxford with Jaycee on her money. I would find a way around this dilemma. On my side, I kept faith by working in a factory the summer before I sailed, earning Jaycee's passage money myself. Jaycee worked as a waitress to get the money to live on while there.

No—I didn't entirely deceive—but of course I did. I deceived in the sense of pretending Jaycee wasn't at Oxford with me. I never confessed to going on with this nefarious relationship while there. Being twenty-one and good at school I thought I was entitled both to a lover and an education. Enlightened people have agreed with me ever since. I could hire an analyst who could make a living out of me for doing the same. But this is to misunderstand the Milletts. Their notion of honor. I went halfway with it by earning Jaycee's passage, packing hair lotion on the night shift in downtown St. Paul, putting Toni Home Permanent kits together on a conveyor belt while listening to bawdy stories among poor women both black and white and then driving home alone at four A.M. But I drove home to Jaycee.

The logic of the Milletts, who lived in the age of Mrs. Simpson and the duke of Windsor—it is even said that my aunt danced with the duke once on shipboard crossing the Atlantic—demanded that I would keep my vow to have nothing more to do with this woman. Or else I would cling to her and give up the chance, poor relation that I was, to go to Oxford to study. I wasn't up to that. In earning money for her I helped Jaycee go there on her own: in forbidding me to go with her they were turning scholarship money into a control over whom I knew or loved. But I was afraid of them. Of losing the chance. Of telling them that I couldn't or wouldn't give her up. Looking them all in the eye. Even facing the family council, if I'd known of it, convened out of airplanes converging from all points to discuss me: Aunt Lucy and Uncle Bob, Aunt Harriet and Uncle La Rue. And Dorothy with her second husband Uncle Walter at her side. In her house. In the great soft gray room where they convene now to say whatever last words are said when the directive from the lady herself is that there shall be no funeral.

So she is dead and I shall never be forgiven. When I called Aunt Lucy this morning the first words she said astonished me: "I haven't seen you since you were here at Christmastime all those years ago. Dorothy was here too. Do you remember?" She is not, or is she, aware of inflicting a wound? No, merely the truth. It stopped then and there for her. I probably ceased to exist. Twenty-five years ago. Yet I was so thick with them down in Virginia that year, teaching nearby in North Carolina, having finished at Oxford and now having my first job. Still living with Jaycee. Who was living with someone else as well. In fact I was now the victim of a triangle, the two lovers living off me and my little salary. Daytimes the two were free to write and paint and make love while I conducted classes. If the Milletts wanted to persuade me my love was a sad mistake I could have furnished them with a great deal along that line. But I was merely living through it. And ashamed, guilty, and in the wrong. What if I had flung myself upon them and said how terrible it had become? An error; close ranks, forgive. But first I would have to confess. To being a lesbian. Or to being a liar. One had necessitated the other.

Or rather cowardice had. And being so deep in lies, three years of them—especially the two years at Oxford—specifically forbidden; a relationship I denied, lied about. Hadn't you agreed to the terms—dishonestly? So that was what I was when I walked in the door at Christmas of the year 1959. Coming from Harriet's. She had confronted me first. Invited me for Christmas and I drove all the way to

Swarthmore to hear myself denounced. To be slapped and told to leave. So the invitation to stop at Lucy's in Virginia was of course a trap. And I knew it. I had no sooner walked in the door, been kissed and given a drink, than the question was put to me simply: did you after all go to Oxford with that woman? Yes. No slimy lies this time.

Of course there had been a spy. A friend of Harriet's and La Rue's. Just passing through Greensboro, North Carolina. I was at work, at the college. But Jaycee and her friend were at home to receive him, to tell him their names. And the name when repeated clicked, Jaycee's name. I think of her now, and wish her well as I always have but I know this morning as surely as I knew that moment at Lucy's that it was for her I lost my family. And it was not worth it. When I could admit to them that I was a lesbian I had already lost them through lying. Denying, being afraid. Bigoted and respectable as some of them were I might still have confronted them with my choice and won. Or at least kept face, honor. If I hadn't lied. In doing that I cut the ground from under myself. And lost them. I think of it again today and know my own folly. No, it was not worth it.

Perhaps it was not for a lover, but for myself. For my freedom. Even the freedom of my cowardice before them. Free of the terror they inspired. Because of everything I was: only half a Millett, my mother's child too; not really a rich person or a noble, not really their kind, bound to be a disappointment. For being a lesbian. Even for later marrying a Japanese they never took notice of. A series of failings underlined by being an artist and writer responsible for books like *Flying* and *Sita*. It was for my own life itself that I lost my family: in order to have that life.

But at the moment when Mother's voice tells me the terrible and utterly final news of my Aunt Dorothy's death I would relinquish those books. Give back this emptiness I called my freedom. Only for the sight of her face, the sound of her voice, her presence, permission to enter that house, to visit, to drink, to talk, to tell my love.

To tell my love is far too much, too outrageous, too risky. Beyond the pale. It is incest. For there were two human beings I loved and desired all my life—my own father and his sister Dorothy. It was thus that I adored my Aunt Dorothy. In every conceivable way, but also in the flesh of her embrace. Her kisses, the softness of her cheek those few seconds, those amazing green eyes that could terrify one as well, their displeasure like death itself. I lived in dread of it.

Somewhere you must have known the worship you inspired in us, in me. Somewhere that too must have passed its bounds and entered reality. Once anyway, once I am sure of. Or I think I am. It was another Christmas and there was much champagne. I remember you kissing me. I will always remember it, the surprise and delight of the first sensuality. For it was not an aunt's kiss but a deeper one, one of the mouth and not the lips. And I was afraid Uncle Harry would see us; I was afraid of discovery. Not for myself, but for you. I was eleven but I understood. Discreet, timid, and I failed you. Easier somehow to talk to you than about you, now that you are dead and I dare to talk at all, even so shyly and carefully, even so secretly and alone. The days of this rocking grief, this terrible knowledge of your end. That you died virtually alone and in pain and after years of pain. Attempts to bypass the arteries in your legs failed repeatedly and were abandoned: doctors considered the amputation of both legs. Which you would have refused. And so it went on: the life of a recluse, the anguish, finally even the wheelchair. Now they tell it, now when it is too late. Forget my absurd and stupid hope of forgiveness, my imagined scenes of reconciliation. The fantasies of having you to my farm, showing it to you, guiding you as you stepped over that little step at the back door of the farmhouse as I guided Simone de Beauvoir last summer. So proud, so happy to have her there. But if it were you, how grand, the perfection of hope. If I could have shown you the place.

"It's just like Aunt Dorothy's," my sister Mallory said one night when we had made a banquet for her there, trestle tables on the grass before the farmhouse and kerosene lanterns and wildflowers, someone's big collie dog in the front hall under a pool of light, the Will Barnett picture of a woman reading in bed with a cat on the counterpane hung over the farmer's desk. We could live like Aunt Dorothy—Mallory's delighted voice discovering a possibility, "Just like Aunt Dorothy." But in fact we haven't: our lives are shabbier, pedestrian; our generation lacked your romance, fell far below it. We are not as close as your generation; we do not revel enough together. Nor are we beauties as you and your sisters were: "From the Three Beautiful Millett Sisters to the Three Beautiful Millett Sisters"—great packages arriving at Christmas and birthdays scrawled with Uncle Bob's witty caricatures—who cares what the postman thinks?

We have lived much smaller lives. Like the times. You were twenty in the twenties, you were a millionaire in the Depression, a friend of Fitzgerald's in the sunny days and of Ernie Pyle's in the war; your husbands owned railroads and were dollar-a-year men for the government in some probably nefarious form of intelligence of which it is just as well I remain ignorant. You were a Republican because you had money, you told me one night when I dined alone with you, myself a college student liberal at that moment. On Mother's side we were Democrat ever since the famine time, her father a delegate to McKinley's convention, her relatives the postmasters of Farmington, Minnesota, for generations. "But Stevenson's better," I urged. "Really a better man, don't you agree to that?" "I think politicians are essentially dishonest people, but I vote with my class interest." "But didn't you carry a card or something at the university; weren't you pretty leftist once?" "Nonsense, that is a long time ago—I vote the way I do because it is logical." And there was no disturbing that sense of logic, no point really in arguing about it. It was one of a thousand points of difference. There was probably nothing in the world we agreed upon.

Except trees. And the last good visit we did trees. Sitting in the gloaming in those pearl gray rooms, the great stretch of green carpeting spreading away behind me to the living room and off to the side to the dining rom, ahead of me to the study. A floor plan I have in my heart and will know the day I die too. They are in those rooms now, those last to say goodbye, the friends and survivors, the "representatives" as the lawyer put it, so arch and stuffy. I am not bidden: instead I am "represented" as are all members of Jim Millett's family, including Mother who lives out there and was not invited either. Instead, Sally and the lawyer have arranged that we are represented by my nephew. Young Steven Rau, Sally's eldest son, a year out of law school. Beautiful, perfect, respectable; I dote on him myself. But it is like a knife that I am represented by a young man who scarcely even knew my aunt while I am not quite invited to attend.

Not in so many words of course. Too tactful, this lawyer. A man named Hank Ransom. Whom I have had the temerity to telephone. To ask for a photograph. He knows of none so far—have I heard of the arrangements? That there will really not be a funeral; just a few friends will gather at her house for a champagne brunch. I remember the urging in Sally's voice, in my other aunts'—insisting that it is pointless to go there. A long way to travel for breakfast, was the ironic family way to describe it. And spend another three hundred dollars on airfare when I was just there the week before and am broke now. But if it were to pay one's last respects, the hell with the cost; if I thought she wanted me to come I'd start now if I had to drive. "You will be represented by a Steven. . ." I hear him search among his papers for Steven's last name. In keeping him busy with Steven's name, I am covering myself: I cannot dare ask if I would be welcome; one gathers from his other remarks that the occasion is really one for her friends in Wayzeta. People like himself; for he is not only her lawyer but a neighbor. I have heard from Sally that it will be stuffy. Rich people. Minneapolis society, the Pillsbury's: bridge partners, club members and other cronies.

I want to get back to the photographs as I go on talking to this lawyer, or rather listening to him. Yet I hardly dare to speak because even to give my address can bring me to tears in this conversation. These awful telephone calls my days are full of now. Listening to him I grow to dislike him, to find the snob behind the lawyer, the distant and disapproving man of money who was her neighbor slipping in front of the correct man of law. And at the same time, perhaps even because of this, I want desperately to say to him—you were a friend of my aunt, weren't you? Thank God that she had friends—Can I say to you how grateful I am she had friends and was not alone in that long illness? If you were her friend you take on a magic in my eyes, like hers.

I shift from one tired leg to the other and shove the debris away from the phone as I stand in the half-finished studio with its chaos of drawings heaped crazily against a wall to be installed when the rack is built for them—confusion on me now—in a pair of army boots and a sweatshirt covered with paint explaining that I live in New York, explaining to that familiar Wayzeta smugness which is convinced it knows how awful New York is and yet has no idea in the world. Spelling my address, the Bowery. Even avoiding my usual, "The Bowery, as in Bowery bum; I'm sure you've heard of it," I begin to hear the disapprobation in his voice. Did she ever mention that rat of a niece, I wonder? But of course the real punishment is never to be mentioned again, ever. Does he know of the prodigal?

He does soon enough, when I stumble, trying to be agreeable: "Sally told me Aunt Dorothy's house was to go to the Guthrie Theater and I think that's a wonderful idea, inspired." "The Guthrie and five other organizations." I ask myself if it won't be a little crowded at that rate: "Sally had said that the Guthrie would use it for visiting directors and the symphony and chamber orchestra for its conductors. It's so good to think of that beautiful serene house going on undisturbed, just as it was, and serving as a home for art and artists. I'm so glad it will stay that way, the way she made it." "Oh no, you're quite mistaken. No, not at all; by no means. It's to be sold. And the proceeds, together with other properties, stocks, and investments, to go to six institutions." "Oh, I'm sorry. What a pity. I had it all wrong; Sally must have misunderstood." "Such a thing would be out of the question. No, no; the house is to be sold. Six months from now. After the personal effects are all assigned."

I am devastated but somehow coerced into sounding cordial, even as I persist in my folly. "That saddens me; I had imagined it going on—remaining as it was—that had made me very happy." "Heavens no, that couldn't be. Of course not." "The upkeep, perhaps, I hadn't thought of that. . . ." Institutions and their finances; of course they'd want cash. "Zoning, for one thing," Mr. Ransom says severely.

I think of that road, her road, "the Gold Coast" a real estate agent once called it when I had stopped at an office for directions, having lost my way to a visit a few years ago. It was so long since I'd been there and already I was late. Frantic for help I stopped at an office by the side of the road and gave the woman the address—"Oh, that's on the other side, that's the Gold Coast." For a moment I was stung; the expression so venal, so plutocratic. But it was reality to this woman—that was the Gold Coast, that stretch of road, probably the highest caste level of real property within her worldview. "Zoning would never permit the house to be used in that way," Ransom is emphatic. Why the hell not—I want to bark at him—are artists, theatrical and musical directors, are they some danger? Seeing the road again, remembering he lives just down that road, a near neighbor.

Farewell the covert hope of buttering up a Guthrie person, making a connection with the chamber orchestra on a visit home, someone who would know someone. Maybe I could just ask and they'd let me—somehow, someday I would walk into those rooms again and they would still be there, her shrine. Without her, but their mere continued existence over time would be enough, victory and memorial enough. I could see it again, now when I know I will never see her. The rooms would be there: the gray, the light gray walls, the carpets, the pictures.

Of course not the Han horse; that was slated for the Metropolitan since I was a child. But now he is telling me that the horse, or what he refers to as art objects and artifacts, the collection of works of art—which are all cataloged and have been actually in the purview of the Minneapolis Institute of Fine Arts for years it seems, while she retained a life interest or something—it is hard to follow—but the Han horse will be packed off there. Horse that I loved and never broke no matter what my other sins, horse that I could greet every time I entered its room, either the living room where it stood fine and dark gray upon the mantel at Virginia Avenue or later on the mantle at Wayzeta. I could talk to it when I was alone, stroking it ever so carefully, knowing that you could do anything in the world but break it; it was that fine, that old, that rare, that beloved to her. And it stood proudly and eternally scratching its ear with its right rear foot all through childhood and adolescence, saluted as I entered the room an adult already in college and her friend and confidante, her favorite niece. The horse enabled me, ennobled me; tenuous as my position usually was, the presence of this magic animal, the force of it as a masterpiece, powerful, declared, self-evident, gave me stature, incorporated me into a charmed life. He was, I realize now, my intercessor: I approached my aunt and her spirit through this totem, using its mane to lean upon, a channel. First contact the horse and then you are centered, fortified—not all that much, but some—so that you can face her, those eyes. And the horse often made me victorious those years, beloved, the chosen one, the scholar, the young woman coming into her own, carefree, confident, easy.

Such a swagger that I hardly ever bothered to notice the signatures on paintings. "Is this really a Dufy?" I asked once in my senior year at the university, finally impressed by art history class. "Of course; what do you expect? And it's not really that good a one either, but I've always liked it—racetracks are fun. Have you ever been to one?" And I hadn't, just the ones at the state fair, the trotters. "You should go sometime." And we left it at that, though such remarks were often a prelude to invitation. The flirt in her, the fairy godmother, the *bon vivant*. I shudder for the horse and the pictures all going in Mr. Ransom's six-month plan, going—the whole damn thing. Another shudder builds and wracks me again, for there will be no more invitations. Ever. Nor has Mr. Ransom invited me to the non-funeral: I am to be represented by my nephew. Mr. Ransom has gotten ahead of himself in outlining his plans, however, and in fact, I needn't even have called him because he is actually sending me a letter next week.

Meanwhile he is pleased to tell me that I am the beneficiary of a bequest. Odd word out of a book. Good Lord, he must mean that she left me something in her will. Her books? All my life I hoped for that. For a split second, elation. To be remembered, even forgiven? No—it might be money. Not money. Oh God no, not money. I didn't want money, I wanted her heart—I begin to say to him and stop. I teeter and am dizzy and afraid: the latter sentiment is more improper than the former. And the bequest remains like a present wrapped with a ribbon—ah, the ribbons of those Christmas presents in childhood—my teeth grit; hold on, as the hurt of recall sweeps over. Lost. Magic they were, wide wonderful colors: orange ribbons with silver paper, plum-colored ribbons, light green, emerald—she had raided Uncle Walter's Northstar Blanket Company—who but a blanket maker would have such ribbon?

So the bequest remains like a present wrapped with a ribbon until Mr. Ransom's letter is dispatched. For he begins now to realize how much long distance has been consumed with my ignorant misconception about the house, my innocent but premature request for a photograph. He is now about to dismiss me. But I have prepared my courage. And I have another question. Even a sneaking kind of covetousness—it wouldn't pry into a bequest, but I must swallow now that the house is to be sold and the furniture taken away—what will become of the books? Let the Chippendale fall where it may: friends and family are supposed to nominate things they like—I do not quite understand how it works; perhaps at the gathering it might be clearer but I am to stay away—never mind it. Her sisters and those friends who know good furniture are the ones entitled to all that, but there are the books. In fact there is a library it used to be my ambition to inherit one day—wasn't I the writer and the scholar in the family? But even without a reconciliation, it slowly became clear to me years ago that A.D.'s library might even be too big and too valuable for me to own or house. There are moments I think I could do it. But her library is a large room, floor to ceiling books, and the books are rare and precious. What will become of them, I ask out of what I try hard to make sound like polite concern; was there a plan for her books?

"She had them cataloged a few years ago and they were doing another catalog of how she would dispose of them. Perhaps to an institution." I hold my breath. "But every time I asked her in the last couple of years, she'd say—'Oh, don't bother me with that; I haven't gotten around to it.' " And for a moment I am convinced that indeed he was her friend; it is her tone of voice: "Don't bother me with that." Even "Damn it, don't bother me with that." The independent old woman, the beauty still having her way, the lady who can afford to cuss and will not be bullied. By tedious homework in an illness. For those were the years of the mysterious illness she would never talk about. So that we never knew. He did, so he simply let her be. "The result is that a lot of this is rather up in the air." "I see." "But when I write you next time I'll describe all this to you." "Of course; thank you for your time. And forgive me for having misunderstood about Aunt Dorothy's house; it's just that I am an artist and a writer myself so it seemed a lovely idea for the house to be a place where artists could come." He's testy: "As I said, the proceeds of its sale will be donated to the Guthrie, the symphony, and the chamber orchestra and the rest of her property will be divided among these and other institutions." "Yes, yes."

"You'll be hearing from me; thanks for calling." "Yes, sir."

I say it before I realize what I have said. I have called him "sir" as if I were still a St. Paul girl, a college kid dropping the smart aleck when confronted with authority. Addressing the rich and powerful, the elder, the established, the member of a prestigious firm. And my high aunt's own neighbor: If you are cheeky, word will get back to her. I am a grown woman alone in a studio on the Bowery and I have actually called this man sir. Spontaneously, a Pavlovian response to power, money, authority, respectability. Only because it's from home. Responding to St. Paul upbringing. I once heard that there is a novel about St. Paul entitled *Respectability*. Nothing could be more appropriate. There is a gentle decorum—both the vice of the place and the source of its charm. And Ransom has failed to invite me to my aunt's own memorial, informed me instead that I am to be represented by a nephew. Snubbed, excluded. When he began explaining the arrangements I held my breath—will he expect me to come: can I afford it somehow, will I have to commit myself this moment? All those bucks to have scrambled eggs—with the upper crust of Minneapolis? Really. But if it were for her sake: she had wanted these people to come together on her behalf. Fine. They are her cronies. But what if she had wanted me there, or left it open so that I could come, the prodigal last in the door? A figure alone in the library remembering her, my hand remembering her on the backs of chairs, my ears remembering her voice, certain conversations, expressions. The scent of her, the sound of a skirt, a scarf, the sight of a sweater thrown over a chair. But it seems I am not welcome. And would look foolish anyway. They will drink and have brunch and visit with each other, a crowd. I would look shabby, morose, out of place.

Instead, let me have a moment with the place to myself, I want to say. To be alone there and invoke her. Before they empty and sell it and it vanishes and the last vestiges of her take flight. So I hung fire while his voice skipped on to my being "represented." It sounded so snotty. As he searched out Steven's name I helped him abruptly, "my nephew." As if that were the last rag of respectability a family of women could conjure up, a young male. And an attorney at that. I dearly love this boy but I resent being represented by someone who is nearly a stranger to her when the aunt I loved so passionately, foolishly, unwisely but never well enough is dead in her great house. All my hopes of reconciliation and reunion a heap of ashes.

A bequest, I say to the board I am attaching to the wall, building the rack for my drawings and framed pictures. All the while on another sort of rack these days, but still dutifully consumed with this tedious yet somehow life-giving project. So utterly unimportant in the face of sorrow, so essential in saving me from it. For I knew the moment I heard the word, heard Mother say she was dead, Aunt Dorothy's dead, that my life would be changed irreparably. It had happened and I hadn't gotten there in time. A bequest: why didn't you just tell him you didn't want it? Money, it was always money between us. Between all of us. Between Mother and the three of us kids, poor after my father left, poor in the face of A.D.'s riches; it was impossible not to compare. Impossible not to be infatuated with her money. It was part of her charm. Not until I was grown did it ever begin to stop being a consideration. After Oxford, where her money had bought me the treasure of my education. And I had betrayed her and therefore knew that money was never going to be between us again—I was not only grown up and therefore entitled to no more—I was a thief and couldn't accept it. Not that I didn't make a touch: just home from Oxford and full of an idea to start an art gallery, in love with the fine arts but without talent or enough imagination to try my hand. She squelched the idea in a phrase. I sat up and understood that all that was over—the being poor and sitting there and waiting to see if someone would give you something.

We had a whole childhood of greed for her presents and she was generous to profusion. Yet it was not only the presents we wanted; it was her love and attention, which the presents represented. But they were too much intertwined. The presents became her love; if your sister got one and you didn't she was loved and you weren't. The preference obsessed us when we were small and continued dividing and humiliating us as we grew older. But that day I thought I had beat it. That visit after Oxford. I sat by while she patiently explained what it cost her to keep this house and why, by the time she died, she would have spent all her money. I sat back in my cushions and looked her in the eye. That's good. That's great, I thought—it will all be for you, no one else. It's yours and you'll use it all up. Perfect. So there will be no question of inheritance or what you leave when you die. I looked at her and was freed. There is just you—alive. And that was all I wanted. That cleared the air forever for me. I would know her all my life now, two adults, two friends. It would just be her and me—never the money, never anymore. It was out of the picture and all that was sinister with it. That perfect visit after Oxford.

Fresh from my triumph, my First Class Honours degree. Which did please her. "Your aged aunt rejoices in your honors," said her arch little telegram. I'd called Mother from England with the news, but I had telegrammed my aunt, avoiding the phone. Jaycee there in the apartment below while I went upstairs to borrow the landlord's telephone in an odd little parlor full of pornographic Dutch prints which made transatlantic calls a still more anxious procedure.

She was not my aged aunt then but a very beautiful fifty, recently widowed by Uncle Walter's death. And when I came into her house for the long visit we were to have now that I was made and had finished school, I carried Jaycee on my back. And the lie. Jaycee would be spending the time in Provincetown with an old love about to become a new one again. But I had no suspicion of that and brought my very married lesbian fidelity with me to my aunt. The one wrong moment to be committed elsewhere. For I was twenty-four now. If I still wasn't fair game, I was an adult at last and I would gladly have been anything she wanted. My magnificent aunt. A.D.—the very initials of my infatuation as long as I could remember what being in love felt like. Perhaps some nineteen years, for I first understood it when I was five. And now I am with her. But for Jaycee. What timing: if my aunt would ever have been more than a friend, I could now only be a friend. And hardly that. Full of another complicity, watching everything I said.

"Why do you say 'we' all the time?" she would ask. "Well, I mean my friends there, there were a bunch of us, mostly Americans who hung out together. Have you heard of an anthropologist named Herksowitz?" "Not that I recollect." "He's very famous; his daughter was in my college. And Dianne Vreuls; she was a Marshall scholar." "Really?" "Amazing girl. The two of us were up for honors in English together but she had more promise, the tutors thought. Then the day of the Schools, the big exams, Dianne fell down the staircase of her boarding-house." "What a pity." "And ended up in a special ward they keep open for Oxford students during the Schools Examinations. "Hmnnn." "But the thing is—they let her write two of the nine papers; it was all she was up to, but you know what—she won Second Class Honours on the strength of just those two essays. Can you believe it?" "She seems remarkable. But you didn't do that badly yourself."

Moments of modesty were fairly uncommon that summer. Even while still at Oxford I would come out of the book I was reading, Virginia Woolf or D. H. Lawrence, the kind of book you could never read while preparing for Schools, since for the Schools Examination in my day literary history stopped at 1830 (an archaism that shocked my aunt considerably) and I would look up from the page and remember, like a lightning bolt—I had a First. I had seen my name printed on the great sheets of fine white paper framed on the college doors, printed with wonderful speed by the Oxford Press itself; you could already see them by eight in the evening three days after the close of Schools. Jaycee and I wound our way down the High Street in the dusk on bicycles, afraid to look. And then by God it was there. Not in the Thirds—I went through them first. Surely the Seconds then: there were times, most times I expect, when my favorite tutor thought I was a Second. Timid and Yankee and unsure, I agreed. Though my heart yearned for a First. Dianne's boyfriend had gotten one last year. He was nearly a figure of romance by now, already a reader of Queens; he might make tutor someday even if he was an American. There was actually a full professor of law at Balliol who was an American. The only one of course, but a precedent. Going through the Seconds, Jaycee already reading ahead and above me—"There you are—you're a First." The crowd around me look up, people smile and congratulate. I am past even being embarrassed. Many of these shaking my hand will have lesser ranks themselves. From that day on I walked on air. Five, twelve, twenty times a day I would come out of thought or a task, wash a cup and realize all over again—

a First; I was an Oxford First. Like being a millionaire. Infinitely better; it was an honor.

If I stayed in England my career would be assured—if I were English. In fact my *viva voce* committee, reconvening in the same bar where I was having lunch next to the Schools building after my oral exam, cast a kindly collective glance and then began to ask me if I had plans for next year. I had already accepted a nondescript job teaching in North Carolina. Perhaps I hadn't dared to hope enough, hadn't held out free long enough for the university call, here in Mecca itself. But I was eager to see America again, homesick. Jaycee too; Oxford had not been a degree for her, only some occasional study with a tutor and time to write inconclusive stories—she was ready for home, had been writing to her friends a great deal. It's true it might have gone differently if I had been alone there. Which is what the family wanted, for me to make friends, contacts, see the world on my own. And I hadn't. I had been a hermit living in an illicit relationship which had to be kept secret from my college and my tutors. Even my favorite tutor, Miss Elliott, must have suspected, deplored or condoned—all was silence. Nor were we the only ones, of course. But those were the days of silence. Outlawed and living in defense of such a connection, one waived all right to criticize it. As a hermit then, I studied. Studied my way to a First.

And came home proud with the prize under my arm. When I enter my aunt's door after a few weeks at Mother's I bring the phony British accent my mother so disapproved of, and my intolerable scholastic pretensions. But a trophy too. That nearly outweighs my deceit. Or it should; I am hoping that the effort and wonder it represents will make up for Jaycee and the crime, that the miraculous stroke of wild fortune which a First is to an Oxonian will counterbalance the wrong she knows not of.

I forgot: I hadn't reckoned with an Irish lady. The Brit accent got lost very soon; my aunt has her own very high way of speaking and references to trollies and lorries, expressions like bloody this and that are stifled right off. For the rest, my own Middlewestern hardly begins to approach her upper Irish American—and as to literary knowledge, my much-touted scholarship is given a very severe testing indeed. Since the then-prescribed Oxford reading stopped in 1830 with the death of the last Romantic poets Keats and Shelley (we didn't count Coleridge or Wordsworth in their later years, which were regarded either as dotage or Early Victorian), she saw to it that no allusions were pitched at me which preceded that year. For two weeks I must answer stupidly that I haven't read and don't know the whole range of Victorian, Edwardian, Georgian, modern, and contemporary writing. And since Oxford specializes in certain set texts chosen for their weightiness, there is a great deal of Lewis Carroll, as well as all the wits and satirists from the turn of the century, fired my way. And all the Irish writers. Which to her horror she discovers I know nothing about. Have forgotten what she has taught me and learned nothing new at all; haven't even been reading them. All this so-called education and the little prig knows nothing important, I hear in her sigh, as I try to get a word in on Spencer or Milton, or embroider some reference to Chaucer.

Such a young dog fresh from school. I tremble to remember how I insisted upon reading aloud from *The Faerie Queene,* Spenser one of my favorite poets at the time. For his descriptive powers, the visual character of his landscapes—which were actually landscapes in Ireland. And because I owned a magnificent set of Spenser in cherry calf bought in New York while passing through on the way to England. The first twenty-five dollars of my aunt's money, since all my tickets were bought in St. Paul. Steamship and rail with a sleeping room: I proceeded across the American continent like a young Isabelle Archer. But the first moment I could drop some live cash on my own was that twenty-five dollars for a five-volume set of Spenser. And at Oxford I fancied myself a collector of leather books, my way to emulate and imitate the great lady.

Alas, also to irritate. For I had no idea I was pedantic, merely thought I was learned, had been sent out like a scout into the very den of learning, ventured even among the English themselves and had run home with their prize in my sack. "Edmund Spenser was for a time secretary to Lord Grey, the lord lieutenant of Ireland—did you know that?" she asks me, her eyes dangerous. "Sure. . . ." "Do you remember what he said about the Irish?" "Yes, from his letters: that they were barbarians and that the only answer to the Irish Problem—he call it that—was the annihilation of the native population." "Have you thought about that?" "Yes. He loved the landscape and hated the people. It's hard to imagine how a man with such opinions could write such beautiful poetry." "For Elizabeth," she says ironically. "Yeah." I am a little bit out of my depth. After all, I was the one who railed against Spenser while I was at Oxford, but it seems I have not absorbed the full gravity of these things. "Have you read Campion?" "They didn't teach him but I read him on my own, yes." I am nearly at the point of, "Yes, ma'am," which is still an expression in use here at home but not appropriate to literary conversations coming from someone nearly twenty-five. "Do you know how Elizabeth murdered Campion?" "I think he was beheaded or something." "He was drawn and quartered. Have you ever read a description of that procedure?" "I did once." "You might look it over again."

"Leave your drink here. William will give us something else at dinner." There's a lot of drinking this visit, but I'm grown up. Also we stay up late. I would like to be talking literature but she wants to talk about other things. People. Uncle Walter. What it's been like since he died. I see her there, lonely beyond limit, beyond her reserve, beyond that decorum the Milletts have despite their sharp tempers and their gaiety—it is naked, awesome, this loneliness in an adult. Why is it shown to me when I still feel a child before it, inept, stupid, with nothing to say? Mumbling dumb things like, "I'm awfully sorry, Aunt Dorothy."

"I have not listened to music since he died. Would you even believe that? It's a year and a half. Without music."

But you listened to music all your life, I was about to say. Classical music of course; there was no other sort for her. "I hear other kinds of music now, popular or something like that. I've been watching baseball lately." "You're kidding." Glossing right over what she has told me about the death of this man, her husband for only a few years but a great love, and a very fine musician whose family interest in a company that makes the best blankets in the world left him a lifetime to study the piano in Vienna or the far west and even here. And a good deal of time to drink as well. When she married Walter he was a reformed alcoholic with his own sparkling apple juice at Christmas and other champagne times, a rock of gentleness and exquisite manners. He even wore pumps to the symphony, which seemed the ultimate gentlemanly gesture in my experience. After I left for Oxford there were rumors he was drinking again. Then he fell, drunk. The bathroom. I know no more about it. If you ask her how Uncle Walter died you are told he was abusing himself. This sounds like masturbation to me: there might be an ironic agreement if you dared to say something like that, but of course you wouldn't dare. So you just listen and go on listening as it gets later and darker and you have had so much scotch your very unpracticed mind cannot figure it out. I have thought about poems until now, not people; I am a library card, quite ignorant of life. At Oxford there was just enough interest in booze to buy a quart of it and drink the entire bottle in one evening once a month while reading one's favorite poems aloud in an eagerness growing with the evening and the tumblers to exhibit an even better Andrew Marvell, a Donne that the others didn't know, or to defend an old favorite like Shelley or some lyric they said was corny—everyone shouting by the end. And then it was over: you didn't touch hard liquor for another thirty days. But here it is night after night and of course I feel obligated to keep up. It's a Millett thing to drink, to drink well, whatever my mother may say about my father.

But not to hear classical music for all this time. When it was her life. When she has studied in Europe, going with Louis to Italy and France and taking lessons to understand even its design, studying composition and theory, honing a discernment over the years into connoisseurship and an attendance at the symphony nearly religious. And I with her in the next seat, those two seats second row first balcony—she had the hall figured out. I was her companion, her date. An eight-year-old at ballets and easy things, a ten-year-old at the subscription concerts, my pocket full of sunflower seeds imbibed surreptitiously, a little pile of shells under the seat when the evening was over—my dread lest she discover that. They helped me not to fidget, because I was bored for long stretches, overtired by sitting still. Perfectly, utterly still—she demanded that, this teacher of concentration and concert going, and only my rapturous love of being with her made me willing to forego the delights of Friday night basketball games in high school and other often so tempting foolishness to be there: her escort, her worshipper.

But it was not always my seat. Only between husbands. Between Louis and Walter. A few other gentlemen intervened but they were so insubstantial I could still go along, grateful for their kindness and generosity, a bit smug that they had not yet threatened my tenure. And then Walter. But by his time I had another way to get into the symphony—I was a university usher and could see her at intermissions. Walter as well. My friend Wash—Janey Washburn—was an usher too and we pooled our intermission guests since they buy drinks for college girls in long-sleeved white blouses and floor-length black skirts who look very orphaned and austere and prefer to save their allowance for books or clothes but really wouldn't mind a drink now that you come to mention it.

The evening of the day that Janey's Uncle Archie committed suicide and she had left his wife's side and the care of his children for a few hours to do her usher's duty, Uncle Walter, having no idea that this girl is Archie's niece, mentioned to another grandee of the town, a buck in a tuxedo, that Archie Ingersoll did himself in today . . . hotel room in St. Paul, gun in the mouth. "Would you believe it—all for a muff?" There is stunned silence; the remark was said a bit apart and not intended to be heard. I was trying to figure out what a muff is. Sounds naughty. A female, pubic hair. I thought Archie was bankrupt. Had he gone and got himself into a love affair too? And Helen in the apartment where I'm going to drop Wash off afterwards. Janey just looks at Walter through her tears and what remains of her pride. And then I think Uncle Walter's inadvertent folly was surprised into sudden understanding and hushed: he apologized and disappeared.

Walter, wasn't he the kind one after all in the family council, the one who said—it's her life; if she wants to be that, so be it. Meaning what the others scarcely ever brought themselves to say: a lesbian, a pervert, and so forth. He even said it to me once, to my face, at the doorway of a room, setting himself apart from the others, astonishing me. But I scarcely understood, a bit too confused and frightened to take it in, though grateful that it would occur to someone in that tribe to imagine my fate was my own individual choice and property. Of course to them it was not. Or if it ever was, surely it was not so in a minor: that I was twenty-one didn't change that. I was still about to take a big step and go abroad to school and it was just at such moments that children have to be watched; she's young enough so that she could be redirected, broken of this vicious habit. For the woman is a habit, an addiction for her. Her mother says she is off with her all the time, turns pale when the phone rings. It's a crush. And of course these things happen. But she's young still and the woman is older, has her in her clutches.

It is always the other one's fault. But Walter looked me in the eye and bid me have my fault. If he were not a mere uncle—wonderful as my uncles are—they are still only in-laws and in-laws do not run a family of women. Harry and my father do not seem to have been present on this occasion. It wouldn't matter if they were. The women decide such things. The Milletts are a family where women rule. A rule generally benevolent, the men a type of willing and gallant escort, protectors once the road has been assigned. Lovers and brothers but not fathers or rulers. They are color and pleasure, joy and company, like knights, and with that estate's chivalry and courtesy, defenders but not deciders. If this were up to Walter to decide, man of the world that he is, he might just as well accept it; what does it matter to him if his niece, Dorothy's niece after all, is a little queer? She's nice enough; he only sees her a few times a year, Christmas, things like that; it's very jolly. This or any other occasion would be as jolly if she slept with a woman when she got home—hell. One sees him shrug under the formal gray coat, a stroller. A handsome man with bright twinkling eyes and a gray beard closely shaven, curly hair still mostly black, and inevitably a Dunhill cigarette holder. I affected one for years in emulation of his.

But of course I am not Walter's niece but Dorothy's and she will settle my case with her sisters. Odd that she should even need that corroboration, so resolute she has always been, the youngest in the family, the baby who grew up to conquer them all with her will, the power of her money, the splendor of her life, their Gloriana. And so they came and sat in deliberation over me and decided upon an ultimatum. I went for the bait and agreed to the terms. I could only go to Oxford through Aunt Dorothy's generosity if I agreed never to see this woman from the moment I left town. They were generous in overlooking the fact that I had moved out of Mother's house and was actually living with Jaycee in an apartment over by the university. When the summer was up, it would be over and I'd be off. And I lied. And cheated. Before she followed me to England Jaycee stayed on an extra month or so in Minnesota for some reason or another of her own, but also probably to throw them off the scent. We did not go together. Instead I took a room, studied my Anglo-Saxon, pined, hated it, tried harder. And sent and received three little blue air letters every day until the day I found and rented a flat for the two of us at Eleven Stanley Road.

Now fresh from that life, from parting with Jaycee at her friend's in New Jersey, I have come by train, even my godfather Louis Hill's grandfather James J. Hill's train, the Empire Builder, with its Vistadome to show me again the beauties of the world west of Chicago: a real Indian paddling a canoe alone on a Wisconsin lake at nightfall, the pines and spruce, lake upon lake of this still pure and wonderful place where I was born and have come home to now. How clear it is here. Clearer than anywhere, fresher than Europe. How the colors nearly echo with clarity on my aunt's lake in the mornings. She is up at what seems to be the crack of dawn; I am surprised by my first hangovers, still more surprised that she has none. Has all this energy, is putting my youth to shame. And in the evenings she is the last to acknowledge fatigue or intoxication as we go through more and more scotch. While I listen to her outpourings, for from her they are outpourings.

After a lifetime of discretion, responsible, even gifted

teaching, information and advice, aunt-like generosity, indulgent playfulness, cautious worldly wisdom. And I am no help: unable to respond to her grief over Walter, I can only offer an ear. For a year she has lived with suicide. I shiver. But am also excited by the rebellious, scandalous novelty of such an idea, unheard of except in history or novels. She cannot mean it. She does indeed. And I shift in my chair. For a few months she's even been seeing a shrink. Good God, a shrink—she doesn't mean it; she has taught me to detest and despise them. Only a terrible crisis would bring her to confide in such a person. She says he's got her past the worst of the desire to die. I relax. But how sad for her to be going to a shrink. If there were anyone in the world who would make fun of the whole racket. It becomes serious to me, also unreal. A.D. in the hands of a shrink: the goddess of wisdom trafficking with a quack. You do not leave the church and abjure confession to tell your troubles to a paid listener—submit your very soul to a charlatan without even spiritual pretensions. I am too young to deal with it; especially I am too young to deal with emotion in one like herself who has always been so conclusively the adult to me, one beyond needing help. Beyond needing anything. And for my own selfish reasons I like it that she is alone now. Much as I like Walter he was nothing in comparison to how I love her and she is now free, by herself, available in a certain way.

But that is the trouble. I am not. I am Jaycee's lover spending a deceptive fortnight with my patron aunt who sent me to a great university from where I am now *en route* to my first teaching post. Where I will still live with Jaycee; maybe her friend will come along or visit us down there for a while, so I've been told. In what capacity I now hardly understand but will find to be in time a little hell. But here now, in heaven, with my beloved aunt, now no longer even married, I am a stick. Unable to do anything but listen self-consciously, holding on to my child self while the very adult self I was supposed to exhibit at last—were we not to be two grown women together—finds itself in bad faith and about to make a false step at every turn. Drinking till the wee hours. As if merely holding on to my glass and not falling over when I stand or collapsing into sleep in my chair were an achievement worthy of being called companionship.

How otherwise would it have been if there were not the serpent of Jaycee and the lie between us: how then would you have swept your lady away with kindness, sympathy, and understanding? Hard to say. But I used to linger over our good nights—for years and in the unhappiness that was to come in the decades beyond, I would remember suddenly and always with astonishment how she would come into my room as I was undressing, often waiting until the modest pajamas were actually on, sometimes not—she is an aunt, family—she who was never familiar, who would always have understood the delicacy or the shame of a child's arrangement, even her possible humiliation in torn underclothes, a gray slip or an old one, or just the fervent wish not to be caught off guard by your own idol—but she came. As if she could not leave me alone, as if she could not stop talking to me, as if she could not finish a story, as if some detail about breakfast was not a thing I already knew. And I started back, as if my guilty secret was about to fall from me, as if the breath of Jaycee were not just about to hurl itself between us, reveal all and take her from me: a finger pointed to the door forever like a Victorian father expelling a pregnant daughter.

But the other horn of the dilemma—were it peacetime, were there no Jaycee—is that at this moment if I was ever to fall upon her neck, my own aunt, and declare my passion—this was it. So watch yourself. And the glory and the terror is that I almost knew that if I were to do it I would succeed. Then, but never again. And my own notion of honor forbade it, kept its bond with a woman who rolled in the hay halfway across the country that night with someone else and never condescended to tell me till months later. For that folly I stood away from the door, took a few steps backwards toward the dresser as A.D. came into the room, this wonderful and beautiful woman who was my own aunt, my first love, adored and even desired at that moment when at last I was twenty-four and could have made my suit or merely received hers. I who was never distant, who was always adoring and waiting, always open with brown worshipping eyes—was now for the first time a little distant. And she who was always reserved and correct and imposing, dealing even with children as from a height despite her kindness, the romp and the friendliness and the occasional and therefore spicier slang—she was now forward, disarmed, helpless, lonely, in need.

When she left I would sweat in the August night with fear. At what I had nearly done, nearly said. Nearly committed myself to, I who was committed already and if she knew—her anger would know no bounds; for the rest of her life she would never forgive me. And she didn't. Once she did know she never forgave. But she didn't know yet. So it would also have been to take advantage of her, to be unfair in the worst way were I to meet her advances, for all that I had wanted them, all the years I had wanted them, all the years I had waited and dreamed of them. And then belong to another instead. I did not even question Jaycee or my attachment—I had made it, it was done; you stick by what you choose; it is an obligation the most basic in the world. Maybe someday if I were free again, my aunt . . . what is there to think? Only that you missed everything. Or what you wanted most. Had what you thought you wanted instead. Never guessing the highest were possible to reach. And under it all, the dragging consideration that my very presence here is a lie. Oxford was a lie, the First. Every golden moment here is built over a misconception. Preposterous and terrifying. The dinner last night, the lake tomorrow morning.

Seeing her at breakfast—she has been up for hours, looks fresh and lovely, young, so appealingly young in a blue shirtwaist. Later by the lake or puttering with flowers she will have shorts. The freckles on her legs, the loafers on her barc feet, I devour and try to look normal. As if I have no hangover and am not still sleepy, my head and throat rife with the stink of scotch. She dresses for me: I can hardly believe it, that the day is a parade of clothes, the kind of clothes someone my age would like. Oxford cloth shirts of the loveliest colors or stripes, chambray, chic jeans, a flannel shirt for the lawn before dinner, slacks of marvelous wool. And perfumes, perfumes smelled and described, tried and played with in her dressing room. A room full of photographs looking down on us, Dorothy in her youth and glory, and here's Harriet, here's La Rue, here's Lucy, here's Jamie, your father.

Once when I was only twelve and staying with her on Virginia Avenue, a house I remember with veneration even as I grow to love this house in Wayzeta—but that was the house of all houses, the ducal mansion—every corner of it I know and remember still though it has been an old-age home for decades now and has died, if a house can stay in one piece and still die—as she came down the great staircase there, I was in a corner of the living room doing a crossword puzzle in a raw silk overstuffed chair leaning on the mahogany card table's green baize top. "What are you doing; you're as still as a mouse?" She came around behind my chair. "Ah, a crossword—can you do it?" "It's hard to know all this stuff: Egyptian word for measurement, five-letter ancient Roman thing and the other. Some I can do, not all of it." "They're tricks: they've got about twenty-five of that Egyptian this and that—they always turn up and you get them by heart. The rest of it you work out with a little ingenuity."

Words are tremendously important. Words were passionately important with the Milletts. Also with Mother who taught us vocabulary as a kind of family game while we housecleaned—words like "perspicacity" were used as a kind of coin, part joke, part ritual, a relish to life. One excelled at words; they were free, they were proof of intelligence, thought, consciousness. So I did not wish to appear stupid over a crossword puzzle or any game of the mind. If I grew timid I was poor at anything, especially sports; against Sally's big-sister, better-player dominance I could even be a bad loser: it was about this time in life that Sally forbade me to try to learn golf with her and sent me home from my second lesson in ignominy. But I am alone with My Aunt this evening and I ask her about crosswords: "Do they really prove you're smart?" "Of course not. Louis could do them like a whiz." Uncle Louis, that was. In the years since their divorce she has never really mentioned him to me. Aside from "Your Uncle Louie went with us to Greece; do you remember him? There he is on the left page." Or "That was when we lived in England and Louie was going to the London School of Economics; you wouldn't believe how the English go on drying their clothes in the living room in that dreadful damp and compound it with all the steam from those woolen things they wear." Or "Of course I've been to Ireland, dear child; Louie and I used to hunt there every year."

Now here is a remark about Louie that she might say to an adult. It is rare that she makes this sort of statement: in fact she is more careful about what she says to us than anyone else we know. Which is less interesting, of course. But it also makes it easier, since if you know more than you should the business of being respectful gets harder and playing dumb the way you're supposed to becomes kind of like lying, which I hate. I could stop her by stretching in my chair maybe, being a kid and drawing attention to that. But she doesn't want me to because now she is really serious. "You know, Kate, Louie was stupid really. Yes. By the end that man bored me to death." "But you can't be an idiot and go to school over there, can you?" "Sure you can. Listen, Louie was so dull he actually underlined everything in his textbooks." I do not yet underline textbooks but I will in years to come and that remark already makes me uneasy. Yet I see her there in England, his consort, her annoyance with the fellow lodgers and their steaming stockings, probably reflecting already on how boring it is to be married to someone who goes to school when you do not, watching him do lessons, aware you could do circles around him. Yet it still seems unkind, even unfair. I already know Louie was unfaithful to her and ran off and married his secretary but I dislike having to assume that he was stupid at school on the strength of that. I have discovered a contempt that could have thrown the man away. And fear it. I look at her in the dusk of the room with round inquiring brown eyes. When you can get a grown-up to look back at you from such a look you sometimes make real progress with them. Because then they have to be honest. Although most of them discover they have to make a phone call right this minute or something.

But the phone doesn't ring. "Kate—I'm going to tell you something I never told anyone before. Your father was the most wonderful man I ever knew." My father is alive and well; he lives with my mother. I wonder what she means. "I would rather have gone to a dance with him than any man I ever met—I still would." Her voice is intensified: she is very moved, near tears. I am twelve but I know something she only seems to be discovering: that she should have married my father. Her brother. "He was more a man than Louie Hill would ever be. Or any of them. Your father." And she takes my hand, her arm coming around my shoulder but still looking me in the eye or as near as she can 'cause I guess she's crying—I am too, I guess, though I don't know why. It's all so complicated. "Your father was fun, the most fun—do you understand—the most fun—there ever was."

And of course I understand what she means. Fun is everything; it's beauty and grace and humor and magic. Even when Aunt Dorothy is mean to us or mad at us or forgets us or ignores us, she is more fun than anyone else except Daddy. In fact she is actually more fun and interesting because we see her less than we see him. Daddy and Aunt Dorothy, yup, I think, holding her hand while I hear her clear her throat a little as if maybe this is going too far, what she said. But it makes perfect sense. So what if they are brother and sister; they are the man and the woman. So what if they are sister and brother; maybe things work out that way sometimes. I have never heard of the incest taboo, merely seen it in operation. And she goes on, tapering off a bit, explaining a bit how when they were at the university, she and Harriet and Lucy, her sisters—then it was Jim they would invite to their dances. And he'd squire them all. The highway man, the student engineer out of his dusty boots and into his best whites. Or the one dark suit. He was sending his sisters, the lot of them, through college while earning his own engineering license out in the mud and snow or heat of the road. Capped off with one of the few professional examinations you can still sit for without first qualifying for it by holding a degree. He had reason to envy them. Instead he was generous as later she would bc.

Now I have graduated and entered the family as an adult, looking at the picture her hand holds out to me here now in the dressing room at Wayzeta, my handsome father in yet another relaxed and quizzical pose, that look of half-conscious detachment he always has in photos. In his engagement picture he resembles a ghost. Also a very light mulatto under his curly black-Irish hair, the fine gray eyes. In that picture, perhaps it was fright. Yet he never looks frightened while posing by a bridge or a cloverleaf or a stretch of highway he has caused to come into being, arms crossed, godlike in his impeccable whites. But for all his good looks you know he is fun, more fun than the devil in his twinkling eyes, a boon companion. Loved by his men, a delight to work with, his laughter in company: a great dancer, warm, the center of things. Would that I had him more. Seeing that face today home from Oxford is an old hurt. That he left us. Abandoned us, Mother says. His sisters have another version and guard his memory fiercely, communicating with him just as if he never went bankrupt, was disgraced, ran away with another woman. All these crimes, we have been made to understand, drove him forever from the serene confines of St. Paul. Dorothy would teach me to go on loving my dad. But to what end? I am his forsaken child. He even has other offspring now.

Wasn't it she who had told me? On the occasion of our great high lunch at the Lexington bar, my own choice of bistro: the moment when she would hand me the check that would send me abroad to study. Later we would pick out a trunk and buy the steamship tickets from Mrs. Davis, her stalwart travel agent in downtown St. Paul. It was a chance remark, a stray reference, maybe even the mention of one of their names. Peggy or Michael. "Who are they?" "Your father's children." "My father has other children now?" The bottom falls out. "Good God, has no one ever told you?" "Who would tell me? Does Mother know?" "I assumed she did." "But how could I know?" My eyes fill up despite the college senior, smart young lady get-up, the striped wool suit from Peck and Peck, the felt cloche hat. The whole outfit hurried into the powder room to curse at myself for crying in front of her. She was a Millett. He was. I was only half of one, down to a quarter now that my father has other children. The very fact of my not knowing it added to the slight. To look silly at the moment you lose so much. The thing itself tears further, tears inside your body; it was to be unfathered, disowned, cast away. He could abandon three daughters to father not only another girl but a boy, a son, two sons, now—she said as I was getting up from the table. James and Michael—shit—each time one of us were born, with each birth, first Sally, then me, then Mallory, we were all to be christened James Michael Millett. And we failed and were girls.

I watched him on the telephone when the news of Mallory's birth came to us from the hospital into our little living room on Princeton Avenue—this moment so like another when I was beaten once for no reason—the two memories are all I have of that house—for we moved from there when I five to Selby Avenue, Mother's house now . . . and the man cried as he listened. For moments, watching, I wanted to cry with him; how much our daddy wanted a boy. How sad it was another girl. And then I turned angry and had no more pity—how dare he cry as if a girl were bad luck or inferior—we were girls. And now he has sons. Now he has everything he wants and will never want us again.

I sit through lunch tasting nothing at all; the whole occasion has backfired, listening politely while his sister argues earnestly that my father loves his children, loves us all still. We never see him. He lives far away. He never sent Mom money. At least not after he got back from Greenland that first year. "He's had difficulty establishing himself." "Mom's had some too." "I know, and I would be glad to help her but she is determined to solve all these things herself." "She wanted to be independent, kind of, make her own way. It's been real hard getting started at selling life insurance but I guess she's doing a little better now—would you believe it—they made her Man of the Year in her office?"

I think it's funny in a different way than does my aunt who has no idea what it is to humiliate yourself fifty-two times in a row by telephoning strangers during their evening rest or Saturday morning leisure, trying frantically against all odds or probability, against pity or patience or courage itself, to interest them in an annuity she is convinced will secure their old age. She succeeded probably because she believed in it, the product itself, security. That together with the terror and need of keeping three children on nothing at all. My mother was as much a lady in her own way: not a great lady, a small, compact, modest, and honorable lady. Galway, not Mayo, Patrick's favorite daughter and his youngest, the only child he bothered to educate at the university rather than at the normal school or the office.

What Mother did to preserve us was vertigo and death, hell and torment. But she did it, day after day, nights and evenings too, policies delivered even in the snow. A cup of coffee, the maternal chat: she insured her clients to the limit, saw after their beneficiaries, checked all the clauses and the figures, had gotten them more and extra every way she could. We went on eating as well, stew, tuna fish, but there were clothes for school, even tuition at Derham Hall and then the university. At which point the great aunt suggested study abroad. Mother had already done the job: one could only embroider upon it. Mother must have decided, when no Millett, not even my father, came forward to inquire about a college for me, that sending Kate to a fancy Eastern school wouldn't be doing that child any special favor, and that the University of Minnesota where she had gone, Dorothy and Harriet and Lucy too for that matter—would be plenty good enough and she could afford it.

It was so cheap I could afford it myself. For I had been busy earning money since my father left. Earning money amused me. Ever since age five when I had an empire in Coke bottle returns and hung upon the bar at Goldberg's store. The bar being the candy case where I stood Tootsie rolls. My wagon and my empties from under the stands at St. Thomas College across the street. Mother's house was on the Selby side of St. Thomas. Not the smart side, not the Summit side, but the back side, Selby. From early debauches that far exceeded my allowance, I moved up over the years to babysitting. Even to babysitting with the dishes and the cleaning thrown in. All for thirty-five cents an hour, a bargain even then. After all, there is always time to read, to dream, to ransack the place for Coke or cookies or whatever they have in the way of birth control devices or other instruments of learning. I was systematic enough to keep a file card system on my clients, complete with ratings. From there I moved up or perhaps down to the basement counters in department stores: Shunneman's, Field Schlick's. Stockings, slippers. After-school and Christmas work. I bought sensational presents, sensational numbers of presents; not even the most remote cousin on Mom's side was forgotten. And sensational wrappings too, professional desk-wrap performances in foil paper done up on Mother's bedspread. But my jobs also paid the electrical bill and the phone bill. In addition I took on the family laundry, iron and mangle thrown in. So I have been through a good deal of the hard times with Mother and though it ill behooves me to be disrespectful of my aunt, whom Mother says only waited to dominate her by taking over our support when we were helpless, I cannot quite fail to explain, in laconic twenty-one-year-old phrases how Mom has really pitched in and come through swell, is going great and so forth.

But also, these years have made me her ally. I am at her shoulder now. I have had to be my mother's emotional support for a long time now. I have had to take sides. The day my father walked out the door I was forced into that. And there were moments I could have screamed out that I was still a Millett and wanted to be one, was of course in love with my dad now just as much as ever, even if he never gave me another thought as long as I lived. He didn't seem to from the few greeting cards, with or without a check. In answer to the urgent letters I was coerced to write him, Mother merciless at this: if she could call every yahoo stranger in St. Paul to sell them life insurance, the least I could do was write my own father. Little Mallory siding with one or the other of us, lonely evenings upstairs after a dour dinner table, that sad and desolate household of women. And would be forced to sit down at that funny old desk I got from a relative and refinished myself into a grotesque whitewash lit by a fluorescent lamp I thought very modern but which gave my whole room a bizarre and unpleasant air, and on a typewriter that was Uncle Walter's cast-off from his days at Yale, fumble through some wordless plea ultimately dictated from the other room where Mother hid her pride but did not conceal her intentions.

Even now, after Oxford and the perspective it was intended to give me upon the world, I am my mother's child in my father's sister's house. By fate, the fate of accident. And how things were done. Not only the barbarity of a divorce which in effect forbade me ever to see my father again—and it is now eleven years—but by the corollary that in losing Jim Millett I was expected to lose the Milletts as well. Not entirely. But a distance was to be made. And held. And though my aunts were fond of me still and I saw Dorothy often, very often (consider the weekly symphony)—it was to be in enemy territory when with her.

If on any of these occasions I could have just come to my aunt and said—"Look, whenever Mom gets mad she says, you're just like him, you're Jim Millett all over—you're a Millett, those cold awful people and so on—what am I gonna do? I am a Millett and I love my dad—I'm still crazy about him and I love you, Aunt Dorothy, I love being a Millett—can I still be one anyway?" But of course one didn't talk. Symphony nights were very ceremonial: there was usually a driver, a butler, a maid for dinner afterwards, my Aunt Dorothy's wonderful and astonishing friends for supper parties. Where do you lay down all these grievances? I was too cowardly and too conventional ever to begin. I had also been carefully educated not to rat, to divulge, or to emote. And you, Aunt Dorothy?

One just didn't drop in on A.D. Because that is how I might have done it. Gotten on my bike one night when I was really sick of it and perplexed and ridden right down Summit, its whole length and grandeur, to where Virginia Avenue meets it on the left and you can see her house as you go by in a car if you know how to look quick. Have I ever gone by without looking? But you didn't just pop in on her: you had to be invited. There were rules; you didn't break them. Not only the formality of all our relations, but their austerity, rarity, divine privilege. The privilege of seeing you was just that, a favor dispensed. A fact Mother never seemed to cease underlining. Mother was always with us: our rich aunt saw us when she pleased and so forth. We were a toy, an indulgence. And of course aunts have by the nature of things a loftier and more distant presence, one inclined toward pleasure: outings, treats, the ballet, a luncheon somewhere, shopping—frivolity. It is their charm and essence that they do not stand duty for the ordinary drudgery of child care: diapers, washing, getting ready for school, blue jeans and ironing and worn-out shoes, money worries, confrontations with the nuns who taught us.

But the grandeur of this aunt stood above all other grandeur. She was famous, baroness of the town. And we were aware of her fame, guarded it secretly, knowing all along the very magic of her name, repeating it only rarely, sure that it was current everywhere, affected even the way that the mothers of our playmates dealt with us. It may have mediated Mrs. Dudley's tolerance when I recited my Uncle Harry's jokes and remarks the days after I had heard them at dinner. Long involved Irish folk tales about Rorry the cat and Paddy McNutt's funeral, recitals whose range of experience in liquor and levity were hardly becoming in her daughter's companion. Hadn't I informed Susan Dudley of the facts of life as overheard in conversation among the Woodruff girls who lived at the end of the block? There Mrs. Dudley drew the line. But my very faith in my Uncle Harry, like my adoration of my aunt, were somehow protected; we were an eccentric family, full of characters, "and her aunt married Louie Hill." A marriage into royalty. And ever after, even living in the twilight of divorce, the manor born having replaced the manner married, far more an aristocrat than Louis Hill, as indeed all the Milletts were born aristocrats whether chance found them rich or poor, A.D. not only maintained all she had acquired but actually refined upon it. By now she had educated herself deeply in all she had known before by natural aptitude, the university, and travel. She had made a personal fortress of her house and her library and lived as a private scholar and a great lady. Not someone a child drops in on. Though no dream or fantasy was dearer to me.

And once I actually did it. Coming home from the dentist one afternoon. Coming from having my teeth straightened, or rather my over-decisive bite tamed through painful metal fittings, rubber bands, and plastic turtles, an operation I usually softened by spending my earnings in the used-book stalls, topped off with a Bridgeman's malt and a huge bag of popcorn for the trolley ride home from the old town up Cathedral Hill past my aunt's and on down to Midway and my mother's house near the Mississippi River. But the day I picked for my spontaneous—in fact wildcat—visit to my aunt, a lurching impulse, a piece of madness and infatuated boldness, was an afternoon when the bookstores had no appeal. Not even Bridgeman's—for I always had enough money for a malt. My own money, not Mother's careful handout which was just enough for two tokens, one to get there, one to come home on. It seems never to have occurred to me until it was too late, that I had no money of my own that day at all. Money was the last thing on my mind—my fear was of ringing the bell and confronting the butler. If he would let me see her. If she would be home. If she would be out. What if she'd really be home but I might be told she was out?

I stood before the great black enameled door on Virginia Avenue. Number One Twenty-One—that was its name, how it was always referred to—One Twenty-One—I dared to come there. Having got down from the trolley after it emerged from the tunnel under Cathedral Hill. The cathedral sits high over the town in the old French way, for that is the type of town it was before the Irish and they saw no reason to change it. The houses of the grandees spring off to one side like a flying buttress of wealth on the brow of the hill. The cathedral round, the houses square: first Jim Hill's house, then Louie Hill Senior's, the Ordways', the Weyerhausers'—all looking down into the Minnesota River Valley and the little structures of the prairie town, the smokestacks, and the river traffic. The trolley valiantly climbs up the hill toward Summit and the cathedral and the great houses and then dives into the bowels of their hill. Each trip I feel the elation with the train, the excitement and the danger through the brave little tunnel. Only a few blocks long but dark, adventurous, aspiring, a feat of engineering that makes me invoke my father's presence for good luck. He has left now; there is only one Millett still here, A.D. He fades into her as we emerge and like a hunting dog I begin to perceive her, the perfume of her neighborhood. You must go a few blocks past the cathedral, even past the Hill houses, Uncle Louie's father and grandfather. Louie Junior's Georgian house is a few blocks more, Rondo next, no Virginia Avenue itself; the conductor actually calls it every week when I come home from the dentist, and every week I want to jump off and make this my stop. An outrageous idea. Today I tense and spring and dare. I felt it coming in the tunnel, I swore I'd do it. But I often do. The longing to see her is beyond endurance by the time we come out of the tunnel. A lover's longing. All later life was mere repetition: your ordinary obsessive behavior—I had known it all since childhood. Even definitely. The business of entering a street only to haunt it—like Tennyson standing before Hallam's house after his death—I had experienced all of this at thirteen. And now I knock. Having recklessly covered the block and a half between this door and the trolley at a run, never permitting myself to think but shivering with the consequences. Her anger is terrible; what if she got so mad she didn't love me anymore? What if I discovered she didn't ever love me? For that was always the lurking emptiness at the bottom of our consciousness, that the Milletts were only nice to us because of Daddy and because we were related. But they didn't love us the way Mother's people loved you—without reservation in the warm family bosom of tribal solidarity. You could drop in on them any time. And I did; I often went to see my Aunt Mary and I was always welcome. But it was not the same, not the romance, not the difficulty, not the challenge. Aunt Mary was Mother's sister and a good woman and kind but she was not glamorous like the Millett aunts, like Aunt Dorothy who was the most glamorous person in the world and here I was knocking on her door without permission. To arrive uninvited was to invite rebuke, to be pointedly and right before your hurt and humiliated little face denied admission. Maybe for a long time. This was a rash thing I did. And I knew it. Without admitting it I must have been testing. As I used to test my father's patience or the catechism.

Foolhardy you are to take that big brass knocker and summon—who—you will have to get him before her, the butler before the lady. Pray that it might be she. That she might be passing the door and open it herself. Or look out the little windows at each side of the door, little leaded windows with a fanlight on top. You have to stretch to do the knocker and you can't do it twice 'cause twice is impolite. But he doesn't come. Nor does she—it is clear it won't be she. I summon her, her face, her perfume, her presence, the sound of her voice which intoxicates me. But if she's cross, the knees buckle and the stomach slips and begins slowly to burn and then you notice your face gets hot and must be red and you are still another kind of fool, your own kind, worse than the stupidities she has chastised you for: breaking something, getting something dirty, not remembering what you were told, not knowing the answer. But this. The nerve of this. That's what they'll say. What Mother would say. Telling me I have no business dropping in like that; don't you know anything about your Aunt Dorothy—you don't just go there, you never see that woman unless she wants to see you. Everything's her way.

And I have dared to brave that, even to knock again and hear the footsteps. His? Hers—could they be hers? No, a man's tread. And the door opens as tall and as wide as the man who holds it, peering down at me. He has probably forgotten me, has no idea who I am. I could be an urchin. "I came to see my Aunt Dorothy"—I had meant it to be brave but it came out as a whisper, nearly a sob. I feel him taking in wind, the breath that will tell me she isn't home. And then I hear her at the top of the stairs, asking him who is there. "Mrs. Hill is rather busy just now," he says. I stand my ground. I am a niece, he is a butler—who weighs more? With my mother's people, where butlers do not even exist, family is all: with the Milletts it could be a far harder struggle. I inch further. "My name is Kate; she's my Aunt Dorothy"—the words taking on glory as I see her past his shoulder coming down the staircase—lady, wonder, the most beautiful woman in the world, my own aunt, her hair like an auburn helmet, her clothes as perfect as she, her hand upon the banister, a bemused look on her face that may end in a laugh or a clipped and killing remark.

It seems indeed that she was busy; she was that very night giving a debutante ball for my elder sister, the candles everywhere, ribbons and dresses and cakes. I was permitted a quick and quiet inspection and then sent home. How convenient that I had forgotten the ball. And had chosen the day my elder sister would be so indulged to go and check up on my own rating. Given the circumstances, I was treated pretty well on my unscheduled visit. Until the moment the door closed I had even pulled it off.

It was only then that I remembered the token. I had spent both the tokens. The first for the trolley ride downtown, the second for the journey back from downtown which I had interrupted at Virginia Avenue. For a moment I felt it was unfair you couldn't get a transfer while alighting for a ten-minute visit. Dummy, I muttered outside the door. Double dummy. "Dummkopf," as Daddy would say: a bit of the family German that trickled down to us. For the Milletts used German as a private family language: forced to learn it as children in Hastings, Minnesota, where the church had seen fit to send German-speaking Dominicans to educate Irish immigrants. Turning this accident into an asset, they used German as a secret language which excluded Mother as well as us.

Now you're really in it. Could you beg a ride from the motorman? Lie, say you lost your token? No, he wouldn't let me on. It is five miles to Mother's house; could you walk that far? You ought to—because if you don't, you are going to have to do the knocker again and ask for a token. They won't have a token; you'll have to ask for money. You'll have to ask for a dime. If you could just find one on the ground. If the ground would just open while you explain to this man in his suit. Then he does a nice thing: he does not go and get a dime; he doesn't even tell her; he just reaches into his pocket and gives me one. Mercy. Wilted, the little debauch over and covered with humiliation about the dime, the extreme strait that might have left me homeless by nightfall, an orphan in the world, clear proof that I could not manage my own affairs and pay calls as I pleased, was merely a child and a poor relation—at least for a moment—and that moment when you are stranded is eternal—I turned back to Selby Avenue, the street of the trolley, Mother's street. Less fashionable. Real.

THE HOUSE ON VIRGINIA AVENUE is gone now—or rather, has been sold and converted to a nursing home, so it's gone to us. And its interior is gone forever. But I have driven there and just sat in the car a hundred times since you left it, Aunt Dorothy. Nearly every time I was supposed to be at Mass. Or learning how to drive. Or doing errands now that I could drive. Or in college having spunk and madness enough to buy old wrecked cars I could never take care of and owned with three other girls who never knew how to fix them either, all of us prepared at any moment to sell them for junk. Alone or with one friend or another, sitting in a car before my aunt's house, telling them about her, explaining her, her importance, fascination. They were impressed or bewildered. Being in love with inappropriate people was not that rare among us, on the contrary.

If I were with Sally and we went downtown on Summit Avenue—and what other way is there to go for a real St. Paul soul, especially when home on a visit—we would always end up before your old house, one saying to the other, do you want to turn down there and see it? Often not saying it at all as the turn on to Virginia Avenue came up. Coming or going, the cathedral before or behind us, the Hill House, the Ordway house, and then that little street—like a call, like an irresistible impulse down to the house on the corner which you do not even see till you turn. But you know; you hear and feel it. Sometimes merely being there suddenly, Sally was so experienced that she could come upon it from other directions, from more remote block-long little side streets I hardly knew, from the back, the other side. For me there was only one way to approach, that turn off Summit. A little before the house where Mother said Fitzgerald was born. And a few blocks past where he lived when he would come home to write. Past Aunt Lucy's first apartment house from long ago, past Percy Carroll's splendid mansion. All the houses have their resonance, each one I have ever been in. As well as the ones whose ambiance I have only imagined, made the settings for nearly every book I have ever read, the old houses of St. Paul standing duty for England or the Continent: rooms, fireplaces, sofas, arches, hallways, windows, the pattern of light. But of them all this was the shrine, a reality whereas they were only a setting. Things happened in that house that were the very marrow of my childhood.

Even that is behind me at Wayzeta, standing before the library fireplace and looking out on to the lake. If I were to say, I loved that house on Virginia Avenue, Aunt Dorothy, I could never convey how or why I loved it or how much, or how loving it was loving you—it would be the effusion of a young person. Who's busy loving every book and painting and passages of music she can't remember the next morning, blinking or rolling her eyes over sonatas, depending on how cocky or insecure she is made to feel. And so there is no purpose in trying to convey my love for that house even though it is my love for her in childhood.

All its parts and places, its nooks and crannies, the record library under the staircase, the powder room where one went to think during dinner parties or in early evening, rehearsing remarks, voiding mistakes, remembering the things that had to be remembered so one didn't make a *faux pas*. The luxury of that little room—one night I even lay down on the rug and hugged it, so dear it was to me to be there, this sanctum of sanctums, the moment alone when one recorded the fact, the wonder of being at her house, at Aunt Dorothy's. A wonder that carried over into life on the back stairs, for there were backstairs as well as the great Georgian staircase. There was, via the backstairs, an entire room for linen, neat and organized as a hospital or the Army. Seeing her in that room once, the surprise of it, linking her to the servants and maids whom I visited in the linen room, chatted with, followed about on long stays when my aunt was busy, was out, was having lunch somewhere and I would be having lunch alone. Teasing them over what was for lunch or even dinner, haggling Cokes from them, even an extra one above the daily limit or the tepid ginger ale which is better for you; your aunt says so. V-8, the sight of V-8 in her refrigerator, or Coke—how much more romantic the bottle appeared in these huge double boxes, wood and metal like a restaurant. The big cupboards where things were kept, finding the cases of Coca Cola myself, or the wine cellar: trips down there, the dungeon-like character of it, the wire screen that prevented theft. And down the corridor there was a ping-pong table, installed for our benefit, for my sisters and me. Although Aunt Dorothy taught us how to play and seemed to enjoy it very much herself.

But even wilder than the ping-pong after dinner in the depths of the huge basement was the night when Elsa Schiaparelli was at dinner and all three of us—the great French lady, my aunt, and I, privileged beyond imagination—spent a long wonderful night in the basement doing finger paints. They'd had champagne and it made them silly, raucous: I was this way on ginger ale. The blue, I still remember the blue as the ultimate blue of all, the purest ultramarine. The rose, for it was not really red, only rose, was lovely too. Even the brown was good if you did the right thing with it—but the blue was heavenly. Lost in it. As they are lost in what they do, for a while all of us quiet and calm, then showing, then laughing, then drinking and changing paper and then laughing again. A big room, each of us in our section of it, the huge ping-pong table and other tables to work on, and the floor when it came to that. The great pile of paper; you could pour it on. And it is all over you: your hands make the painting. Their hands. Hers. Schiaparelli's. The laughter and gaiety. Look, let's see—look—no, look at this, now look, look at this one. That one, the one over there. It's a Picasso—hell, it's better. It's a hat. No, a whole outfit. Here are the eyes, I would say—and they would begin all over again, a peal of delight. We were at times not even two adults and a five-year-old child, but three adults, three women, three children, three sisters, three friends.

Schiaparelli made me love France and the sound of her voice was France, the lilt of her laughter, the expressions she taught me, her amusement when I said *tais toi*—I knew something French that I had heard at home but I was not supposed to say that. And the rapture of saying *Oo la* the way she said it, and *oui* with a little whistle in it. She was small, somewhere between my size and Dorothy's and this tied us together as the child and semi-child. But she could inveigle the child in my aunt, make her merry and foolish and able to run and shout. Champagne and more champagne and more pictures and the floor full of pictures, finger paint all over our aprons. For we had, thank God, aprons especially for the mess and so could feel free in it. This is what I go on remembering of that night, because of its enchantment—and its vision of camaraderie, of art as something done as a game with other people, social. Not lonely but hilarious, approved, the approval of cohorts egging you on to grander and more terrible but also more wonderful excesses. This is how it could be with grownups, I thought, this is how fun it could be. If they relaxed, permitted it, stopped scolding and punishing and diminishing one. If they would do childish things, permit themselves to do childish things, really permit themselves: then they would permit me too. I could even stand by and watch them, admiring them. For their designs were wonderful, inventive, ingenious, witty. Schiaparelli's of course, she was an artist. But my aunt as well. For me she was also an artist. Of life, of everything.

Now I deal with the tired widow. Here in reality, in Wayzeta. But she is also up at the crack of dawn, her mornings a flurry of decisive activity. The evenings ruminative, lonely, given to explaining, in need of comfort. Something in me holds back. I am as afraid to be the comforter as the seducer. They are one and the same, perhaps. Or perhaps being the deceiver, I am as dishonest in giving comfort as I would be in following the elliptical little signs of favor, the odd beckoning in the late nights, the quantities of scotch searching for friendship or more. What more? How does one even think of more? Feeling it only to be more dishonored and dishonest. It cannot be felt or followed. Ignore it. Properly. You are a niece on a visit. The restraint of family, especially this one. Given so to kisses upon meeting and great extravagant phrases of affection, but never to tears, never to loneliness or need or lack of any kind.

This is the first and last time I am ever to see her lonely. Though she must have been lonely often in the years after Louie and before Walter: the attention directed toward us, her nieces, was perhaps proof of that. But we were children and one does not project that sorrow onto them. Though there may have been times when she looked for something beyond our greedy admiration, our infatuation with her as the dispenser of presents and astonishments. I kept my quietude for that side of things when living in her house as a child, turning my companionship into a kind of rest. Then too I had little to say, was shy, was terribly afraid of making an error or offending. Being there I was not too far from tears at certain times of day: the late afternoon for example—for the temporary happiness of being there was so easy to lose. One could be told at any moment that William would be driving you home tomorrow, even tonight. Whether for an offense or merely because that was the original arrangement, you didn't know, you didn't dare ask.

One afternoon she found me reading *Peter Pan* in tears. The real *Peter Pan,* not the simple storybook at home. Over which I had already wept copious and repeated tears. But this was a new version, complete, a grown-up book, long and without pictures, part of a set of J. M. Barrie I had found on a shelf. Remembering his name I began to drown in it for an afternoon. At the end of which I was overwhelmed with grief. At first she laughed at me, but when I cringed, she was not as she was so often, cold and scornful of tears. She was suddenly kind—the very kindness made me cry harder and harder as she sat down with me and finished the book, reading aloud, wistful herself at it. Though part of her must have loathed its sentimentality, part of her forgave it, failed for once to deny it. And I ended the day happy in her arms.

There are all these things to recall as your eyes go over the books. Barrie still in its place. Even *Tristram Shandy.* A first edition. My mouth dries up and my forehead grows hot with shame for an instant to see Lawrence Sterne's wonderful book, eighteenth-century Dada, its old leather binding. That I had the nerve, the gall, the stupidity—not only to beg that Jaycee be invited along with me to lunch here that spring of my senior year—dumb enough to think if my aunt meets the one I love she will like her, tolerate, permit—what? But then having brought Jaycee along and seeing that my aunt was frigid, polite, maybe only barely polite, but tolerating while detesting—I went one step further and asked permission for Jaycee to have a look at the first edition of *Tristram Shandy*. And then, let the heavens fall—they do this moment being forced to recall it—I trotted out the folly of my love, enthused about how well Jaycee read aloud and how much she admired this book—which was a kind of bible between us, though I had first read it through my aunt: hadn't it been our bible too? The perfidy of it, to make my Aunt Dorothy listen to this person, as she would call her, reading aloud from her own book, a first edition at that. A book she had taught me. With less pretense about the prototypical Dada business, for Jaycee and I imagined we were deep scholars of the eighteenth century and were both taking Samuel Monk's yearlong course; indeed, it was our rendezvous.

Jaycee read as well as she could and I held my breath for her. This was her greatest gift. Beyond teaching me orgasm I had no higher proof of her ability, intelligence, sensitivity. This was the limit. And I could hear without even raising my eyes that she had failed to impress my aunt. That the whole thing was a stupid mistake on my part, that I had only given my aunt a glimpse of what she would have no difficulty in opposing and destroying. And that worse, I would go right on in my loyalty to what she could look upon as *déclassé,* a misalliance. I loved someone she found contemptible. And in Jaycee's sensible buckskin shoes, her worn charcoal skirt, her impossible bright red shirt, I saw my aunt's contempt and blocked it out. I still wanted the being in those shoes, that skirt. Part of me was furious too. It seemed unfair—I could not have my aunt, so why could I have no one else? And the fury of the student, the poor relation—if the money is for going to a university, why the hell does it matter who I sleep with when I'm there? Am I not twenty-one, will I not already hold a degree when I enter Oxford—how long can these people run my life?

Ah, but it was their money. The *Tristram Shandy* on this shelf is much the same book in the modern library edition after all. You could have gone to graduate school at the University of Minnesota and lived in colorful poverty with Jaycee in your sordid amorous rented room. With the dog that barked continuously because you were only beginning to think maybe he was deaf and couldn't learn commands. And the toilet down the hall shared by four other parties, a landlady who minded the barking, the front porch and its swing, the bush in the front yard where you went to sleep drunk on your graduation night because you didn't have to go home to Mother's. Mother, who wept at the sight of the rooming house, sat on the bed and took out a Kleenex and looked about her at the one room, the roaches in the kitchen, a gas ring behind a door, "my

God," her voice as if she had seen a ghost. We lived on leftover steak from Charley's where Jaycee waited tables. And artichokes. I'd buy artichokes around noontime when I got up from sleeping off the night shift in the factory. We always had wine; it was a very romantic existence. That whole summer long. Jaycee had lived in Greenwich Village and she knew about artichokes, about wine and candles stuck in wine bottles, about roughing it and *la vie bohéme*.

We would soon lead the same glorious life in Carolina when I wasn't teaching. Maybe even with her friend the painter. Jaycee was a writer. I was only a scholar, now demoted to a junior instructor, lecturer actually. But I could assist the arts and the artists. That was the notion behind starting a gallery. A.D. says nix, but I could do it myself, from my teaching salary. Because a teacher is somehow incomplete, less than an artist. Since I cannot become an artist, I can devote my life to helping them.

I have secrets then to hide. Jaycee. Her friend. The artist side of things, a commitment to another world, frowned on. So watch out for slips; she has asked three times who you mean by "we." The urge to tell her, to confess, rises up again in my throat and then turns to panic in my head. And be thrown out, lose these precious days? But living this lie—imagine what a rat and coward you are, every moment you are with her. Then remain a little distant, figure out some way you can be decent, what little honor or kindness is available. Because it will pass someday. Either she will not care anymore, permit you to be grown up. Or you will be alone again, without Jaycee and then . . . free to admit this to her? It would still be admitting to a lie even if it were twenty years in the past. What can you do then beyond confessing, getting thrown out, losing her entirely? I can imagine almost losing Jaycee but not my own aunt. She has been my aunt all my life. She will always be my aunt. Family. Nonsense, she's a Millett; they don't forgive like Mother's folks. You could tell Mother and she'd carry on and cry and raise hell and revile you but she would never throw you out. You wouldn't lose her. You would lose A.D. And her anger, so terrible you couldn't live through it. You are so afraid of being called a liar and dishonorable that you go on in this situation, giving nothing, being nothing. But a lie. Here she comes.

The hypnotism of this presence, always the wonder and the fear before this, even if she were to say the most commonplace thing about the sun on the water or going for a swim, that it was time for dinner or time to dress for dinner. I hold my breath in the old expectation before this radiant assurance, the command of her voice: her cheek, her shoulder, her step upon a rug. Even mellowed with age how fierce and nearly alien are her eyes, that mysterious pitiless green flecked with gold: so suddenly cold, so judgmental, so full of examination and dismissal. Everything here is hers, is her, each picture and rug and book, all speaking their undying allegiance to her personality, her choice of them, their loyalty before the entrance of any stranger. And I am dumb before her power.

Her power over me, which has not diminished one jot

for all my travel and study—I am as humbled as when I was eight before her: more so, I no longer have childhood to blame. When she squelches me with a glance, a lift of her head, a look turned away from whatever sophistry, pedantry, youthful prejudice I have stumbled out with, I am as paralyzed as then, way back then. There is no progress in life, I think. I admire her and fear her, adore and idolize her just as in childhood, am as obsessed with her, captivated, controlled, mortified, rendered silent and naughty and foolish. But with this one difference: she does this time indulge me. More than ever before. Or was I always indulged and never noticed it? For all my tremblings and hurt feelings as a child, she may indeed have been spoiling me with kindness. But this time there is a greater indulgence—she treats me more as an adult, a friend, a comrade. The late-night drinking. The confidences about her widowhood. Everything to which I cannot respond adequately. Because I am still a child before her, still a niece. Desperately clinging to that in the face of any other temptation to confidante or comforter, positions more false than an errant young relative.

The sun bursts onto the lake outside the window over the boat sofa which has come here to the water's edge from Virginia Avenue. If it were to bob slightly like a ship at a mooring I would hardly look twice, so directly do all the windows here seem to give onto the lake that the water nearly enters the rooms. The windows in the great sitting room where we rarely sit, so big it is, so formal; even they look like ship windows onto the ocean, the windows of a big square room in a ferry or tugboat. For all the Chippendale, the silk and linen upholstery, the serenity of the Han horse over his mantel, the very intensity of the light and the water fills the house so there is no need to go outdoors. In fact I have unconsciously refused to and swim very little here, which is odd for me. Occasionally we will walk on the lawn or in the garden among her trees and flowers, but it takes coaxing to get me outdoors. Indoors is what I crave, shunning the world of fresh air and distraction. To be indoors is to be with her, or more closely and intimately with her. There are servants here too, but out of doors there are neighbors, the lake, all the people who live on the lake, the world beyond: Minneapolis, St. Paul. Everything that is not her. Inside there are only the two of us, interrupted by the man who lights the fire or brings the cocktails, the invisible woman who cooks the dinner. Their comings and goings are usually predictable, but it is only late at night when they are sent to bed in the cottage next door, that we are really alone. Those moments. Tantalizing, terrifying, compromising, full of every pitfall of discovery—they are our intimacy. Itself full of pitfalls, compromises, and discovery. This fine edge.

AS SHE COMES TOWARD ME she could be about to announce that she has discovered I was at Oxford with Jaycee. A friend has informed her. A spy. She is a sophisticate with friends all over the world; why not a spy? Some unconscious bit of information she could add up for herself, some innocent contact with a don or a tutor there, and it would be all up. The green eyes would blaze. It would be over in an instant. She would have William deliver my things at my mother's house tomorrow, but I should go with him instantly. Maybe she'd tell me to take the bus—I grin despite my dry mouth. Watching her arrange flowers, happy, singing to herself, chattering over the sound of her own scissors. Lady—I want to cry out, my heart sinking into my stomach, God, what have I done. What an impasse I have made of my life. That I should be here with her I love best and could lose forever in an instant if she only knew who I really was, who I had really lived with all these two years away from her, whom I return to in a few weeks.

The renegade life I have sold myself into, like some secret society banned by the police. The first forbidden act of sex, so far better than my huddled experiments with boyfriends, wonderful, the entrance to life itself—this had brought me across a line my aunt would never step over or know, made me an alien, a freak, lesbian—a word I still could not pronounce without blushing, hear without wincing. That word in the mouths of my near and dear, my tribe and family, had been a forked sword, a wand of lightning, the sting of a shame more profound than ordinary wrong or the law code or the catechism. I was henceforward a secret leper, secret everywhere except with two or three other souls in history or books. Gertrude Stein was dead, Sylvia Beach was maybe one of us, Proust, Wilde surely—the very name synonymous and mocked—otherwise characters from Jaycee's past in the Village, the friend she visited now and one other whom I would never meet for years. All had been each other's lovers, an incestuous microcosm into which Jaycee was my sole introduction.

I might love my aunt but she was not of the sisterhood; loving her was folly. For two reasons: she was far too sane and discreet to regard her sophomoric niece in the light of a lover, and my own love of her could never fit into the lurid circle, the byzantine intrigue, the risky business, the leap of faith past the doors of astonishment which sexual declaration meant among these damned whom I knew. Otherwise, what hindered? I had loved my aunt sensually all my life: her smell, the kiss of her skin under my kiss, a child greeted and held and hugged, a little mouth searching for just the softest place of her neck or throat, inhaling perfume like incense, the sacramental wine of the enamored. The sexual? Of course I knew nothing of it then and now I knew I could not let myself think of it. Or even remember the kiss that Christmas Eve. Probably I invented it. But I knew I hadn't, nor my perfect response. Which was both to react with an utterly new emotion, passion; and at the same time to protect my lover from discovery. The gallantry of an eleven-year-old.

Much less gallant now, only craven. Responsible. Made so by my own errors in having betrayed her with another whose existence now was a bar, another commitment, another kind of honor and morality. And having betrayed, not only in loving another, but in lying about it—there the Milletts would get you, would never forgive—but hadn't my own father lived a lie for six years between a mistress and my mother and been forgiven by his sisters if not by his wife? He was a Millett and their brother. You are not: you are only half a Millett, a half-breed to them, mixed with your mother's blood which they never permit you to forget—now in lying to them you have breached faith and lost honor so completely that if you were to answer any invitation to whatever intimacy now from her, your Aunt Dorothy would have two crimes to charge you with. You deceived and then deceived again.

How then do you stay here and not deceive? Not easy. Whatever innocuous boon companion, dutiful daughter combination you come up with in the late nights, you are betrayed by your own exhaustion in the bright morning hangovers where you are twenty years older than the woman you love and avoid. She drank and talked in good faith last night. You didn't. In fact you drank and listened because you cannot talk at all. Not only the old shyness, but you cannot even tell a story, any silly anecdote of university life, without tripping over your unholy alliance to someone she detests and has forbidden you to see. You not only went to Oxford with Jaycee, she was your Oxford. Now you begin to notice it, when quizzed about the people you met, your friends, the places you went, travels: did you stay at any English country houses? I am flabbergasted even by the notion. I hardly knew anyone English, let alone people with country houses. Travel was travel with Jaycee, where she wanted to go. Little journeys in the old car we bought. I bought with your money—but not her steamship ticket—that was my factory job. Never mind, keep your story straight, journeys through England and Scotland, a trip on the ferry to Ireland. Try that then. Ireland, what did I see? Hoping to God it is the right thing. Connemara. I should have known this was too much in Mother's line. Galway, the Irish poor, the exodus. No, I missed Kerry and the places she must have jaunted. "Did you see Mayo?" A direct question: it is the Milletts' own county. "Well, just a bit of it actually; we were running out of time on the rented car and had to get back." "And who are we?" "Well, a bunch of us were pooling together and the others weren't Irish and didn't want to pay extra on the car." Almost true. Jaycee looked at Ireland like a photograph or a storybook, liked it well enough, but was not touching down on the pure electricity of race memory so that it was a different trip for each of us. But we had come to the same conclusions about the goodness of the people by getting gigantically drunk in a pub in Galway one night in Lent and were neither robbed nor raped nor murdered. In fact the proprietor drove our car out to our own hotel himself the next morning, complete with our money and passports, shared a Bloody Mary for breakfast and smiled at us both—"Didn't we have the grandest time in the world last night?" This being my best impression of Irish virtue (compare it with travelers' tales from anywhere else)—it was still nothing you can tell to your aunt as proof of the broadening effects of travel. Many vacations I just stayed at home and studied, tense and afraid of the approaching wall of examinations. One summer I read all thirty-seven of Shakespeare's plays trying to keep them straight. I did not see the world: I did not ski at San Antoine; I did not become the polished young lady it was supposed I would become. Instead I got the prize and came home without a great deal to say for myself. Unable to mention Jaycee, I had little else but pedantry and opinions.

I did not ski San Antoine with A.D. or without her. Jaycee didn't ski and I avoided the places in Europe that were my aunt's, feeling I knew them already a little and must learn others. Like the Paris of my friends at the Sorbonne. Paris was most of the vacations. Hardly a vacation to be living seven stories up in cheap walkup hotels, the toilet on floor three, the bath on floor five, the bidet a place where you did your laundry or washed the lettuce. Most of the day spent in cafés arguing about surrealism or Shakespeare or Gide or Sartre or de Beauvoir. I was reading *The Second Sex* and would take on anybody over this book, which women as well as men harassed me for: some of the Communist boys were even on my side. We ate the free sugar the café grudgingly left on the table, ordered coffee every three hours, made calls from an impossible phone in the basement next to the loo, and waited for yet another Chaplin movie to start at the flea pits or treated ourselves to the *avant-garde* films all in puzzling French.

It was before one of these trips to the other city, for Paris and London were the poles we lived by—like the characters in Dickens's novel we were back and forth at every possible juncture—that my Aunt Dorothy announced out of the blue that she would descend on me with Uncle Walter. Fortunately it was not quite a direct descent. They would be at San Antoine; they would not be here in Oxford discovering me. Still I was struck with terror even though I had squired my mother's relatives through Oxford a day or two, Jaycee vanished to a friend's house. First you met the visitors at the station and showed your flat, which hardly needed adjustment, then took them to dinner, a trip around the colleges and back to the train. It's true I slammed my fingers in the car door in a moment of diminished confidence after seeing them off and required a number of stitches on the way home from the station. But I managed it. Easy enough, simple good people on a tour, old women with swollen feet from twenty-eight days of bus travel where one European country smudged into another and they could only welcome the idea of Farmington, Minnesota, and the good old U.S.A.—but pulling the wool over Dorothy and Walter would be impossible. Also just too low-down. She'd sent you here; are you going to show her your flat—the place where you live and sleep with Jaycee, the woman she abominated and forbade you to know—and pretend this is your solitary existence? Cheap duplicity. But they would not come here, it appeared; they would be on the continent—why didn't I join them for some skiing? If it had been her alone, yes; there would have been no refusing. But Walter too. Who would have read me, found me out. I wrote I had already made other plans. They were nice about it.

I could not have abandoned Jaycee to a vacation by herself either. So I thought then. Yet when I finished the

Schools Examination and had three weeks before the *viva,* the oral exams, she urged me to go to Italy, alone, even have an affair, why not? In fact I did, with permission. While she had I never knew what back at Oxford, I met an Italian sculptor who whetted my growing appetite for the fine arts and was charm itself as a companion. We had our theories, our freedom theories, and our other life in Paris with our great friend Phyllis and her troop of young French student leftists and starving artists. Of course a corner of me yearned to be at San Antoine. It seemed so churlish to refuse such an invitation. This is the aunt who had sent me here—I had never refused an invitation from her in my life.

Perhaps once, perhaps once in high school, one Friday night I may have chosen the charms of a basketball game at St. Thomas where my high school crush Mary Quinn would be that night—over the symphony. But not often; Aunt Dorothy came before everything. And then a time came when I could dismiss her and her husband as just boring old bourgeois adults you could do without on vacation. Who wants to ski anyway? I gave it up after Sun Valley, a whole season as a ski bum on the mountain all day long, braving it, beating it. And then down below again for a few years you lose the knack. At Sun Valley for a while it was all or nothing: give up college, never go back, ski forever spending your tips to party; that or never ski again. I only broke my vow once, accepting an invitation to go for a weekend somewhere in Wisconsin with Dorothy and Walter, humiliated to have forgotten so much, I who had skied the exhibition hill at Sun Valley perfectly was back to the snowplow the first day. "You'll remember in time," Walter said, "you'll have it back tomorrow." But that night, I stayed up late talking alone with my aunt. It was that night she brought it up: it was my senior year in college and she must have been hearing the rumors of my perversity already from my mother, so she steered an innocent conversation about the military and the Second World War into forbidden channels—she had known a woman who joined the military during wartime; she had joined sheerly out of patriotism: "She became an officer and did a great deal of good—but she was not like that, not like what people imagine of women in the service." "And what was that?" I asked, my breath like an icicle in my throat. I could feel myself shaking and tried to control it. "Well, you know what I mean." "But what exactly?" "Well, I mean mannish and perverse."

I dread the word lesbian, which must come. It is poisonous, a lethal word to me: if I hear it I shall be paralyzed. I have been with Jaycee, a few afternoons in her arms by now. The great longed-for afternoon has not come yet, but will—I have already embarked down a road I cannot turn back from. I am already that thing in secret, that terrible unspoken word. Part of my mind is still rational enough to object that to make love with a man or a woman, one of the same or the opposite sex, is still only an act, a thing done—it needn't be this disease, this way of life, this series of maniacal prejudices my aunt's words call up. But the very inflection with which she has spoken, "mannish, perverted," annihilate me. What if I were to say to her—"You mean lesbian, why not say so? What's so very terrible about that?"

But then where would you go? Hold up Gertrude and Alice? What does that prove? Did Gertrude write better or at all because she was a lesbian? One could argue otherwise: in fact most of her work is a disguise for her lesbianism. The writing's original and baroque qualities, its distinction, may have lain in the fact of her sexual difference, but that fact is not there on the surface. Proust and Wilde—what does it prove that perverts have talent; every group has talented members. And your aunt could give a damn about that stuff anyway. You may kid yourself about these little literary gods of yours, you may hide your shame and insecurity by bedding them down, but they will cut no ice with her. If Walter were here with us, instead of asleep, kindly making this conversation possible, would you have appealed to the man of the world in him? He might even agree with you. But it is she who cares.

Being a coward I said nothing that was on my mind. And once at Oxford I did not go over to San Antoine. Because I did not want to be caught in a lie. It was after their trip to San Antoine that Walter died, some months after their return. I had missed my last chance to see him alive, but I read in the news of his death too that she was alone again, more mine than before. And a year later I had finished and come home again. To find her still devastated by Walter's death, by the loss of him, by the great emptiness at the center of her life. Fool enough to imagine I could fill it were I not declining out of a chivalrous intention not to mislead her further. Not to mention my earnest marital ties to Jaycee.

At any moment when my aunt entered a room she might say to me, "William will be taking you back to your mother's; I have a luncheon engagement with Mary Cornelius today," or "William will be taking you back to your mother's just before lunchtime; maybe you should give her a call." And it would be over; I would never have this chance again, be this close to her, be close enough still to school, to the schooling she has treated me to, to the position of being at home and in the family. And she still doesn't know. It is maybe only a matter of time until she does. The better thing would be to tell her yourself. But how can you? Even as the sun crosses the carpet and you hear the words that will be your dismissal, even then you will never have the nerve.

PART THREE

Now if I come to think about it (and it is never out of my mind; waking it is my first understanding and clouds the day) perhaps this shadow will lie over my life forever now, a permanent misfortune. For I have no doubt that the whole course of my experience is affected and I write partly out of self-defense, to fight off a sense of doom. What is it, then? What are you, A.D.? An old woman unforgiving at the end? Mean, spiteful, selfish, and alone. Isolated from nearly all who had mattered to her once. Her brothers dead, her nieces exiled or estranged—my sisters as well as myself. Her own sisters far away in the South, her only companions the rich of Wayzeta: admit it, these strangers were her world, her friends and cronies. She saw you once or twice from inside this circle, but over the years nothing worked. You were not permitted to step back into her life, or you simply did not come often enough, try hard enough. She was wise perhaps to guard against you. No, no, for behind this there is always the shadow of the great aunt of childhood, the beauty, the wonderful commanding and fierce glory of those eyes, aunt and godmother and fairy godmother. Lost. Maybe you lost her by growing up. And what you mourn in her death is merely your own childhood. At the moment of her dying, of my hearing of it, of it happening to me.

What in fact had happened the day before? My day before was an odd empty afternoon when I had tried to draw and was overcome with ennui and anxiety which I wrongly attributed to some trouble at the farm: broken pipes, plumbers, a failed furnace, money troubles. Over which I grieved far out of proportion and realized it as well, so despondent I gave up even trying to draw and went upstairs to the fifth floor at the Bowery, the floor where I live. I built a fire, unable to do anything but read for consolation. On that afternoon far away in Minnesota in the great heaped snow of this winter she died. A doctor present, death from a curious internal bleeding that could not be stanched. A surprise and sudden, despite the long circulatory illness I had never been told of and still do not quite understand. Years of unsuccessful operations to bypass the failing circulation in the legs, to introduce artificial routes for the blood to come up through the thighs to the heart. The last attempt was simply given up: there was no useful tissue to graft onto. They considered amputation, which she never would have permitted. Then what? The condition remaining stable though really declining into death, known and foreseen. And still I never turned and ran. Was never alerted. So the word came to me like a thunderclap. With it the realization that I could have tried one more time. Having just been home in Minnesota, I could have called her, telephoned from St. Paul over to Wayzeta. You can call Wayzeta from New York City too, but she always resented long distance as an intrusion, perhaps a false alarm—why call when you are that far away? Write. Writing intrudes less; it would not interrupt her at luncheon like a siren. There might have been a last conversation then, if not permission to visit. Surely she was too ill—she died the third of January. But what if she had said yes? What if she had admitted her illness, admitted what she so proudly hid from all, concealed in varying degrees, but from me entirely? The final reconciliation lay just within my hands. This will go on forever.

Or if the notion is too fantastic, too optimistic, too much against the grain of all those years of isolated and chilly visits, then there is the mere filial piety of the African violet in the snow. Which goes like this: Sally and I hear from Dorothy, through a slip of speech, or by accidentally getting the butler or the maid whom I still imagine as William and Bernice even though they have long ago been replaced by another pair at the cottage, dialed in error, or even at the house—because one of them, contrary to custom, picks up the phone there—and we get wind of her infirmity, are told she is being given a bath, whatever. We pull it out of them or they provide the truth, the fact that she is ill now, gravely ill. And we go. Forbidden to see her, either because she forbids us herself or because her loyal protectors do not encourage it, advise against it—still we go—just to go. Stopping by Holm and Olson on the way for the violet. My idea, stupid, sentimental, a quixotic gallantry. Her favorite flower. She might throw us out but she's never been known to be cross at an African violet yet, we chuckle as we speed along. A joke between us or we treat it as that, being as tough as we can be, as determined. Having borrowed Mother's car, with the truth or a pretext, or even against her advice that the trip is pointless. The roads are icy; it is snowing again; it may even be dangerous. It will certainly be long and cold and perhaps all too late and too little. Of course we won't leave the damn thing in the snow but we could put in on the front steps, ring the bell and run—that would assure that William got it. But would it? "Listen, Sal, you're not going to have her open the door to find this idiotic object left by runaways?" "She won't open the door—silly, she's really sick—William said so." "Okay, what do you propose then?" Sally of course would have a sensible idea—"We get to Wayzeta, we call William or Bernice, being sure to get them by phoning the cottage first and only if they are both at the house, risking that phone, let them know something is being delivered for Dorothy and then we'll drop it off at the cottage." "At the cottage—not at the house?" "They are next door, goose." I see the cottage, I see the house and its front step. How many times I have crossed it: in hope entering, in despair leaving. I had wanted the violet to sit like hope on the step, a proxy. I see the house and I see the cottage—but not its interior: I have never been inside it. It is not her house but theirs.

The house, the house, those fields of emerald carpet, the sun and the lake booming through each window, her presence like a shadow in every room stretching from the Han horse to the fire in the library. Up the stairs to the room where she slept, the room where I slept. Even the English prints in the bathroom, even the powder room downstairs by the front door where she slipped once and broke her pelvis. The only illness I knew her to have and it was years back. A few years ago she told me she was fully recovered from it, though her face was ravaged, older. She wore slacks and a big sweater and seemed middle-aged, ashamed of her age, afraid her beauty had gone. But it had only changed. Would she be that woman still? Or the one I saw the last visit of all, who dismissed me after an hour because she had to rest a large part of each day? An excuse I imagined to be a snub because I had arrived late. But these women were not dying, they did not even seem ill, only slowly growing infirm, still beautiful, still in power.

So not even to put the flower at her door, to leave this token with others and not give it into her own hands directly—how poor. But of course Sally is right, she is discreet, she is not an attorney or an elder sister for nothing. I have obeyed her for so many years I do not really think to differ. Or rather, differing—I nearly always differ—there no longer seems any point in expressing the difference, since it is so likely she would be right and I would be wrong. Despite numerous instances to the contrary. Only when it is too late to undo have I any confidence in my own opinion.

And so we never called, we never learned, and we never went there. Either to be cast away or received by failing hands for the last and perfect blessing, or just to leave a violet, a posy in the cold—a token, a gesture, the least damn thing one could do for a woman who was our second mother, our idol, the light of our young lives. Even if the unattained and estranged love of adulthood, perhaps actually the neglected love, the easily satirized and despaired-of great lady, the rich bitch, the cold old woman and so forth, all that our shared rancor could create: the emblem of cruelty and stodginess and respectability, rigid unimaginative bourgeoisie, *rigor mortis*—living with a butler and a maid in this day and age. Let her sulk out there and eat alone, one would say and the other would grunt assent, the entire cussing-out session a bluff. Either of us, Mallory too, would have obeyed a call from Wayzeta all the way from hell itself. But none ever came.

That is the wonder of it, the admirable determination on her part or the sheer oblivion into which we had fallen. We were never called about anything; no pretext ever arose, no change of heart. Slowly Sally fell into nearly the same disrepute as I. And Mallory fell out of favor suddenly when from Manila in the Philippines she wrote A.D. of her coming divorce and her loneliness and a sudden need of being in contact with and supported by her family. Dorothy took this, unjustly, to be a request for money and read the letter over the phone to Mother with jeering laughter. That did it for Mallory. My sins were known. Sally, as Dorothy's health failed and she drew more and more into herself, maintained the only line of connection, mostly phone calls rather than visits; they were brief and on family matters such as my father's death, or Mother's cancer surgery. On that occasion, the last time Sally had spoken to Dorothy and only ten days or so before our conversation about calling her at Christmas, A.D. had been sweet, remarkably compassionate, approachable. Maybe with this success behind her Sal didn't want to press her luck again so soon at Christmas. But all around the three of us, there had been an emptiness for many years, the aura of love that had once been our aunt and was now withdrawn.

FOR OUR CHILDHOOD had had two figures, two great women for its poles, Mother and Aunt Dorothy.: We lost touch with Dorothy: now there was only Mother. Poorer now, we huddled around her fiercely, bewildered, stricken. With this one left and how dearly to be guarded, Mother's illness in early December had us in constant telephone contact, hourly around the surgery, each voice tense and afraid to lose her—all we had left.

And that other flank unguarded, desolate so long, nearly forgotten. The sudden attack has left us with no defenses. In a second we lost Dorothy—all that we had lost before when she turned cold towards us—lost all over again and absolutely now in death. And that which had been once, the loving aunt of our childhood, returns only in a more anguished and permanent loss. Which goes on day after day in the cold snow of January. Yet grief dulls itself finally and this grief will too, disloyal as it seems to acknowledge it. Disloyal to one's own sentiment if not one's sentimentality and as it dulls her figure should recede. But the loss only grows. The impoverishment. Having lost the beloved lady long ago, I have now lost all chances of forgiveness, reconciliation, the gift of her friendship again, her affection, the happiness it would have been to see her often and in joy, to be her apple, her pride, her companion—I lose both what I had once and what I had not but might have had. What now can never be.

Isn't there some way to convert her shade into a friendly spirit? At the moment I heard of her death I had a wild second when I felt this might finally be my forgiveness. For don't people forgive when they die, let go, open their hands of all grudges and wrongs, bless or at least attain neutrality towards all the wrongs of life? I know she didn't die cursing me only because I know I was the last thing on her mind, an old woman bleeding to death internally whose doctor could not even find a remedy. It might have been years since she'd thought of me, and the me that she thought of might have been eight or eleven or twenty.

Or the forlorn fool who visited her, the last visit of all, the one I can't bear to remember, the one when I was not only an hour late but "crazy"—or said to be so, and, furious at the accusation, shaken by a plot two days before in New York whereby I had nearly been actually committed, I rambled on about how Mallory was trying to have me locked up at Payne Whitney Hospital. As Sally had rather more successfully put me away six years before. Mad or not, I had the fleeting impression of a tear on A.D.'s cheek once during this recitation; was she eternally patient or impatient with my vibrant paranoia? Was the tear out of pity for my troubles that summer—or out of sorrow that I was so disarranged in my mind? Did she side with me or Mallory? Surely I knew it was wrong to bear tales. Such inappropriate ones for a reconciliation—but I'd been struck again and needed comfort. Still more inappropriate evidently were the pile of books and manuscripts I would foist upon her as proof of my worthiness. And that was the last she would remember of me—that awful occasion. The summer of my discontent, having steered clear of capture and gotten off on my journeys first to St. Paul and then to an exhibition in Europe, I was still shaken, shaky, outraged. How foolish I must have appeared before those always-censorious eyes, how lost a creature. I cringe to remember, remembering as soon as I heard of her death, that this was the last time we met. This was who I was the last time she saw me.

Problematic offspring: first she is queer, then turns artist and throws away her education, writes those dreadful books, and now it appears she is mad as well. Or suspected of it. At my previous incarceration, under Mother's aegis and on the advice of a heroic doctor she had located at the University of Minnesota, I had the gall to telephone my aunt at a point when my sanity trial was going well and I could look forward to a life on the outside, dialing her up from the public phone booth in the ward with a dime that had escaped supervision. With Bemelman's *Fifi,* a book that my aunt had given me in childhood, clutched under my arm as a crutch while I dialed the number. Calling from a loony bin. I had found this old relic at Mother's while staying at her house the first night I arrived in town and rejoiced that it still existed, the great scrawl of "To my adored niece Katie from her Aunt Dorothy" on the flyleaf. The next morning the white coats came at Mother's behest: the wonderful doctor thought it was wise to take the full step of committing me since I had proved so devious and uncooperative at our interview the night before when I told him to be on his way: if I needed a shrink I'd find one myself in New York. By seven A.M. he had persuaded Mother to sign the papers and consign me to the state for good.

By the afternoon of that same day the civil liberties lawyers arrived to save me and I signed the papers demanding a sanity hearing. Then came days of the mad trial, a strenuous and humiliating procedure whose greatest ordeal was keeping silence while one is discussed for six hours at a time. One evening, after a day of this when things were looking well for us—I was not out yet, but I would be—I gathered my courage one evening with Bemelman in tow and called my aunt. Her voice spun firm and calm at the other end. "Perhaps tomorrow when you are 'up' you should call again. And when you are 'better,' that is when you are out, you should come to see me."

It was equivocal of course. Holding on to Bemelman or letting go of him and depositing him on the floor while I organized the cigarette and the match and the dime and the phone book—remember not to call the cottage but the house—it all seemed simple. Mother's side had put me away. Starting with Sally who did it last month in California. I got out of that by falsely swearing I was a voluntary patient, a ratty little game I played with the bully in charge who was afraid I would make trouble for having been involuntary to start with, ambulance drivers having nearly broken my arms while I looked on in amazement. Sal had told me we were going to visit a psychiatrist: I presumed in an office. It turned out to be a locked ward. And then Mother takes the ball—when coming home from California to New York I stop off at her insistence in St. Paul—and she has slammed the gates of hell closed again, maybe permanently. Until the good guys, the lawyers come. Then the folly and chicanery of court, the fustian and comedy of proving one's sanity: I go off each morning like Joan of Arc on her way to the stake. Even prepared to be quizzed on the multiplication tables since the trial is in St. Paul, and sanity in Ramsey County is established by statute as having the multiplication tables in thorough good order.

The evening I called my aunt it was part of a strategy to keep or restore or retain my sanity against all this confusion. First I took a wonderful bath: the baths at the university hospital are both marble and glorious, the veins of the stone as old as time, as pure as sculpture, as hard as history or the ancient world, the very memory of the planet's passing through the ages engraved, inlaid in deposits of fossil with petrified metal material running through them, the remains of another world. And then a vision appeared, an old woman who was Sita and not Sita, who was an Egyptian and a gypsy, all the poor of the world but nobility in disguise—probably simply another patient or more likely an attendant, dark, mysterious. But suddenly fraught with enormous meaning to me: a profound compassion suffused me; the day in court vanished, the place itself. Or rather it converted itself from a hellhole crazyhouse to something as innocuous as my sorority house at college, here at this same university, only a few blocks away. Pass over all this present unpleasantness and congratulate the place on having decent bathtubs anyway; real marble, that's class. Basic materials, you can't beat it. If the whole place disintegrated or were demolished, including the bars on the windows, they ought to leave this intact; this is worthy of a real hospital.

And I emerged feeling fresh enough to tease the nurse about hopscotch and the Charleston, and the similarity between the two, and the checkerboard floor tiles before her desk, demonstrating a step. And no doubt persuading her of the congruity of being her prisoner at the same time.

My own good humor has persuaded me that she is not my jailer, merely a convenient presence like a hotel clerk, someone who knows the time and what day it is and the weather, someone to say hello and good night to. So I go off to my room for the dime. I have been waiting for the moment to spend this dime. It is time to call in the Milletts, I think, the other side of the family. We are winning in court and it is now time to check out the other team. If one team locks you up, the other team is likely to be on your side. After a lifetime of their rivalry and the division of loyalty, this is a logical conclusion.

It is possible that the lawyers have even apprised the Milletts of my plight through Aunt Dorothy. They are in fact rather fancy St. Paul civil rights lawyers, do lots of *pro bono* work for the Indians in the state—my own case is to set a precedent in cases of lifelong commitment imposed upon Indians all the time here. The rationale being that if the state can put me away—despite my education, publications, reputation, etc.—how very easy to do it to an Indian in the north country: poverty, alcoholism, record of delinquency, lots of psychiatric drugs, no opportunity to demand a legal hearing. The attorneys are in fact very good men, but they are also an upper-class outfit from an old family, my aunt's own world; the head of the firm is one of her very best friends. Though they came to my aid for my own sake and for those who may benefit from the precedent, there may also be some other support or obligation deriving from her. The man in charge is Stuart White's own son; I knew Stuart in my childhood. He met my plane once in Chicago as I was being sent by my parents from St. Paul to my Aunt Harriet in Philadelphia. It had been a rough flight and I had been very sick, so the good man was presented with a shaken little tyke who had not dirtied herself but, far worse, had vomited all over the army sergeant who sat next to her and been held back in punishment as the plane emptied, the hostess having decided she was dangerous. Not sure what to do, Stuart filled me with malted milks and hamburgers and put me on a plane for San Francisco. An error discovered on the runway. My life might have been very different indeed. Stuart White himself is in Sweden just now, but his son had sent another member of the firm, Donald Heffernan, to save me from the state. Mother's attorneys, our opponents, Pierce Butler III, St. Paul's fanciest lawyer of all, is another one of my aunt's closest friends and a squire in her divorcée days. When Mother went to Pierce to divorce my father, Dorothy turned up her eyes in pique: to use her own lawyer to divorce her brother—so she is more likely to be on the Stuart White team this time. And anyway, doesn't it stand to reason that if your mother's people put you away, the Milletts with their usual contrariness would say you weren't crazy and be for getting you out? It is politics of the two families: even the sociology of St. Paul.

So I will knock now on that door, dare to call her up and present myself, make it sound funny, another one of those family things: "I'm doing just fine, have the nicest lawyers, a wonderful guy from Stuart White's. This way we can test the law, don't you see, get a precedent. They are hoping in fact to introduce legislation this fall so that on one can be committed without trial. The hospital's not so bad if you overlook the iron grating, that sort of thing." And then her reply. Then my stunned, dazed disappointment. Which is not entire: after all, you are to get in touch if you make it. Did she know, did she expect this call, is it a fetch? Her mask of not helping is preserved: after all you are under a bit of a cloud just now; responsible citizens don't open their arms to maniacs. Or is she merely perplexed, bothered at home in the evening? I was careful to call before nine-thirty, the prescribed moment beyond which you do not trouble a lady, rules learned here in childhood. Does she even remember who I am after all these years? A scapegrace. A figure in the phone booth of a loony house, carefully repossessing a children's book and trailing off to bed. To practice Mahatma Ghandi's patience or Buddhist prayer or tomorrow's arguments in court.

And when it was all over, the champagne in the room behind the courtroom, long-distance phone calls of rejoicing, they took me to Stuart's beautiful house where the paintings made me cry for the sheer joy of a red Mondrian or of a Chinese line on a scroll after the emptiness of the bin. Which now the sight of a real house made me realize might have gone on and on, years, a lifetime shot to hell in wards behind bars; then I rested. And in a few days I went over to Percy Carroll's house and spent some easy days on the porch. It was from the porch that I called A.D. again. And was given an invitation to dinner some five days hence, clear into next week. I thought I'd be going back East very soon, probably the weekend, returning to the farm. But she steadfastly maintained that was the first day she was free. Moreover there was the attraction of a certain witty priest also invited for dinner that Tuesday; I'd be sure to enjoy him. The last thing I need in the world is an amusing cleric. I feel the pull of any invitation from her—and then withdraw, pull away. Just out of a loony bin, my life in ruins around me, I want to see my aunt.

And the last obstacle I want to struggle against for her comfort is some ordained pedant, the charm of his erudition, that sort of thing. Yet I feel its pull, talking to her. Perhaps these are the delights of civilization; where else in the world would you find them but out here? The soft lull of Percy's porch, the comfort of it, home in St. Paul, a place you might try to describe to someone but give up after a moment. So foreign it is to New York, the blistery desert of Poughkeepsie—what do you have to go back for anyway? Everything has fallen apart with Fumio, every soul you ever knew in New York has decided upon hearing of your "nervous breakdown" that you are mad now and permanently disabled. A casualty if you keep silence but if you call them and enter upon your troubles you are merely a nut. You have lost your name and reputation. A natural circumstance of losing your mind. Here Percy and Sheila treat you as a normal human being; your aunt even seems to want to see you. On her terms of course, five days from now. But the invitation is real and warmer than years.

Why then plead you must go home? Because you have

a farm and must take care of it. Because you might still patch things up with Fumio. Because you can't hang around five days for a meal. Because you don't like being put off. And maybe you are not too sure you want to impose for five more days—Mother's is out. Having lost her suit against my liberty and for my "treatment" on an indefinite basis, Mother is vexed indeed. I had a friend bring me to Mother's to collect my clothes, a professor from Macalester who specializes in St. Paul writers, a penchant that stiffened her sufficiently to accompany me to Mother's, for she is a friend of Mother's as well. Still Pat Kane stood by my side against Mother's wrath and even Sally's furious curtain line about how I had "better get myself together pretty damn quick." I think I managed to keep my mouth shut and limit rebuttal to a fairly gentle remark that if Sal intended to finish law school and enter the bar it might be a good idea if she looked into civil liberties a bit. Sally became a fine and sensitive attorney and we became friends again over the years. With my aunt too, I figured there'd be time, the next speaking engagement or reading that brought me to the Middlewest. There was ever so much time then. Especially for the people out there; they would always be there, always had. What was necessary was to rush back East again, plunge into my own life, re-establish what I could.

And when I came out of the wreck, depression followed in the fall growing into suicide in the winter; the urge to die was overpowering, the hatred of life. Depression, if not the partner of mania, was certainly the partner of incarceration, the shame of it, the loneliness. Fumio gone, the old Bowery studio condemned to demolition for structural reasons by the City of New York, the eviction, the limbo of being without a studio in the city, a home, a place to work, being exiled to the farm in winter or taking shelter in Ruth's little room, for Ruth was the only friend left—it had been as I had predicted about friends. Except for Washburn who buoyed me up and suspected the suicide plans and suggested calling it plan A. Why not try plan B first? Lithium and so forth. Then the long struggle out of depression, back to productivity, to having a few friends, something of a name again, a little reputation for honor or sanity or intelligence.

Years of recovery blasted in a summer when I went off lithium and according to Sophie, my companion, acted odd. In no time I was awarded the status of crazy again. In no time the rumor spread, calling forth the *sine qua non* of commitment—a family member. So Mallory was informed and by the end of the summer a little cabal faced me. Which included even Washburn. Mallory of course indispensable. And a perfect stranger billed as a psychiatrist—the bunch of them confronting me in my studio a few hours before I was to take off for St. Paul to see both my mother and my aunt. The last time I would see her.

PART FOUR

I knew when I felt it in my hand that it was trouble. That kind of envelope. Even before that address. Them. Him. It. The will. Money. The judgment. The bad news. Whatever Ransom had said about a bequest—after all, a bequest could be an old covered chair, perfect in its age, antiquity, well-worn elegance. Its value like gold as a memento. But this is the will. Money. The whole tribe yelling in my head, the old disgrace, the old sense of losing out, the old certain understanding of the poor relation.

Idiot to have waited for the mail, opened the front door

at the Bowery again upon seeing the postman. The car was ready at the curb—we are going to the farm. Carefree. And you were stupid enough to fetch the damn mail out of the box. The usual everyday hope—finding money but getting bills instead. For the fourteen years I have been a writer my agent has sent me checks in cream-colored envelopes which are the first thing I look for in every mail. Then the bills. Con Edison, things that have to be paid or else: ignore that stuff at your peril. But there are other wonders that arrive in the mail: little checks and money orders from folk who want autographed copies or a poster. Letters from friends that can make your whole day and would be fun to read on the road.

And instead this thing, the big telltale gray envelope with the green border. The lawyer. He had said we would be getting something about now. It was the only civil thing he did say, in fact. I had called him to ask again about A.D.'s books. Having written but not heard from him and spurred on by Uncle Bob's encouragement. Bob and Lucy had liked my letter, approved the idea, wanted me to have Dorothy's books. "And you should call this fellow, the lawyer—you should probably call him right away in fact. It's in his hands, not ours—but we're behind you." How kind Bob's voice, after all these years. Sophie had called me out of the darkroom to talk to a Mr. Kissack. "Ah, but that's my Uncle Bob," I said, feeling like a child, a niece crossing the studio to take up the phone: the old excitement, the old timidity. Compounded by twenty-five years of ostracism.

"If you are going to be like that, we cannot know you," Bob dismissed me in the driveway after the terrible Christmas, the discovery of my crime, infamy, recriminations—on his part a farewell. If you are going to be like that. A queer, a homosexual, a lesbian, the word too awful nearly to think out loud—a word no one ever said in all this turmoil. Or a liar? Because of course I had lied to them and they had me there. I could hardly argue whether my kind of love were right or wrong: nor indeed would discretion permit them to, either. But a liar, lying—that was against the code of either of us. Clearly wrong and more than wrong, sneaky, base, dishonorable.

And twenty-five years have passed since this favorite uncle bid me adieu. Yet his voice is warm and kind as ever: it does not seem to age or hardly at all, still velvet, sexy, intimate. This uncle taught me the tango—this courtier, this consummate gentleman, the word congruent with that voice, its amazing gentleness, its depth and music. Representing him in the one dimension of sound so accurately that you see the great mustache and the height of the man, the European manner, the childhood spent in France as the son of a painter who became an art historian and held the first chair of art at the University of California. My uncle was an English scholar himself who did Chaucer at Oxford and then became an early documentary filmmaker, finally an army officer in some undisclosed function, now a retired colonel in Newport News.

How can Sally keep saying he was CIA? Walter too—the lot of them, what a family—nights when Sal and I drink together on the phone and try to figure it all out over long distance, a martini before each of us. Sundays taking advantage of the rates to be extravagant. "Walter got drunk once toward the end—you know he was off the wagon, it's what killed him—but I suspect that indiscretion did him in even more than booze. Because you don't admit you're CIA, you know; they'll do you in for that." "Couldn't they just fire him—he only cost a dollar a year." "Nope. He knew too much. He was drunk one night and I think he told Ed." She is long divorced from Ed. Ed's far away and it's the cocktail hour and Sally relishes a good gossip, is Irish enough to love this kind of talk: part mythology, part supposition and the other ninety percent the sheer bravado of telling. The virtual outrage of what is said, the unspeakable. Abomination in daylight or under scrutiny or with other listeners—strangers. Ed was a lieutenant colonel in the Strategic Air Command and it is probably true that as an air attaché for two years in Afghanistan he fulfilled some fairly customary intelligence function. Or knew that others did. Or something.

It's all very vague to me; I live on the Bowery, am a Bowery artist drinking as night comes down with my big sister the lawyer who knows the world, knows the family, knows a million stories I will never remember in the morning or keep straight in the retelling. I am chiefly enjoying her voice, the companionship and affection of these confabulations. That fact that Elder is confiding in me, giving me the lowdown. Also the mischief, that as the pillar of the family and the mother of four and a member of the bar she is speaking heresy, letting her hair down, divulging scandal to me the sinner, the writer, the sieve.

We veer between sentiment and scandal, enjoying both equally, experiencing with each an equal release. We now mourn our aunt in long painful silences which do not very successfully cover tears, spaces we laugh at or admit to. We create the past again in humdrum remarks, sarcasms, practicalities. Sometimes we just cuss our luck. That what we had as children we no longer have—A.D. and all she represented: the sense of wonder, the recklessness, the love and beauty which we now believe money destroyed. Mother's version. Our own understanding, which we veer toward and then away from, that we destroyed it ourselves. Either through being a disappointment to our idol, or simply betraying her. My case. Sally's is different, one of immense angry frustration. Elder will not accept death. She was older and closer to Dorothy and to Dad. With both of them she chose to be outraged by neglect or absence. I only presumed to be hurt. "A bitch, she really turned into a bitch," Sally grumbles, gin trying to put out her tears. And then we begin the refrain of her coldness again. That they are all heartless people, the Milletts. Being Mother's children, we condemn them, pick them apart, look for flaws, find scandal with a Millett interest in tall tales, unlikely irreverence. But the scandal has a special complicity in it that returns us to our closeness in childhood, stamps us as rebels, sophisticates, heretics. In her sauce my elder sister has heretical tendencies that are alarming and very lovable. Lovable—and I suppose these conversations are an expensive kind of lovemaking between us as sisters.

Cheaper than airfare, she would say canonically. Safer too, I think—we won't even quarrel: a tone or inflection will ward us away and we are not there in person to tire of each other and finally lose patience. I with her conservatism, she with my radical righteousness and impracticality. And the tale spurs us on. "I'm pretty sure Walter got so drunk he talked—Dorothy invited the two of us to have dinner with them at the Radisson one night and Walter made a fool of himself: I looked at Dorothy—you know she was incapable of embarrassment in that highhanded way of hers—well, she was in agony that night, she could have died—or better yet killed him." "Mother says she did," I laugh. "That's baloney." "Sure it is, I said it to make you laugh. But I wouldn't be surprised if Mother still believes this. Or she used to." "I know it; it's still baloney." "There are about three versions of how Walter died, I think. Dorothy said he fell in the bathroom—that's the official version. Mother says she pushed him—that's unofficial." "I know, Mom says A.D. had a black eye at the funeral." "That's the third then—self-defense." "All baloney—Walter was so drunk that night that he told Ed, actually told him—they went into the bar for a while so Walter could bang down a lot of scotch—Ed says Walter told him, one way or another—but in no uncertain terms—you know that jargon and code crap—Walter admitted to Ed he was CIA." "So how does that kill him?" "They rubbed him out." "Oh, Sal—you're too much." "Listen, Walter lost control entirely by the end and they do that sort of thing. If he talked to Ed, he was talking to other people too and he wouldn't have been safe." I hear paranoia, she hears innocence. We laugh, I light up, we both sip a little gin.

We have had a great many occasions since our aunt died to rehearse family history, resentments, inequities, character failures, and funeral procedures. And this lawyer fellow. With whom I fell out of favor early, but that is to be expected. He has lately denounced me for inquiring about my aunt's books. But didn't he tell me on the phone that we should all help him—friends and relatives as well—his first letter reiterated it—because Dorothy had not made sufficient arrangements for her personal belongings? So if there were a chair or some dishes or whatever, friends in Wayzeta and even relatives at a distance who had a fondness for something should speak up. I was fond of the books. I spoke up. Dorothy's sisters Lucy and Harriet were executors, together with the lawyer in charge of requests, I thought, so I petitioned all three, and had Bob's and Lucy's vote—Bob said I should notify the lawyer at once, before other arrangements were made. So in considerable trepidation and with a very small frightened voice I telephoned the great man, Hank Ransom. Never mind that I don't know him: he is in charge of the books I loved as a child and have wanted to inherit all my life. Moreover, he is something I could not become—a close friend of my aunt's. It seems Sally called him this week as well and now he claims that "all of you" are putting him under great pressure: "This is a regular lemon squeezer and I will not put up with it."

Why not, I wonder, though I dare not say it—you are being paid a very handsome sum to handle these matters. Your own instructions bid us make requests and these things were my aunt's. But the man talks as if he were himself the heir. All right. I accede to that; you are a Minneapolis swell, my aunt's friend and neighbor: I'm a Bowery artist she perhaps didn't like. You win; you have always been right: you inherited and own the town, I'm an exile, even a pervert—have it your way. But must you bully, hurt my feelings so? I have written you a charming letter, asking for your friendship, for reminiscences of my aunt, even a foolish lover's line asking if she had ever spoken of me to him. He gets to that right off. His follow-up letter will say it in indelible linear type: My aunt mentioned me only once in his company and the reference was perfectly neutral. I don't dare ask what it was: that I wrote, was a feminist—or just the reference in her will. I rigidly refuse to discuss wills—my interest is books and photographs. I have won a nod about photographs. Can I win one about books? Non-monetary things: however much he may despise me he can at least get it into his head that it is not money I want. Did I not scream at him—at least in my mind—that very first phone call when he mentioned a bequest—that I did not want money.

Now, at last here is the will. Money. Finally you will have to deal with the money part. Probably you will have to deal with it all the rest of your life. As permanently and thoroughly as you will have to live with her death—you will now have to live with her will. Because that's what's in this damned gray envelope that you were unwise enough to return for. Never meaning to get this—meaning only to get the mail out of the same idle curiosity that makes one open it every day. Now you have ruined the weekend.

Once it is here, once it is on Sophie's lap as we drive away, turning at Great Jones and coming down the Bowery to take a right onto Houston Street, heading for the West Side Highway, off and away to the farm, the clear road under the George Washington Bridge, Westchester and Yonkers and then the high lonely beauty of the Taconic State Parkway—and you are not even out of town before you must ask Sophie to open it. She does and then hands it across to me behind the wheel. "Here, take a look, but you'd be wiser to forget it all till we get there." And the first look, still driving, is rather wonderful. Reading inaccurately with one eye on the road the paper appears to inform me that my aunt left two thousand dollars. Sum total. Rather modest it seems—maybe really she kept her promise and spent it all. That day on the boat sofa and she grinned me out of all residual avarice by stating simply that she had it planned so that she would spend every cent by her death. I was delighted: how wonderful if indeed she would spend all her money on herself, appropriate it entirely to herself. That removes all temptation, erases the past, all the predatory urges of my upbringing. If she really uses every cent before her death there will no longer be any money between us. We will be equal. She will have hers, just as much as she needs; I will go out into the world and find my own. Meanwhile I will deal with her on an equal footing, no more dependent, no more someone casting an eye, proposing and hoping and receiving or not receiving. Oxford has capped it all; her generosity will cease here and now and we will be peers. I was twenty-four years old and already employed, contracted to a college for an annual four thousand five hundred dollars, a magnificent sum it took years to understand was actually underpayment. We are on the same plane at last; however much money she has, she needs it all; keeping up this house takes a fortune, she had said, waving a hand about toward the rooms. Right, I think, of course. It must take ten thousand a year to keep her house here. She will need every bit. She speaks of spending it out, spending everything before she dies. She describes this with utter relish. Good—in fact the best. We are friends now finally. There is nothing of money between us.

SO THIS DREARY DOCUMENT, trying to interpret it while behind the wheel, it seems to say—papers like this are deceptive, dangerous: you must read them many times and consider—but here it is plain: two thousand is the whole amount left. Wow—she really did spend it all. But of course that's the money for her relatives and so forth. There is also the Guthrie Theater. And the Minnesota Symphony, as they are now calling the Minneapolis symphony, our hometown team, where we sat in the two sacred first balcony seats, second row, all the enchanted Friday evenings of my adolescence. The Minneapolis Institute of Fine Arts too. Even the St. Paul Chamber Orchestra—they are all inheriting as well. The proceeds of the sale of her house and so forth. Maybe even the books too—well that's how it goes. The choice of the Guthrie and culture itself, fine ideas. So two thousand, though it seems comically small, is delightfully small. She'll divide that equally among all her surviving kin. Maybe it's more, maybe even two thousand apiece—whichever. It's fair and kind and it's a terrific idea.

I hand it back to Sophie, delighted. We proceed in silence as she reads, "I think you better look at this again some other time: you're mentioned here." "Yah. I guess everybody gets about two thousand: it's a really very nice idea. There might be a bit more for her sisters, Lucy and Harriet, that would be the right thing." "No, you haven't understood at all. It's not two thousand dollars on the first page, it's two million." "Good heavens." "And it's divided differently. Not equally." "Well, Lucy and Harriet should get more: they are her own generation, her sisters, closer than anyone." "They did very nicely. Don't you want to know what you got?"

Suddenly my throat closes and I am a little sick and very afraid. "You got twenty-five thousand dollars." "Good God." "Here, see it. On the second page." I look and see my name, the second down on a list of the decedents of James Millett, Sally the first name: but a fabulous sum, far more than mine. I'm hurt, furious. My own name Kate, twenty-five: my younger sister, Mallory, twenty-five. Feeling outraged on Mallory's part as on my own, maybe more. When you come to think of it, she did less to offend—and this is the punishment list, as well or instead of, the Christmas bonus. This is what we are being told at the end: after death comes the final statement of our worth.

"You should be glad to be on it at all, after everything." "Sure, but what did Mallory do to deserve this insult, this inequity? I was a liar or a queer or whatever my Oxford folly and disowning meant, but what did Mallory do?" Remembering but still hardly crediting Mallory's bitterness when I called just after Aunt Dorothy died: "Don't cry; she was hard, she was cold and cruel to us all these years; why make yourself miserable?" "Mallory." "I mean it; when I divorced Ron and was all alone out in the Philippines I wrote her a letter. But not for money." "Well, maybe you needed some." "Listen, it was not for money, it was for some kind of support. I lost out there and I wanted to reach out and touch my family so I wrote her a long letter. Will you believe what she did?" "Well, she was always on Ronnie's side; she liked him. She liked his parents. Mother said she liked them as drinking buddies." "Listen, I'm perfectly serious—what she did with that letter is this—she called Mother and read the letter over the phone, making fun of it." I realize that this is Mother's version, but say nothing—Mallory is in a fury and an actress cannot be interrupted in a tirade. "She made fun of it! Every loving thing I said she ridiculed." I listen and say nothing, remembering A.D.: that voice in insult, in sarcasm, in sheer annihilation. Yes, she could have done that, probably was angry at what she took to be a begging letter from a twenty-year-old: the style, the handwriting, that college-girl printed scrawl, the cheek of her leaving a good man and so forth, even a good family—she thought in those terms.

"But I was not asking her for money," Mallory shrieks into the phone. Hurt, so hurt, my little sister. Will she be hurt now again when she reads this? "And she has never forgiven me or seen me or spoken to me since. She doesn't give a damn about Kristen"—Mallory's daughter, also an actress. "Yes, she does, Mallory; the last time I saw her she said she'd been watching Kristen in the soaps and adored her. In fact—do you want to know what she said?" No mother can resist praise and Mallory will come around—"She said the family had a real one there." A silence. "A.D. said that Kristen had great promise. I swear she said that." What will Mallory feel when she reads this, my urge to protect her as strong as in childhood? Of course it is inevitable that I should get less if I got anything. But shouldn't Mallory have what Sally had and not be lumped with me, outcast and bohemian with a fraction of Sal's portion?

Moreover, Mallory has a child; I have none. If there is any justification beyond a favoritism that condemns others in rewarding one, it is that Sally has more because Sally has four children. But Mallory has a child too; Kristen is nowhere mentioned. Nor Sally's children. Although our cousin Claire's three sons are. Each of them inherits a quarter of a million. So does Claire. Altogether one million dollars. "Staggering," Sophie clucks. I stay on the road. Claire, my same-age cousin, nearly a sibling, my childhood buddy; we spent summers together, were best friends, the dark cousin and the fair. She is Harriet's child. It is something less to be one of Jim's. What on earth has Claire done to be so beloved? But I know. Even living all the way in Hong Kong the last twenty-five years and visiting rarely, Claire has, besides a fortune of her own, married a great banker and raised three sons. I'm outclassed.

But my very hands on the steering wheel agree with the slow realization forming in my head—a quarter of a million dollars would fuck you up entirely. Utterly. You'd never work again. At anything that made sense: writing or pictures or sculpture. For you a quarter of a million would mean only one thing: Sleight Farm. A women's college there, a new women's college, not just an art colony. Big stuff, utopian schemes. You'd pay cash and end up sitting on a lot of new acreage you couldn't even farm without personnel or machinery. All by yourself, land poor as a maniac, scrounging for mortgages and loans, someone to administer this half-baked megalomania in a noble cause. You would run from place to place in the external world and never write another word. Fortunately Sleight Farm, which a few years ago was going bag and baggage for a quarter of a million, lands and manor house, enormous barns begging for conversion to studios, two hundred fifty acres of prime farmland dressed and tilled since fifteen years before the American Revolution—is now off the market. No suitable buyers. Even horse breeders wouldn't make a good offer. So the Sleights carved out six building sites for suburbia—one small section of land. The farm is broken up now and may go on being sold in little pieces for big prices. Piecemeal's a better deal for them: their original price was only a thousand dollars an acre—disregarding valuable structures—and now an acre lot costs thirty thousand dollars and up in our neighborhood.

Without Sleight Farm to buy, you wouldn't want to buy anything. Live on the interest? The interest on that kind of money—my God, that would be enough to live on. You'd never have to worry again—set for life. No surprises. But how boring. To have it known, set out in little bank certificates—the future. That could be dangerous. So the actual bread might make you sick and lethargic and lost. Haven't you seen plenty of artists wrecked and impotent from family money, even a little of it? But the gift of bread—that's the rub. That others got and you were refused. Hard enough that Sally, my own elder sister, should outshine me so many times over in my aunt's love. For that's what it comes to. There is no way around it; the voice from the grave, the paper drawn up, as Sophie notes, in 1979. Revised in December, 1980.

What was I doing that year? But I saw her in '80. A whole year late for the meeting I missed by going to Iran; that day she might have forgiven me if I'd shown up. Was even prepared to take me to lunch at a restaurant in her village she said was "not that bad." The idea was forbidding—why not her house? It was also her rooms that I wanted to see, to see her in those rooms. And then never saw her at all, saw the revolution instead, then at the end Khomeini and the triumph of reaction. And was arrested and tossed out of the country. Did she worry for me or only find me rude, bizarre? I was surely so that August afternoon in '80, arriving at last. Of course I couldn't just get up and go there: too busy, too thrifty, too pessimistic. I had to tag this visit onto a reading at the university that could pay the ticket. But once there I had summoned my courage, called and gotten permission to drive out that day. She would see me at two o'clock. In fact seeing A.D. was the real reason I had come at all, to make peace before I went to Europe that fall. Being crazy at the time, or thought to be, the pressure of opinion all through the summer had probably made me strange by the time I arrived. The meeting burning back into my mind, in shame, in folly, even ironically perhaps it seems now, in lost opportunity. Imagining it was only a love affair I pursued when in fact I was possibly doing myself out of a fortune too. The hell with it.

But you were still so stupid, arriving late, getting lost. It had been that long—that you could get lost going to Wayzeta, forgetting the turn by the mansions that begin the lake drive. Some familiar, some strange, bewildered everywhere, stopping to ask the real estate agent. Showing up with your hair brushed at least—when I was a block away I stopped the car just to brush my hair—that kind of thing was crucial. But the outfit was wrong. I had thought a dress, sandals, a straw hat—since A.D. now wears pants I thought this was not only dressed up but even chic. Straight too; maybe there was a touch of one-upmanship in that. It backfired.

"I wouldn't have known you; you look like a gypsy," was her greeting. With a lifetime as this difficult woman's niece behind me, I braced myself under this remark, tried to reply with humor: "I'm staying with the Heffernans and had to use their clothes dryer; like most things in St. Paul it moves slowly and that made me late." Of course I had gotten lost: my enormous sorrow and shame that I would not appear eager, polite, civil enough to be on time. Knowing her time was rationed by her illness.

She was old at last, yet still beautiful. Whatever was wrong with her seemed to affect her legs but she refused to discuss it. Beyond the fact that she had to rest at four. It was now nearly three. I had lost one of my two hours. Talk fast. And I did not tell her what I meant to say: the apology, the love, the long passion. Or did, but did badly, offending through frankness. "I have loved you all my life," I said. "Even been in love with you." Her look back at me challenging, forbidding. "As children are." I side-step. "And have never lost that adoration." The piercing green eyes, terrible, meaning yes, meaning no, meaning all and nothing at all.

What happened? It is even hard to remember. There were tears. Mine; maybe hers. I do remember bitching at Mallory for having tried to have me put away in Payne Whitney only a few days before, my outrage still fresh and furious. But you do not complain of your sisters to your aunt: we know that, all of us. Her eyes discouraged and disapproved. "You must be in control of yourself," she intoned. My tears were proof I was not. And then the oddest thing, toward the end of my account—which I should have made funny and fully intended to—indeed it is obligatory among us, the Millett thing, to turn any tragic experience into giddiness, gaiety—but I had been unable, talked with the tears in my throat if no longer in my eyes—and I had the strangest impression of having seen her finger remove a tear from the corner of an eyelid when I finished. What else could it have been—an Arab gesture of disbelief? Perhaps she was laughing to herself. It was probably impossible she could be moved for me and yet I imagined it was possible, fancying that, fantasizing as I have fantasized her love, imagining a secret reciprocity all these years. The romance I pretended to myself during the visit after Oxford, the kiss in childhood. Now here near the end, in her age and illness, what if she still cared for me? The scapegrace who should never be encouraged, but was still in a hidden way cared about, followed from afar.

Mad fantasy that she always knows where I am. Between her money and her contacts there is always a way to know whom this niece lives with, if she is in jail or a crazy house or about to be summarily expelled from some distant theocracy. And she would know. She would simply make a telephone call or receive one. Did she know when months later I was busted into a madhouse in Ireland? The American embassy knew and the FBI made a report that I was stirring up troublesome support in Southern Ireland and among Irish Americans and feminists and other elements on behalf of the rebels in the North and the political prisoners in the H blocks then on hunger strike. And did all that pass into her ear from a discreet voice somewhere? Did she get me into scrapes or custody or did she get me out? Or did she just decide in December of that year that I was a lost cause entirely and knock me off with a sum small enough so that it didn't matter if I squandered it?

Who knows? On the other hand, she might have written you in on the 1980 revision. After you did come to see her and say you were sorry. Though you didn't say it well. She even asked you how you did for money. And your answer was something brave about how you did well enough, a little miracle of living from one gig to the other that was always an adventure. Moreover you had the world's most beautiful farm—wouldn't she come and see it? The last fantasy of all. First forgiveness, then friendship, then the hearth at the farm in her age. You would take care of her: you could be martini cronies by the pond. Imagining her in each room of the farmhouse, her foot crossing your threshold, her taller figure leaning on your shoulder. Splendid dinners.

That visit you were off to Europe with Alex and for once you did not mention Sophie or a lover, made it clear you and Alex were merely friends by calling Alex your "curator" as a joke—"Alex is an art historian and she helped me set up this show in Amsterdam; she's going along for the museums." A.D. raises an eyebrow. But how pompous you were, how overblown you were for having just had your first show in Europe the spring before in Berlin. Now this one in Amsterdam. As if you were taking the art world by storm. When, like Mother, she would probably only believe in your books if she even believed in them.

Not much. She makes friendly ironic reference to the footnotes in *Sexual Politics,* but the rest are anathema. I had sent her *The Basement* that summer but she found the book incredible. Life on another planet, too terrible. We had been trading puns on the nature of tragedy over the telephone when I called to ask permission to visit and tabled the discussion only to forget it when together. So *The Basement* failed. But before I left I tried to foist my books on her with a bovine lovesickness. If only to validate, give proof, that whatever I did or was said to me—I had done this. I had not made children, nephews and nieces, not made money or a good marriage, but I had these real and tangible proofs of my existence; I had produced these objects and these alone. You could hold all I had done in fifteen years under one arm, or both arms, counting the mass of *Going to Iran* which I had the temerity to present as well, mere typescript, still not even in print. But together with Mother she was referred to in the text and she should know beforehand, if only to object before publication. She wouldn't bother. She wouldn't even bother to accept it in its black spring binder. No, absolutely not. Then the *Elegy for Sita;* this is a rare edition. There were only three hundred fifty copies printed; each is signed. Isn't it lovely paper, the edges haven't even been cut. "No, I detested *Sita* and I do not want this either." "Really—" stung past tears, the sheer surprise of it, this slap. I clutch at the notion that perhaps it is jealousy of Sita, as I have told myself for years that perhaps it was jealousy that made her so angry to start with, over Jaycee, that I had gone to Oxford with "another woman." When she should be my all—this invented romance of mine.

Though it hardly suffices at this moment, it does help face those few more seconds until I am out the door. For I began the book attack even as I was leaving, being made to leave early, being ushered out unceremoniously—it was time for her to rest. A moment before, the telephone had rung and it was the order to rest. Who gave it, I wondered, the kitchen, the butler who brought the martini? Young, too young and good-looking, I thought, and a very poor hand at making drinks. There will be a new couple, not William and Bernice anymore; they've bought a farm and moved away. So will it be the cook from the kitchen? Or do you telephone from the kitchen to the library? Only a wall and a few feet separate them. She had to get up and go into the library even to take the call. Is there a nurse or a therapist hidden away? What is the nature of this illness? Apart from the slowness in walking (but then she fell in the powder room years back and broke her pelvis: that might account for it). What else is there she is not talking about, refuses to talk about? Preferring trees or her garden, or even my subjects. And adamantly refusing to discuss her health, making it a gaucherie to ask after you have asked and been ordered to desist.

A moment before she was telling me there was a performance of Oscar Wilde tonight in Minneapolis and she was being asked to attend as a backer. Did I like him, would I like to see it? So in my folly I imagined I would be staying for dinner and the theater. Why not overnight? When I left Alex I had joked that I might not be home for dinner if I was found worthy of being fed. What a pleasant and sympathetic choice, an evening of Oscar Wilde. I wonder idly if my old friend Percy Carroll will be there tonight; it's his kind of thing. I may even know other people there: it would be like being home as one accepted and belonging. Rather than the hurried trips where I stay with Mother and see no one my own age, no peers and cronies, nothing cultural or social. I would be a writer coming back to town: I fantasize a place on the St. Croix, old hopes and illusions having a foot in the place still, making new friends to fill the lacuna of all the years I have been away. The afternoon light in my glass, the tears of reunion and acceptance dried: perhaps, I think, perhaps.

And then in a moment I was out the door. Her nap—it is time for her nap. It is stupid to offer to go down to the village and shop for a bit while she naps, then I could come back. No, it's over. You don't say things like that—you don't suggest that you could come back again tomorrow. You know the way now and would be on time, could see her during the appointed and approved hours then. If only. No, you say nothing; you only try to hide your shame.

You know what you are in this family: outcast, sinner, poor relation.

And mad to boot. Since you were mad enough to tell her so. And the old crime of liar, atoned for in dogged honesty all these years, before the press and in public life—you have that around your neck still—for all the books you are trying to gather up to offer. So the books were the last possible gambit, a forlorn hope. You had brought copies of each one, pristine and with fondly inscribed flyleaves.

She has *Sexual Politics,* has read it, needs no extra copy. *Flying* was already sent to her with an inscription, she claims. There is no evidence she has read it. She insists she reads them only if I send them. What temerity to send *Flying;* what a cocky thing I must have been to engrave my love and dispatch it to her from Alfred Knopf's own personal desk, set down there one day to send off copies to important persons on an afternoon when he was out of town and his office was open to visiting authors to pad out the list of critics. This was a critic indeed. She has nothing to say about it—how I would love to know what she thought. How much I would dread knowing. So I dropped it. She has *Sita* too since I sent it. Again, I am staggered I actually had the nerve. As to *Sita,* A.D. volunteers how much she hated it. And rejects the *Elegy.* The woman is dead, I say to myself, Sita is dead; why not accept her *Elegy?* Never mind. Then no to *Iran* too. No, no. Out the door. I stand dizzy and alone on the front step.

How little I thought it would end like this when I crossed this stone I stand on, the door shut behind me.

How little—even ten minutes ago, relishing the evening ahead with her. What is she doing now? Does she cry as I do, fumbling in my rented car? I think not. You imagined a tear on her face twice today. Both illusions. She has rid herself of you as if you were an ill-mannered dog. A typhoid carrier. There is no chance to be angry: I am too hurt, battered, insulted. By the time I reach the village I am angry enough to spend two hundred dollars on a lifetime's supply of rubber boots for the farm rains and fleece-lined slippers to wear by the hearth this fall. Idiot—you thought she would ever visit your house. And now to show you are not a poor relation but a big shot you have pissed away all this bread: wild extravagance in someone just leaving for Europe with only a thousand dollars and planning to stay for a while. Consoling yourself with sheepskin at fancy prices.

It was all over and lost. And that was the last time you saw her. All over, the big ideas of reunion, acceptance, being taken back, a friendship, companionship in old age that would exceed, because it was real and adult, the casual wonderment of childhood. Negating, forgiving the errors of your twenties. All past now, all gone like water under the Marshall Avenue bridge, washed clear down to New Orleans under this new disposition. Dreamer. You went to her mad or said to be mad, were rash enough to show up then. The last crime of all, the final indiscretion. How with someone as uptight and rigid, as utterly the soul of convention as she is, how could you have been so foolhardy as to make an appearance at that moment? The other time you were not this crazy—when you got out of the madhouse with Donald Heffernan's help—you passed up her learned clerical dinner (the Irish priest who was so entertaining; come and dine with him Tuesday) and went off home to the farm without even seeing her since you were not about to wait five days for an appointment. But this time you thought you had beat the rap by outwitting Mallory and the posse, complete with psychiatrist, who waylaid you in your studio while packing to come here. "If you go to Minnesota they will surely put you away," Mallory scolded me. "Remember what Mother did last time; just come along with us over to Payne Whitney and take a rest." But I was too smart, too up on my civil rights formulae—in fact I called the police. Who helped me out of a tight spot; nice black cop lighting my cigarette, checking my airplane ticket, ready to flag me a cab. I was within my rights, refused to go willingly and therefore could not be forced. The posse in consternation. I in triumph, a short-lived little victory, but a victory nevertheless. I proceeded to Minnesota, did the reading at the university which had paid for the ticket. And called my aunt for permission to visit.

And then blew the whole thing. Being late. Being crazy. That is, upset. Telling her what had happened, weeping, unstrung, etc. The woman only sees you every couple years and you are always getting put into insane asylums or escaping them or being expelled from places like Iran—what the hell is she supposed to think of you? And she is ill too—have you given any thought to her illness, her fatigue, wanting to consume her always with this perverse passion? Of course she shows you the door. But that moment when I thought I was staying, going to the theater with her, staying for dinner—the two of us at the great table. What happiness. Let us hope it will not be some strange dish like brains tonight, things I used to endure so badly in the old days, a child set before some mess of animal innards, a young relation dreaming of steak and finding the meal was lungs—let it be real people's food.

Cheer up, you're not staying for dinner. You were invited for a drink, not dinner, because you are only worth a drink; she made that clear over the phone. Be a sport and take Alex out for prime rib at the Lex tonight; your mission in St. Paul is accomplished, over, a failure.

And that was the last time. That was 1980, a dark year, an all-star loony bin year. You saw her last that September; by December when your depression set in she was revising her will either to put you in or to knock you down to a fraction of what Sally got, a tenth of what Claire got and so forth. Love's score, the sums of affection—not really money at all but ratings, grade point. She sent you to Oxford and you went with Jaycee. And she found out. And she never forgave. And now she is dead. So when the day of reckoning comes you are knocked down to a fraction. Any sensible aunt with such a niece would do the same, dealing with one so unreliable, unstable, and with so little to recommend her. Crazy and queer; maybe not so crazy but queer. Queer then and still queer and she undoubtedly knows it since you write those notorious indiscreet books. Which shock and implicate and permit reporters to say damaging things about your family. You are someone who has left years ago and scarcely ever returns, a stranger unknown at home now, living in a strange world, a New York artist. Not St. Paul, not one of us anymore. Someone who does not even have an accent.

IMPOSSIBLE for my aunt to believe that I think of her often, almost daily, that she forms the subtext of my mind, that my wrongful erroneous love for her and her anger over all these years are the subjects of my dreams, the fabric of my unconscious, those still-painful moments upon waking which color the morning and darken the first hour of consciousness day after day over long stretches of time. That this sense of being judged and still unforgiven was—is—so pressing it brings me here to plead again for absolution. And finding none, I know my life is in some large portion doomed and condemned. Like fate, like Mother's voice over the phone telling me she is dead, Dorothy is dead. And in that instant I know I will have to live without forgiveness now forever. That there had always been a chance and now there is none, will never be any hope.

And in sleep the mind goes to her over and over. All these years: sometimes for months on end, great dreams of reconciliation, even consummation—why not—these are dreams: the mind without a halter or rein will over and over put me in her arms. Beds, there are beds; we lie upon a bed. Her house, it is never mine—always the unconscious protects me in giving me the role, not of the seducer but of the persuaded. For the essential point is that she be willing. Since I am the lover. No—the beloved. She must announce her desire, secretly, after a lifetime's discretion, reveal her passion. Give in, the one nod or look or touch or outreach of the hand, that final admission. That she too loves a woman. And then the rest is a pact. In which we are equals at last. Past age or authority or money or even old age, we are then peers and companions. Her hand reaching toward mine but not touching it as we lie together across some enormous bed. That is the proof, that assurance, that final and absolute trust. Between two persons who in life had none or so little or it was all demolished, first by me in dishonesty, then by her in obduracy. Now these two hands at rest, in perfect harmony and friendship, touching but not touching, at ease; they become us, the final agreement. Platonic and elevated and then somehow beyond the flesh as is this dream. But there are a thousand other dreams of the rarest eroticism, the perfume of her flesh remembered with a child's tenderness and adoration still mine, but adult. Utopian, transcending every taboo.

We are one then in being women, in being wise and intelligent women, in being humorous, in knowing places and times and years of propinquity and kinship. In knowing the world as well, Paris or Rome or the best streets in Dublin: restaurants, fountains, books, and pictures. And we bring all this to our rapture, to the scent of her flesh as I kiss the soft skin under and behind her ear as she embraces me. The same embrace as childhood but adult and sexual and without ignorance or innocence, our selves looking frankly into each other's eyes. Two women, neither aunt nor niece but that as well, and the green eyes do not turn from me nor do they grow cool and treacherous as in life: those little glints of yellow in the green—utterly terrifying in life. Suddenly angry or contemptuous, the fury of disdain. But in dreams she does not turn against me; she is without guile, frank and trusting. And I am trust itself for at last all that I had cherished is given me. There could be no greater happiness; nothing the psyche has longed for more could come to it. This is the mind's paradise when in hidden hours it invents, completes its hopes, draws its full circle of wish and pattern. This.

In dreams then I have you, there in the quiet waiting corner of the mind. Remembering as Sophie and I pass the ski place on the way to the farm, the mind fleeing the hurt of the paper on my lap, your last will and testament, the overwhelming judgment of it dissipates at this point of the road, the highest moment, the crest of the small mountain one must cross in coming to the farm from the city. The tail of my driver's right eye reading the sign "Fahnstock Ski Area," gauging the slope again—pity it is never open, a park and public funds but never even used—I do not, could not pass a ski slope without you being present. For you and Dad taught me to ski. But you especially, you for whom I skied, a ski bum, page and knight errant of your craft and sport out in Sun Valley, another railroad resort. Not Glacier, which was the Hills' and yours, coming to power through winning young Louis. No, another railroad, another resort. A college girl imagining I was being original, skiing away my terror of skiing, down the exhibition run and every other vertical terror I could find until I could ski behind the American women's team at practice. Still without breaking a limb—I went on escaping the great fear, for skiing can kill you—not just that great young skier girl Jill at Aspen that year—but your back, it broke your back, A.D., all those years healing and you were skiing again. With Walter. When I came home from Sun Valley the three of us went up to Telemark together—but I was suddenly no good. Had forgotten it all. Spent the day alone on the baby slope, the bunny run. And that night while Walter went off to bed you lectured me about lesbians and the danger. You knew this woman who had been in the Marine Corps during the war, out of pure patriotism. For of course you would never know the kind of women who were in the army. She of course was not a lesbian, but had told you such things existed. The army, worlds like that: people one wouldn't really know. But that such things did exist. I should know.

Or should I only know the correct from the incorrect, the mysterious and acceptable way of Sappho, not the clumsy and obvious path of error? God knows what was intended. I had no idea whatsoever, was mystified and embarrassed beyond any amount of scotch. But I knew it was up because I already knew Jaycee and Mother had already put the question to me as I stood at the top of the stairs in Mother's house, a mirror before me surprising myself with my own face, its own lie, its own truth—the mirrors in bars after plenty of beer that senior year and you go to the washroom to commune with the truth that is dawning this moment alone: you are different from the others. Oh God, is it that difference? Doomed semi-inebriated moments of understanding like the news of liver cancer or lupus—my face in Mother's long mirror at the top of the stairs as she calls, still holding me with her voice though I have fled it—"You're not in love with that woman, are you?" "Oh Mother, really," the bored collegiate answer is already Edward Munch's painting, a figure shrieking, open mouth agape by a bridge: he too has just found out the bad news, the sentence of solitude.

What if Mother had meant Dorothy rather than Jaycee? How apt. For of course I was in love with that woman, had been all my life. And Mother had to endure it. A mother is a mother; Aunt Dorothy was a romance. Mother could swallow hard and attribute it to Dorothy's money, her flirtatiousness, her hot and cold affection, her will-o'-the-wisp attentions to us, her treats and expectations, the ambition she would encourage, making us dissatisfied, potential snobs. Every moment of her life Mother was a good woman struggling against that, the Milletts and their arrogance and money. Mother battling with a peasant's realistic appraisal of their shallowness. Shrewdly calculating their incapacity to achieve, even to survive. Observing that beyond matrimony they achieved very little. Dorothy and Harriet married money and Lucy has never done anything useful a day in her life. As soon as she married Bob she became a Southern lady supported by a maid and the adoration of a husband who waits on her and spoils her like a child. What would Dorothy Millett be without Louis Hill's money?

It has been a terrible ordeal for Mother to watch these beautiful and charming young people who were at the university with her, the Millett sisters, watch them a whole lifetime and their fun-loving brother who became the man she married and was broken and nearly destroyed by—becoming in his case a drunk and a failure and his sisters growing into high hard cold obdurate rich people. Airs, pretensions. What is their learning but snobbery, what money bought them: the time to know one aria from another, the names of Persian rugs, first editions—going on like connoisseurs, grandees, baronial Irish on robber-baron money.

We know it all, all three of us, her daughters; we know because she tells us. And we know it on our own, seeing from the corner of our large soft child eyes as we enter and are ushered along by a butler and then must sit quietly and wait for our aunt to descend the stairs—she does not come running hell for leather to pick us up and exult in us. It is a play; being there is a play, a solemn, often very boring play. And we are fascinated, solemnly playing our parts; we are seduced. By everything: the music, the pictures, the witty talk. The sight of adults drinking champagne which makes them so happy and funny they say such wonderful things. And laugh and dance and are so carried away that Uncle Bob has gone to the attic and found lady's clothes and lamp shades and now they are dressing up. Because they are children too. Big children.

Mother's relatives are never like this. They talk prices and wheat and local elections—the men. For the men are different and stay in the living room and the women wash dishes in the kitchen where it is all who got married or is going to. Or still more awful, when they sit around the big table after it's cleared and the dishes are done and the cake and coffee, then the important ones, Mother's older sisters, talk very deadly talk about Joannie—will she marry? She is sitting next to me and I am in agony for her. Or cousin Ellen, thank God she wasn't there that Thanksgiving, but when will she quit Northwest and the airline hostessing and settle down? Prospects are raised and discussed. The dread of old maidhood: the final truth of kinship. Then on to what a nephew named his new boy. "His wife's folks are from around Rosedale; I think they knew the Olmsteads," distant cousins and outlying places as Swedish blood creeps in through marriage, welcome as this clan settles and assimilates in Minnesota.

Ireland is never spoken of save in a family reference—Billy Jackson's rosewood walking stick, a shillelagh in the corner of a room, or the wool of an old sweater. "This was Mother's," Aunt Mig might say; her own mother brought it when they came over. As if speaking of saints. John McCormick's "Auld County Downe" is in their voices then, like the tears in my mother's eyes at the unearthly melodic line of the tenor himself singing the

"Rose of Tralee." Her own one tune on the piano when we were small, "The Wearing of the Green," is an atavism by now. They are American now. They have joined and are eager and patriotic. Have forgotten. Ireland is a tourist place now. Not spoken of as an immediate part of them. Or never its politics—which the Milletts speak of always. Though mostly through books, the new books of Irish culture, the Irish Renaissance which was the meat of Mother's college days, especially John Millington Synge. But for the Milletts it is Yeats and everything about Yeats: biographies, critiques, even memoirs from his circle, each book landing on the shores of Minnesota's Lake Minnetonka where Dorothy holds court for her brothers and sisters on high holidays.

Mother's people do not drink; they go through Christmas dry. The Milletts drink. And Ireland is alive with them. Though there are parts that are hidden. For they who hide nothing from children become discreet at moments. But the monuments are eagerly pushed upon us; knowing Yeats and knowing him well is holy and fine and important. There are other moments, when they argue, or when Harry, having different levels of daring or outrage, may say—why not?—the English being that way, it has to be violent. When Harry who always knows the most for reasons Mother disapproves of, wants to report what is happening and needs to do it circumspectly. They want to speak and they do not wish to send us away, and so they resort not even to their childhood language of German, but simply to an English so arcane, both so Irish and so learned, that we comprehend nothing. At least nothing precisely and that is all they wish for anyway. It would not be well if we knew enough to repeat things. Even in confusion we enjoy a complicity—we know the great battle out there. It is as old as we can remember. "Seven hundred years under the heel of England," A.D. looks at me hard but says almost casually as if it were not in itself a sacred phrase, the fury of centuries in it, the outrage, the humiliated pride.

And the Milletts, these lairds. Even my father, the youngest, and a man who actually worked for a living. His elder brother Harry a man of leisure, his sisters rich women in the manner of Fitzgerald who was one of their circle when he was in town, living lives of pleasure, elegance, ease, and delight. Harry was often poor, for all Dorothy's generosity; it mattered not that much since he was still a gentleman, a type, a kind of coat—like cashmere. His days spent in conversation: his shirts, his hotel, his afternoon walks, his lunches at the old Angus Hotel, its bar where he held court with the drinking priests, the gunrunners, or the partners to whatever disputes he settled as an unfrocked attorney, a failed lawyer who never passed the bar but arbitrated in one instead, and celebrated a lifetime of inspired raconteurism.

Everything about the Milletts is frivolous to Mother's people, good industrious folk rising from farming to the grain elevator, the postmasterships in small towns and then the women to teaching, the men to branches of business culminating in insurance and lumber, a few cousins still running dirt farms. With the exception of Grandfather Millett who was timekeeper for the Hill Railroad, capped by his daughter marrying its heir, I can think of few Milletts who ever worked at all except my father. And even my father's engineering was understood by his sisters to be the practice of an art form and never intended to be the backbreaking labor or the heartbreaking bankruptcy it became. That he should be on the roads in all weathers was part of his apprenticeship as a young man sending his sisters to college. But that done, he could settle down to civil service for the highway department, a nice house, a good maid to make his wife's lot easier, three well-groomed daughters, endless happy discussion about the best way to make coffee, white flannels and white suede shoes polished by his admiring little girls and then set to dry upon a windowsill out of sight but ready for Sunday. There was a music to his life, the excitement of his work, the skill and intelligence, the innovations in design—his cloverleaves accepted now and used throughout the state—until he grew restless, angry, frustrated.

And then Dorothy gave him a company, a business of his own; her thirty thousand—imagine what thirty thousand could do once—then and there and together with Gene McDonnough's money. So now my father had a partner who was a business man, while he was the engineer, brains, designer, and builder. Very happy days at first. Probably too happy; Mother and Sally are full of tales of his extravagance, improvidence, and folly then. But at Dorothy's house that day, the younger son, standing a little easier than usual beside his brother and sisters, the stigma of a working stiff falling away from his handsome shoulders—he was loved, the beloved of his sisters always. Even Harry, his lordly and stately elder brother, the laird, senatorial in his fine coat and beautiful white hair, even Harry was kind to Jim. With an elder's kindness, but never contempt. And Jim deferred, admired, defended his brother, who was never a *roué* in his eyes or a gossip or a notorious character. Nor a sinister rebel nor anything else whose echoes sometimes reached us. For Jim, Harry had not only passed the bar but had taken the bench as well.

When Harry came for dinner we listened, each of us in astonishment and wonder, to his tales. They were the food of the evening and more than food. He was never interrupted but always encouraged, gently led on from short story to prose poem, each of us utterly attentive in our chairs. Mother no less than the rest of us. For he was fine and she knew it too, and adored a story: Harry was a professional, an entertainer, our entertainment. Better than strawberry meringues, rarer and finer because he was art and an artist. And that was holy. He is gone a long time now but how much he taught me; how much more I could have learned if I'd had the wit to listen harder, remember more, ask him questions once I was grown.

My eyes smart passing the summit of Bear Mountain. And now this paper, the final judgment. Harry was the eldest, Dorothy the youngest, the two poles. With my father in the middle. Dead too. They are all gone from me but Lucy and Harriet, voices of estrangement coming out of twenty-five years' distance over the telephone hearing my choked embarrassed scapegrace grief. All too late now to be absolved by their dead sister. And their own grief is too terrible to bother with mine, though each was kind, Lucy so ill she can barely speak, but Harriet came right out and forgave me by proxy, forthright and soft-hearted always, definite and cheerful. Harriet had never suffered a moment's guilt in her life, Sally would say—it's her gift—imagine that good fortune. But the paper on my lap, the final word, the last will and testament.

And by measuring out money, it has measured out affection. You know it. You can fight it and perpetrate your family romance forever, blathering away to yourself that you loved her best, out of all the horde of admirers, past your rivals, your elder and younger sister, your cousin Claire—you loved her best. And she knew it. Somewhere she knew it and loved you back, the best, the favorite—were you not the clear and declared favorite those high school years, Claire far away in Swarthmore, Mallory still a kid, Sally safely away at college—weren't you the one for the symphony and the dinner parties? And in college weren't you taken more seriously, the promising young scholar, the great achiever—Oxford for you, not Mills or the University of Mexico like your sisters? You brought a first-class degree from the highest British school in the world back home to your family. And then you went wrong. Wrote books and painted pictures and went still further wrong. We hardly hear from you for decades and there you are throwing yourself on the grave. Well—here is your report card.

The damn sums of money are not just money—bad enough, I could use some money—I have two thousand five hundred dollars in the world right now and not enough gigs, no other prospects of any kind, no advance in the offing for the next two years or so and no clear idea how to survive. Just how broke is cousin Claire today? She was already an heiress when she was twenty-one—her grandfather's will; her uncle will leave her everything else and her parents as well. She is also married to a very rich man. This is silly—was the point to leave money to people who had so much they didn't need it, would not even find it useful or interesting? "That's the way with money," Sophie murmurs, "it seems to cling to itself." But the point is not even the money—though money is like beauty or food or time—delicious and empowering—the point is that here is a rating system. It is how she rated us. Mallory and I flunked. We are told our worth in dollars and cents. We got a twenty-five percent rating, Sally got much higher marks and Claire is so adored she's a cool quarter million—in fact she is so wonderful even her kids are worth as much, the only members of their generation even mentioned—and that family unit walks off with a million dollars. That Harriet and Lucy each have half a million seems right—they were sisters and worth twenty times what we are, Mallory and I, nieces. But why is Claire, another niece, worth ten of us? Dorothy never saw Claire;

she lives in Hong Kong—could they have been that close? What has Claire done or got that I haven't? You will drive yourself crazy this way. But it isn't love, it's money—no, it isn't money, it's love. You and Mallory are as loved and worthy and honored as her two favorite servants; they each received twenty-five. "Your father's eldest child by his second marriage got fifty—how do you explain that?" Sophie asks. "Guess A.D.'s into primogeniture. As the eldest Sally got more than Mallory and I." "Does it bother you about this Margaret Millett person?" "Not at all; it does bother me about Sally."

It hurts the most of all. More than the inequity of Claire, which is so disproportionate it is merely silly; but for A.D. to have left one of us sisters so much more than the other two—what if it had been you? I'd split it. People never do. Well, I would; I'd have to. "You probably would," Sophie laughs. Thinking to myself that it would be easy to split the money: the favoritism, the mark of favoritism would still be all my own. Does Sally feel that blessed and kissed by being so chosen, or does the whole thing simply make her uncomfortable? As we begin the many hills descending down to the farm, I'm calculating divisions—if we three sisters threw our money together, we'd each end up with—Pointless even to mention this. Sophie has said people never do this and she is probably right. But what if we used it or a bit of it, each of us, to buy something at home, along the river, the St. Croix, the family landing we always talk about, or I do anyway—something that bound us together instead of dividing us apart as this might do.

Mother will be worried tonight. The understanding among us all is that she alone holds us together; were she to die, we would be flung apart into the separate and inimicable entities we have been all along. Mother alone is our tie; we know it and fear it, each of us afraid of the moment she dies as the moment we lose not only her but each other, any pretense of a family, the last vestiges. It is Mother who keeps the peace, Mother who is our cement, our entity, integrity, and essence. Real as we are false, honest as we are selfish. And what if we quarreled now, if the money drove us asunder, if over Dorothy we bit and clawed as we did all through childhood, each envying the other the new dress, the pretty book with the inscription in her writing, the magic of her signature? Each material object proof of her love, her better love for the other, younger or older, her favoritism. Finally indelibly clear now. How can I not be angry, how can Mallory not?

AND YET, AT THE END OF THE WEEKEND, near a phone again—for the one at the farm had been mercifully shut off, saving much in long-distance financial discussion—Mallory is the soul of quietude, calm, magnanimity. I would have thought she would go off like a wasp. Remembering her bitterness the night of her aunt's death, I am astonished by her contentment as an heiress. "Listen, we were lucky to get anything—don't you realize that? And twenty-five grand—whee, it's terrific." "You don't feel put off that Sally got so much more?" "Hell no, let it be. In fact I could hardly sleep Saturday night I was so excited—do you know what kept me awake—it wasn't the money—it was that she left me this, that she thought of me at all. Listen—what I feel from these bucks is confirmed—I mean it, confirmed. Like my aunt just told me you're swell; you're great, Mallory; I believe in you."

She had made it her confirmation. Mallory is an actress who has worked long and hard at her craft and never had the applause of her family or a cruel industry; but she has somehow converted this legacy into a blessing, a final approbation of all she has endured, all the hard times and auditions and lost parts and good plays without reviews, the tough breaks, the unfairness of the theater. A world she has lived in without help or support for fifteen years now. She has by the magic of her optimism converted the philistine old aunt who showered money upon the Guthrie Theater and the Minneapolis Institute of Fine Arts and the Minnesota Symphony and disapproved of both artist-nieces—into her patron. I must too. Never mind the portions and comparisons. Mallory has just canceled their meaning and converted it to one of her own. She has made it goodness.

There's Sally still to talk to. A conversation with Mother gives me opportunity to gripe beforehand over the inequity and be reproved into following her advice and Sophie's—"What do I say to Sally?" "Congratulate her—just that." A little sheepish and embarrassed she is. And then strange. Bitter, even disrespectful of the woman who has just left her so many thousand dollars. Angry somewhere. That it was not more, I wonder—for we all think of Claire. Or that it was too much, more than her sisters, and she must now live not only with the money like an admonishment but the finger of that favoritism which the money represents? Yet it bores her; she is indifferent. And says unkind things just at this juncture. Hearing her, like a lover hears the beloved scorned when out of favor, I defend, remind. Weakly. "A.D. was cold; she was a miser after all, and you know it," she says, her voice held down with hurt. A mean hard rich person—it expresses me too—a mean hard rich person. Who had never worked a day in her life. Yes, that for Mother who did work so hard. Even Dad. The starving artist years, maybe the cold old years ahead. "Sal, I decided to make this my little-old-lady fund—you know of any real smart investments, any magical double-your-money things? Mom's looking into an annuity for me." "Not a bad idea, but you can do better. When we're not drinking I can tell you about some municipal bonds." Right now we'd rather just drink money. Philosophize. See the humor of it.

In fact Sophie and I spent most of Saturday in bed at the farm, the richer relations finally forgotten, propped up in pillows and drinking coffee, adding with paper and pencil and without the pocket calculator which had been left down in New York, wonderful mad totals of what twenty-five thousand becomes at ten percent (eleven is too hard to do, so let's say ten; it's a nice round figure): in one year you get two thousand five hundred. Add that to the total; you now have twenty-seven thousand five hundred. Ten percent of that is—my God, compounded and left in and your twenty-five become forty thousand in five years.

TERRIFIC, THEN I CAN BUY MY STUDIO. I can put a down payment on it if the city will ever sell me our funny old building. And the next week in town, Sophie out for the evening, I am carried away with a good dinner, a fire and most of a bottle of wine and have one of those great "thinks" where I plan or discover my life. And decide that what I want to do with my windfall, my inheritance, my one big chance, knowing or thinking I know that there will never be another big book advance—and anyway that is money you earn and must live on—this is money from heaven, the big break. So what is most solid, appropriate, and perfect to do with it? You could buy land—enlarge the farm—but how would that give you any old-lady money? Think about taxes for the ten whole years it takes to grow a crop of trees. And how many more trees can you stoop over, mow, trim, clip, fertilize: No, you can't do it; it's too hard a way to earn money; you're getting on in life, forget it. If not land, if not the farm (which could swallow this sum in a momentary glut of machinery and be no better off), what is it you want most, need most—what would be the best buy? Your studio, a house in town.

A house in town—wine and remembrance bring back the little bank book titled "*Sita* buys a house in town." The money from that book, eaten up so long ago, that awful day in Franklin Square just after the income tax had finished its final punishing assessment and cleared me out of six thousand. The little bank book in my lap. Cursing them and smoking a cigarette to steady myself for the bus. Upstairs I had asked if I could pay in installments. "Do you own anything?" the woman said; God, she was cruel. "A farm." "We'll put a lien on it; if you have savings you better turn them over at once; you'll be paying plenty of interest otherwise." Fuck it, the soul said, take it, here take *Sita;* it is all that I have saved. To buy a house. To buy my piece of the rock. Six grand, all that was left out of the twenty the book earned in America. But now suddenly here's twenty-five. If *Sita* could not buy a studio in New York, your aunt can. Odd, for Sita used to hate New York, and then loved it the last time, would have been pleased to see the book make that studio secure, a magical place, she called it. And your aunt—how would she like to buy you a studio on the Bowery and make you safe as a New York artist? Maybe it's revenge—Sophie laughed when I told her. Or forgiveness at last. A final blessing, permission to be everything I wanted to be. All that she once disapproved of.

I have lived here for ten years on a thirty-day lease. And fifteen years more on the next corner down in an 1806 Dutch house the city threw me out of so they could demolish it. Twenty-five years on this street. My entire adult lifetime has been on the Bowery. If I could buy this loft I could stay here forever. No more meetings to run to, just to save our houses from the wrecking ball or now from the speculators. Deal with the city and we could all stay, artists and the Puerto Rican families—my friend Ruth's scheme, our committee's stated objective now—to dig in and insist on keeping the places where we live. Thereby saving them from demolition, speculation, gentrification. And the neighborhood, this wonderful collection of Hispanic family life, struggling artists and writers, the Cooper Union Arts School, the cafés, the cheap restaurants, the Bowery merchants of lighting and hardware, the little shops on Second Avenue, the Jewish and Ukrainian historic base with its new overlay of Spanish and black and the recent graduates, the poets painting pictures with the bathtub in the kitchen. We would stay as we are, the greatest neighborhood in New York, the Lower East Side, the salt of the earth, the last bastion of the old town and low-storied brick buildings, streets full of people, writers and children, punks and newspaper vendors, delicatessen and ice cream, nights of music and crowds and winos, fruit stands and the lines for the cut-rate movies at St. Mark's. I will never live anywhere else—I love it here.

And I could hang on to my piece of the rock and be safe from eviction or exile. Lose this and you have to live in Poughkeepsie because you are far too poor to pay the going rate for a loft, the sucker's price, the newcomer, the mark. Even an old-timer like you cannot afford studio rent these days—so it's this or you cannot live in New York at all. Death for a New York artist. You have a gallery here, are a founding member of the Noho Co-op, are showing soon. Buy your studio. That silly annuity would take forever to earn you just seven hundred a month, thirteen if you wait twenty years till you're seventy—screw it. Boring and safe, not what I want. Even Mother isn't pushing it, worried as she must be by whatever folly I will find on which to piss away this sum. How little they realize how scared I am to lose it, to do the wrong thing—the check is still in a drawer; I'm afraid even to put it in the bank—even the initial decision. So now you've lost several hundred dollars in interest. Interest is not really money to me; one doesn't earn it.

But you can't buy the house now; it's not for sale. It will take four or five years of maddening negotiation to get them to negotiate with you, with all of us. So squirrel it away; when the time comes, you'll have more, maybe forty thousand. My downstairs neighbor Michael—our old dream of buying our building together—when I mentioned it to him today as we swept up the little balcony after we had tarred it—"I'll go for that—we can get it cheap too 'cause of our sweat equity. We've been those city bastards' caretakers here for years."

Even say you just had the twenty-five and had to take a mortgage to buy the house? But no one would give me a mortgage; I don't even have a job. Last year's earnings were ridiculous. So okay—for this—to buy your own studio—you could mortgage the farm. For my two floors then, what will they want? Michael will buy his floor and maybe another. We could split the rent on the ground floor and use it to pay taxes, water, repairs. Will they hit us with code? What shape will the building be in when it's on the rent rolls again and subject to real inspections versus the casual kind we get as a city building whose landlord is beyond the law and whose tenants take care of it on their own? If you mortgage the farm—which you should never do, but for this you could do it—you'd be okay, unless you got in a crossfire and lost both for lack of cash, for lack of money at all. Never mind—you will dare and venture it.

On the other hand, if the city got the market value, you could be paying a mortgage all your life. No way. But think—you're already throwing money into rent—at your negotiated price you could have bought the joint by now with ten years' rent. I can do it. I can do it. I can have my sliver of the rock, a pinpoint on Manhattan. A final safety from the marshal's sign upon the last loft: entrance forbidden upon penalty of arrest. I called to the workman to get the shutters I had built for those nine beautiful windows with my own hands. But he could not let me enter, finally would not even tear them off and throw them to me in the street. The dark days of last time, the suicide trip. Own your own studio and that will never happen to you again.

So my aunt would make me a made artist. Would she like that? Admitting of course that she gave me the money to do what I liked with, would she like what I did? Is that to ignore who she was? Or to pretend that death has made her something else, some free spirit that approves of living on the Bowery, spending your time writing those books, making those pointless pictures, brewing those dangerous and meddlesome political notions? That she now approves the general raffishness of this life? I try to reach her and test the water now and hear nothing back.

But, given this decision to make, to nail down my studio is the best thing I can do. In terms of survival and morality it insures my work and also that I do not either risk and lose money or enter into uses of it I cannot approve. That's it then. I have nearly finished the wine and perhaps in a great many years will finish the mortgage. Which won't even begin till five years from now when I've nearly doubled my money through the bank while waiting for the city to sell. And when it's done and paid for I can rent it out over the summer which will provide me a little-old-lady fund at least as big as an annuity would give. I am not a bad businesswoman either since I would have equity too in owning the studio with Michael.

So you'll neither starve nor be homeless in your old age. Because suddenly, perhaps with the arrival of this money, the inheritance itself, I have become obsessed, not with how to get through the next month or the one after that, but with the bleak vistas of old age unsupported by Social Security whose pittance I have forfeited already. This being winter in the city I foresee years without even the occasional forty-five-dollar royalty check. And no further advances: who would ever give you money for a loony bin book? *Basement* is out of print. *Going to Iran* too. Someone told me even *Sexual Politics*—or so they thought. *Flying* is for sure.

It is five years till the first Christmas tree is cut at the farm and that money should go to the women's art colony you're making there, not to you. Not unless you're starving. But the way it's been looking, you might be. On your next birthday, you will be fifty. Time is marching on and your career as a writer has either dimmed to obscurity or entered upon an interesting literary phase that is purely private. You will never get rich as a painter or printer; you will never make a dime as a sculptor. How do you exist now? Lectures. The gig. The great uncertain phone call that North Carolina or Nebraska or some place in New Jersey urgently needs a speaker for Women's Week. And sometimes forty-three phone calls later it appears they don't after all. But only sometimes. Mostly gigs are a wonderful way to earn fabulous sums of money—enough to last a month or six weeks in a mere forty-five minutes of oratory, meeting and greeting, pleasant travel; put it all together, it's four days, two for travel, one for composition, and one for doing the job. Even throw in three or four classes to teach, as well as the address itself, interviews, press conferences for small-town and college newspapers, it is still real fun and excitement, contact with students again, a look at and a link with the real world—and you get paid too. Plenty. Only of course there are never enough gigs. Or so it seems. Actually there are almost enough. If you live with maniacal frugality and never go to the movies you can, with real luck and terrific gratitude, get through the year. Having few debts each month—and they are being whittled down, having schemed a way for the farm to support itself and pay its taxes through winter rentals. The bills you forget about till they come: health insurance, car insurance—making lists a month ahead of what disbursement will be made in June when I take out the money for the month of May, hustling a poster here, a silkscreen there, an autographed copy somewhere else, pride swallowed in simple need or the exultation that with this ten or twenty bucks there will be food in the fridge.

And suddenly you have got twenty-five grand to worry about and you worry. Right away you shrugged off the possibility of living on it. "Looks like your Aunt Dorothy by dying has saved your life," Sophie said as we headed up the highway—"You could exist for two years on this; by then you might have a new book finished and an advance." I am finishing a book pretty soon, but I'm sure as hell not going to piss away A.D.'s kind of money, a whole chunk of money just merely living on it. Never. How could Sophie know how dear it was to me, both in the sweetness and in the bitterness? This sum represented my entire expectations in the world, a poor relation for a lifetime on the edges of money. This was my chance to do something smart, to bet on what would win, what might make the difference between a hard old age and security. As Oxford made the difference. A.D. had given me my education; now when I'm fifty she had settled on my sufficiency. A judgmental settlement, the bitterness lies there. But having absorbed that, there is the sweetness too. It is still an artist's idea of a whole lot of money and it will make my fortune if I play it right.

A GREAT MANY SCHEMES have come to mind besides the usual certificates of deposit, annuities, or my sister's municipal bonds. My eye always goes toward real estate. If not land, then a building. This building where I live not being yet for sale, the idea is to park the money from my legacy until then and increase it meanwhile. Sophie, who wants to renovate buildings and has no capital, considers the Lower East Side with me. On Eleventh Street the city will sell you a ruined building for a dollar if you rehabilitate it with your own money. We look at it. A lovely shell, Italianate detail, shelves for statuary. A neighborhood of toughs, needle-park children. Some white bourgeoisie who have bought another ruin across the street arrive to work on it as we watch, only to find that the junkies have locked them out. The police are called and break down the door on behalf of the rightful white owners, brandishing their blue paper deeds from having bought the shell at auction. "Not for us"—we look at each other, parked in a car observing it all.

Later on Ruth tells me I made the right decision: the Puerto Ricans want artists to stay off that block; it's their turf and they still resent some city program for "artist's housing" that was so elaborate a renovation it would end up costing sixty grand a floor and would displace Hispanic families as well. Shells in Brooklyn then? More ruins and neighborhoods where you feel like an intruder. The dangers of renovation: lose your shirt and the place may be still uninhabitable by the building code. Give up a year's writing to sweat in brick dust in order to produce some shabby thing to rent out and become a collector of rents? How much of the smudge of speculation would still adhere to the dirty clothes and exhaustion of your own hard-earned labor?

It comes down over and over to the very shaky morality of buying a house you don't want to live in. Because you live here and this is the only house you want. Are in love with. And it's not for sale; the city owns it and it is scheduled for demolition or urban renewal or something—for many years now, though no one even remembers the days when there was money to destroy whole sections of a city and rebuild with federal subsidy for middle-class high-rises. So we wait for another bureaucratic decision. Less in fear now of demolition than of sudden speculator takeover, the day Mayor Koch sells us outright to Helmsley-Spear and we hit the streets. But no, never give in. Fight, organize, stay and win. Meanwhile why glance at other buildings? This is the one you love; you would never even consider living on any other street. The Bowery or nothing. But you can't buy it yet. Maybe never. So you fiddle with other buildings; your eye examines them because they are there.

And then Sophie got the loft in Brooklyn. Frustrated beyond endurance by fixing faucets for Upper West Side types, dying to build again, to renovate, to make new and over and wonderful. Doing it nearly for the fun of it, alone. The little character, her landlord, a jive guy who got hold of an old feather factory, and worked out leases so that his tenants would make over the building for him at their own expense. And for a while he was in so deep over his head he offered her a partnership. Since she plainly had so much more sense than he did. He was dishonest and lazy as well, promising things he never came through with. But she was sure it was the break of her life. If I would buy one loft floor with my legacy, another friend who is a professor of medicine at New York University would do the same. Sophie would have two other floors and part of the original mortgage; the landlord would have in return for all this the cash he needed for his second big down payment and title. And then he decided he'd rather go it on his own. Get all the money the building was sure to gush out for him over the years. It probably irked him to be partners with a woman. After the first disappointment, the perfect little-old-lady fund, the equity of a floor plus its tenants' rent to repay my investment, which having replenished itself would then earn a profit to be ready at hand to buy my own loft when the city could be induced to sell—and so forth—I was relieved to be out of this scheme. Further acquaintance with this landlord convinced me he was hopelessly crooked and irresponsible, a plague to be associated with in any way whatsoever. Still less desirable to be dependent upon him as a business associate.

Sophie lost the big break. I lost the sweet deal. She'd put in two months' work; I'd put in a week or so helping her with the grungy labor of clearing the loft, making it ultimately a beautiful space. She will get out with her shirt, I hope. Mine actually, since I loaned her the money to do it, three thousand that came in from Germany which I had saved up to live on for the three months of next fall. Beyond that she got a pittance for her labor. But plenty of experience for the next try. Real estate is in her blood, renovation her passion. All those spaces we have done together at the farm. But do I want to write or go about with a dirty face pounding floor nails?

A great deal more fun sometimes, a wonderful challenge. Yet somehow only when it's my own roof I'm tarring can I justify it, my own floor, my own walls—rented or purchased—my own shelter. And with my kind of money you can't buy labor; after a down payment you have too little left to renovate, let alone hire. And knowing how now, I can't justify employing other people to do the things we can do ourselves. Finally, I don't really want to own any place besides my own studio. And I cannot believe in investment, somehow cannot justify it. Then you have to do something as unimaginative—and safe—as putting your money in the bank. Till you can buy the Bowery. What if you never can? And years go by and by and you never ventured anything at all—you who love houses.

So this legacy has brought you great anxiety, even terror that Sophie would make off with it into the crater of her schemes, the thing disappearing gamely along with her newest venture, her gallant and enormous projects, her screwball landlords, a string of Iranians she knows with money to invest in projects that sound vague and alarming: houses in distant Brooklyn, lofts on the East River that will never be granted building permits while the years languish and are consumed in lawyers' fees—versus a skinflint nightmare of crouching alone and defiant and hugging your one mite, your talent lodged with you useless or about to be squandered and lost. And all you wanted to do was to buy your own home. Well, stick to it, nitwit.

Your legacy—surely you cannot fail to notice this—your legacy has made you rather miserable and anxious. The nature of money. Of course. In two months you have not even managed—so indecisive you are—to get it into the bank. Since you trust no bank but that funny little outfit you deal with in the country where everyone knows your voice on the phone and they transfer and cover and take care of you like a cousin. This entire winter you have not even reopened an account in New York. When Manufacturers Hanover Trust annoyed you one last fatal time by closing an inactive account, you looked around the neighborhood and decided they were all rude and computerized and uncaring, had long lines and unpleasant manners, and refused to have anything to do with them at all. Henceforward enormous ingenuity is required to keep you afloat since you cannot get cash unless you drive all the hell to Poughkeepsie. A frugal but labyrinthine way to live.

Go back to the Bowery Savings Bank; give your money to Joe Di Maggio. It was at the Bowery where you started off, all those weekly trips from Sixth Street and First Avenue down the Bowery in shocked horror at the bums. That's how you got to the Bowery to start with twenty-five years ago, simply because you banked there when you first came to New York. It was one of Jaycee's better ideas. When you asked her the name of a bank in New York—she of the years in Greenwich Village—all she could remember was the Bowery Savings Bank. Those awful walks down that avenue of sorrow, those sights that had to be erased by afternoons reading Victorian novels on Sixth Street. Just out of Oxford, so precious. But one day, nearly inured after three months of this, you noticed a "for let" sign on what became Bohéme, your first studio. Twenty-five years on this street—to stay on it you better scamper back down to its premier bank, its grandest money temple. Back to the Bowery then—it's decided.

PART FIVE

I have brought you here at last to Provincetown. My haunt at the end of summer all these years. A spirit, you are portable, even tolerant now of this sort of place. And gay people: Richard who owns the place where I stay, Harvey the painter who has his shop on the roadside out through the garden on Commercial Street, and Stephen Fitzgerald who is my dealer here and will give me a show next door at his gallery—a week from today on my fiftieth birthday. I'm a regular here and know lots of people, have already run into six friends since my arrival late last night and the second cup of coffee this morning. I have come here season after season just at the close of summer when the cityfolk disappear and the weather stays fine in early September, the ocean clear as air, as washed glass, as Meyerwitz's Cape Light photographs. As clear, they say, as Greece or the Mediterranean. But for me Provincetown is finer yet, clearer, more lucent, more acute, this blue of air and sea before me out my windows on Richard's Landing—I am in one of my favorite places in the world.

Only for this could I leave the farm yesterday, the loosestrife still lavender around the pond, the sunny grass, the big barns to draw in, laze in, even read—the busy summer's over. But not really, not until you have seen the ocean once. This ocean, not the one I saw three days ago in California on a hurried trip to a west coast women's musical festival where I sold pictures like a happy fool, one print of each of the prints we made this summer at the farm. And in half an hour paid all our debts: the old tractor, the new old tractor, new to us but still with four hundred due to Reardon Briggs over in Millbrook, couple hundred for the little Gravely tractors, three hundred fifty for H. G. Page building supplies, the last outlays in renovating the farmhouse, charged in desperation, all other sources having dried up—even paid the bill at Adams for seedlings and plants—clean. Utterly out of debt. Having ended the season in the red, the prints, as if some divine force were following our fantasy hope of supporting the colony with the art made there, put us in the black. With a thousand left for planting, or maybe to cover the thousand from my savings I threw in when the house was half-finished and the money set aside for the job—a little bit left over from the winter rents, a dash from a good stroke of luck in May—all run through. So I coughed up one of my winter months, gambling there might be a gig come along to save me when the time came to replace it. It works. Something happens at the last moment. Or miracles occur and people buy pictures. I tie it together.

You once asked me how I lived. My crazy visit. I bluffed and said the books did it for me. And didn't I have a fine farm—did I bore you with my utopian scheme to make it a women's art colony too? How bizarre my life must have seemed to you. Those terrible books, the shocking disclosures that compound a lack of respectability with unnecessary candor and scandal that redounds even onto your relatives, an act of treason. Almost inexplicable in its wickedness, its incomprehensible tastelessness, its flagrant want of tact. And to grow Christmas trees to support a bunch of lesbians and women's libbers, Lord. The eyes roll.

Cousins and friends' offspring used to do all sorts of things that were signs of gumption, supernatural cleverness, and ingenuity. Various Ty-tys and Deborahs and Jacks and Berts would have something to do with goats or climb mountains or settle in the Caribbean or the south of France and do over houses or invent some new toy or cleansing cream and it was regarded as a wonder: their feats were recounted for hours while one fumed and resented these merry rich brats' achievements. But I would come dark and quiet into your house, the lover, the outsider and outlaw. And stutter about recovering fields, planting so many thousand trees, rebuilding the barns into studios, and wonder if you heard me at all, desperately pleading my case, urging my accomplishment, bringing it fresh and alive for your inspection and approval. And failed. Trying to make it interesting, an adventure. Yet practical, not a waste of money, not a nutty idea, not another dumb scheme like that art gallery you never went for. And mine—I had earned it all, owned it all, on my on. Taking a run-down go-to-hell farm and making it a good one, working it myself, months in the field, now years. Your eyes glazed and tried to focus. But of course I could never remember to bring photographs: it is one thing to say an 1830 farmhouse in New York State; it is another to have a smart-looking photo of the same to convey the thing itself.

And now, having failed to bring you my hardworking practical finally flowering farm world, I have forced you along over here to Provincetown at the end of America, the last tip of land before Ireland, the final footing. And full of queers, those people we have always differed on. Artists too, the other difference. Alive I could never have persuaded you to set foot here. You never saw my farm but it might not have been beyond possibility to go there—if I were in favor, if I were cousin Claire. But if I were cousin Claire—never mind. Provincetown under any circumstances "not your style," to use one of your expressions and by far the kindest. Now that you are dead, I have the impudent ability to summon you everywhere.

And you're different; I have made you so. Not permitting you your old and characteristic prejudices, typical and ingrown and of a piece with you as they were; they have not survived your demise. You know more, being dead; your spirit—for you must now be spirit alone—cannot afford that baggage. Took one look at the world from its new vantage point beyond death and jettisoned the snobbery that was once your life and breath. You may even have renounced Republicanism. You have surely gotten a better grip on world economy, the facts of poverty, war, class. You're about as cool now, as tolerant and open, as you were in college, I expect. And a good deal wiser.

So you might not be as utterly adverse to this place as once you were. There's been the refiner's fire so your spirit is on its own, your self transmogrified now by death. I say this to escape whatever culpability I may take on for bringing you here. And converting you from a cranky old snob to a kindly disposed and broad-minded sophisticate, a woman of the world. From a Wayzeta Brahmin with an icy edge to something mellow and approaching serenity, as philosophical as your favorite authors. I have made you a companion, even a superior. Of course you were always superior—so many reasons: age, family rank, your fortune, even your arrogance. But your superiority now is quite a different affair. For once I've given you the moral edge, full enlightenment. I who always had a better take on the poor, warfare, and class struggle, on the cruelty of your caste and its privileges, its philistinism, its piggish proprietary attitude to the arts, its contempt for artists. From childhood, with whatever little leg I had to stand on when facing you, I sure as hell knew better about right and wrong, even if I lost the argument by not being as clever and sarcastic and nasty about "people who wore clothes like that" or "couldn't manage their affairs," Or whatever hook upon which the unfortunate were hung to dangle helplessly. Their fate like fabric ripped by some nearly invisible nail one had never noticed until suddenly the flesh bled or the cloth gave way with a little scream. And there was no pity.

It is that which made you frightening. So I've given you at last—compassion. No, I don't mean sentimental pity, Irish whimsy and tears—of course you could fill your eyes with tears as they all do, your sisters, the tribe, the very race itself. I mean the pity of justice. Which will not have its mean fun, which will even keep silence. I am aware of your finesse with servants, not only the generous bequests at the end but the skill that kept them loyal and adoring you for forty years. I'm sure you were polite to saleswomen, up to the point where they annoyed you. I remember your comment—you who were a lady—upon the linguistic anomaly whereby salesgirl had been changed to saleslady so that salesladies were in fact now the only ladies left in correct usage. Often arch snobs themselves as well, we both agreed. And very formidable people. Rather more formidable to me than to you, I suspect; you were a big account. As a scruffy artist I was a pushover for the clerks at Bloomingdale's, could be squelched instantly with a long painted fingernail despite my own years behind the counter, and humiliated into buying something out of sheer gratitude that such an arbiter of female correctitude and fashion would bother to take my money. I was my mother's daughter and knew how a penurious housewife feels before the power of the corporate snub. You never did. So I have entered you in a short course of this.

Almost to shake you into humanity, dead or alive. Having loved you. Loving you still I insist you cut it out, that part of you that was corrupt and corrupted me—or would have if I had not run away and yes, disowned you just as much as you disowned me. For twenty years I never mentioned your name when sober, wrote damn few letters, sent damn few presents, tried—as hard as I could—to forget you. And sat on the present you gave me, an education, hardly seeming to use it. In becoming an artist I made it appear nearly superfluous, making sure that what was left was my own. I was not made by you, I said. I was not even from St. Paul. "The Middlewest," I'd answer blankly when asked, and watch Easterners grow restive hiding their condescension. Forget it, buddy, I'm from nowhere: have no town nor family. You wouldn't have any notion; if I tried all night to explain St. Paul I could only weary and mystify you. It's another world. Fitzgerald wrote about the East. I would write about nowhere at all or only where I was. Never about there, never about home. Or the family. Or childhood.

A word or two crept into *Flying,* the hardest words of all. But then nothing. I had given up the idea of ever doing it at all—hadn't the book on my father gone aground wordless? Out of gas. Literally wordless, the empty page, every writer's terror come at last, the ultimate horror. So try the larger subject, political prisoners, torture. First tell about the loony bin trip, find whatever dragon kept you silent: the shame of "insanity," the strangulation of being mad or said to be mad—so much the same thing that the difference is hard to define. But not the family, not home, not those years, not back then. And then—you had the nerve, the power, the bad timing to die—before reconciliation and forever preventing it. And you have forced me to go back. When I was doing another book, didn't have time, had a show to do and another book to begin after the previous one was finished. Out of nowhere, out of a gray January afternoon, your death has impelled me into this unplanned pregnancy of a book.

Fighting these six months now with you—difficult, impossible, arrogant, unforgiving old woman. Haggling over a mystery, the spirit of honor. Did I not lie? You bet. I might still, lie, steal, and kill to get out of that time and place and its respectability, the cloying authority of that neat mean-minded intolerant place you would have bound me to. Mother gave all she could and it was there and its limits were there. But you actually invented limits; you created and appointed limits, rules, shalt-nots, sins, and crimes. Nothing I was, was permissible—you bet I'd get out of there again and fast. And the "honor" was cheap and easy and made out of money. Snobbery. Old names. Old this-and-thats, objects, discreet drinking, amiable falsehoods, hobnob, flummery. Big deal. I ran away to see the world and saw it.

So I gave you a real quick kaleidoscope view after death, whizzed you through African famine, Asian cholera, hot-rod aesthetics, bohemian ease, a few foreclosure and bankruptcy sales, the afternoons of the senior citizens who live in Florida and do not drink out of crystal, the fun of being seventeen again—I did my best to bring you back to when you still had a heart—prenuptial times before the fortune hit and began your paralysis, the cirrhosis of your soul.

AND I WONDERED parenthetically, because I must—if Jim Millett's sisters countenanced his abandonment of his three daughters (I, being one of them and therefore curious)—because, by marrying again he could try once more to father a son? Three attempts with Mother produced only three girls: that was enough of a try and more children than he could finally support. So another gamble with another lady? Could his sisters, being women, accept that? For what? For their goddamn crazy name. Their royal family obsession with the last of the line. Which Jim was. His bachelor brother Harry produced no children or none that one could lay claim to. And each of Jim's issue merely a girl. Who cannot carry the name. I do; I'm the only one who does. But I have no children. And promptly upon remarriage Jim produced, with the aid of his former mistress, no less than two sons: one Michael, one James. Names once bestowed upon each of his daughters in the womb, born only to disappointment. And his sisters went along with this patriarchal crap. I went along with the fantasy of being the last of the line at least to the extent of a lust for immortality. And despite whatever immoralities in love and art got me kicked out of the family, I went right on using—they would say abusing—its name. Fumio's name, Yoshimura, could have offered an alternative solution, however improbable. Kate Yoshimura—has quite a ring to it, suggests a *nisei* painter. I too use a *sumi* brush: the name could very seriously mislead. But of course it never occurred to me. I was a Millett. Whatever the hell they said.

And now that you are dead, the last, the highest Millett of all, the dictatress of the tribe, matriarchal for all its fawning toward male heirs—now that you are dead there is no one to oppose me. Shall I wither and imitate you, buy silk blouses and conservative suits and alligator pumps, play the stock market? Impossible. The only possible course is to convert you. And to this I have set my mind. I have even come here alone and without the usual lover simply to have your company and only your company at dinner and through the day. Unconsciously or perhaps even consciously—for I came here to write to you and of you—I have severed myself from Sophie at this convenient juncture, told Skippy Dakota it's just as well she stay in Los Angeles or even make it to the family reunion back home in Sisseton since after all her aunt is ill and dying—an ounce of prevention that would have improved my case—all in order to spend good vinous evenings before the moon upon the sea alone with you in this room. Rituals I neglected during your life, and during my own to date. So now when it's all over and too late, I take the time. Now when it profits nothing but the mind. In life, having botched the material, the relevant or warm or possible, there is now a communion of nothing but the mind—and the soul. Safer to assume it's all in the mind. Haven't I dined alone but nevertheless in conversation with Simone de Beauvoir? Even Sartre. In expectation of that next trip to Paris, for it would be on the next trip that Simone would introduce me to Sartre. "The next time, for sure, and we will all have lunch; meanwhile it's so nice for us to have dinner, just the two of us." But the next time he was dead. The same with Violette le Duc. On the phone in my agent's office she regretted that her house was too far from Paris for me to visit this time. "But surely next time, the next time you come and you must plan to stay long enough so you can come down to the country." I came home from Angela Davis's trial in California and Bookie read me the newspaper obituary; le Duc was dead. Always the next time. The time after Iran, the time after that.

And never having done it at all in life, I do it now afterwards, after your life is over. Since we both know it might have been impossible to do it while you were alive. Mad as hell at me and never, I mean never, going to give in and forgive or know or like or trust yourself to love me again. Therefore I take advantage of you. Saying the phrase with some uneasiness, some sense of bad faith. I cheat and lie still, I suppose you would say. And you are right. How else could I ever get you to eat steak with me before a window full of moonlight over ocean, the moon one day short of being full, in a rinky-dink former Portuguese fishing village, now a largely homosexual resort town on Cape Cod?

If you were to come frail and ill along our boardwalk here at Poor Richard's, or young and beautiful, would Richard himself greet you with gallantry and compliment, big and gruff in his huge wool shirt? Deliberately crusty—he even imagines I have broken the wicker chair that was already broken when I got here and reminded me twice not to leave on the outside light and waste his electricity—but would he stop everything and bow to you if you arrived like a being from a different sphere, remembering his river manners? He's from St. Louis and is really a very good fellow after all. How wonderful, how like an apparition, a ghost living or dead—were I to watch you approaching my little box over the water, walking, your feet and legs walking well or ill, young or old. The simple planking that leads from Harvey's and Stephen's shops on Commercial Street through the little swinging doors that create our privacy back here at the landing, along the brick pathway through the garden and finally the boardwalk and decking out to Ten and Eleven, the furthest little houses. Built on pilings, really right over the water. At night and in high tide I sleep and wake imagining I am still on shipboard going to Japan, so constant and pervasive is the sound and the movement of the waves around the pilings under the floor. I sleep above in a loft on the second story of my little house and can still feel the vibrations of the sea under me even in sleep while the bed rocks and the house sways. A storm here is rather sensational.

Last night Stephen came by for another drink when I was drawing after dinner and told me a story that may explain Provincetown to you. Assuming your new sense of humor, your devil-may-care nonchalance, your saintly tolerance of lives you once so adamantly opposed. Stephen was staying right here one year after the season ended, concluding his business affairs and probably paying Richard something nominal for the discomforts of an unheated house in late October—when a grand storm came, a nor-easterner. "Waves right the hell over the window ledge, and then right in the windows. The floor was a foot of water and rising. And it's freezing—I'll drown in here." He points to the floor, the windows now full of moonlight. "Then a big one right smack the hell over the roof. Now you know Richard can't make that skylight work even in a summer rain." "Hm—he told me yesterday he was going to give up on it finally and do a big dormer." "Right—I mean right over the roof—a solid wash. That was *it* for me—it's coming in on three sides and I headed for the door before the planks went and the boardwalk back to the land and the whole thing went to sea with me in it. And you know what, I got out on the street—it's raining dead dogs, you can hardly see—but there, under the lamppost, going right along to a party is this goddamn faggot in a costume. I mean heels, big skirt, and this huge silly hat. The umbrella falling all around her, him, it, whatever—this creature couldn't for the world miss a party. It was only my first or second season up here but the whole thing together explained the place to me."

Is this fag courage and valor as well as frivolity? Or a nice mix of frivolity and *joie de vivre?* Or just further evidence of perverse aberration—I ask you these things because I want to see how you are doing, how near we have arrived toward rapprochement. And of course I am not budging an inch. For all my chivalric little gestures: my taking your arm over the doorsill, my readiness at uncorking the wine, my flair in serving the new potato confection: parboil, slice into thin rounds, fry slowly on what passes for a frying pan up here in olive oil, and when golden switch to butter. Rather than butter from the onset as in potatoes Irish renaissance . . . which are a bit too rich for our age. Am I not swiftly approaching my fiftieth birthday and you your eightieth, or thirtieth or whatever you have chosen for the occasion? I would maintain a niece's respectful deference in keeping your wine glass full of Côte de Rhone—metaphorically—since what was still left in the bottle was there for Stephen to finish, downing it like Seven-Up after a hard day selling posters, still open at midnight while Joel Meyerwitz signed the last prints before leaving town—though of course I would be unearthly happy if you were really here and had a real glass to fill. But whether you are material or not I am still holding my ground against you here. And about time.

Fifty years toadying to snobbery is long and overlong. Nor will I tolerate your prejudices a day longer. I am here in my stronghold and bearding you. As I must have somehow all these twenty years I have run to the sun and the sea to be among the outlaws and the artists, sticking out my tongue at St. Paul and my stuffy aunt and the family edicts against me. But this time it's different.

ONLY BECAUSE you are dead and can't fight back? Probably. Also because you are dead and I can no longer make peace and be restored to your bosom or that of the town and homeland or region either—so I will stand and fight. In order to make peace. Quarrel and talk back and defend myself. Better yet, look your bigotry in the eye. Coming out is saying "so what?"—call me a name and I'll grin and agree to it. And you can do nothing further to me in the world. Unless you slug me, but then we are at war. "Sticks and stones may break my bones but words will never hurt me," we used to chant in the alleys of a St. Paul childhood during apple fights between Irish and Swedish kids. And I knew the truth then but have had fifty years to forget it and lose my way, be bullied and shamed and chicken and wretched. Made miserable by a rejection which was for the most part only small-minded and nasty. Yes, I told you a lie once, since you made telling the truth so difficult; I was not then good enough to do it. But doing it later only compounded your coldness and disfavor.

So arguably, I really ought to say the hell with you. "Why do you love your aunt?" one of the volunteers at the farm asked after I had read them all a few pages of this. Brought down hard from the euphoria of testing new work, the private audience, the intimacy of reading aloud, I wanted to throw the book at Sara but limited myself to pointing out how my aunt was beautiful and smart and glamorous, even her money a glamour, everything about her miraculous to me in childhood. "Well, I mean she gave you such a hard time . . ." Sara muttered. Seeing I was exasperated and undercut as well, deflated in a moment of enjoyment after a reading, Christian piped up—"There is no morality to love." I looked over at her, knowing one of her loves, one who had utterly failed to appreciate her. "And especially of course when we're children." Christian knew.

Sophie tried for years to enlighten me, to point out how mealy-mouthed and disastrous to pine over those closed women in the Millett family decade after decade, how pointless and mistaken in the case of A.D. to continue an infatuation which clearly goes nowhere but into remorse and guilt and now in death throbs like an infected limb. We got past the moment of Sara's question, but later, as we lay in bed and talked, Sophie insisted with an irritating Scots Canadian pragmatism, returning again and again to the pith of Sara's remark. I felt a writer's exasperated insecurity: "Jesus, Sophie, if I failed to convey what was lovable about my aunt—at least when I was a youngster adoring what was magical—good God, I surely must have got down something of her charm. . . ." I light a cigarette. "No?"

The question remains: "Did you ever—so far in the manuscript anyway—say how much she hurt you? How unfair and narrow-minded all this time in exile was? Do you challenge even how they think, these people?" "Sure. I've spent nearly fifteen years working in gay liberation. I'm an activist. I have memorized and even lived my propaganda." "But with your family. . . ." "With my family there is still the unresolved moral issue, the fact that I lied to them. That they can always say I lied and that is honor." She sighs, turns a beautiful shoulder composed for sleep. This is too silly to bother with. Perhaps at this hour it is really too complicated to enter upon the upper-bourgeois concept of honor as reimagined through a Norman Irish heritage, a structure of married money and immigrant recall. Mother's honest peasant world of telling the truth and keeping the faith with blood kin is clear and untarnished. Whereas the Milletts are a creation of their own, too unsubstantial, too different, perhaps even too familiar to Sophie's own Anglo-Irish aristocratic ties on her mother's side, those British cousins she found tedious and strange. And she would far rather turn out the light and sleep.

Honor, I can fancy Sophie examining each ironic twist of pretension, starting with the Empire Builder's cash. I was raised on my mother's passionate interpretation of that Protestant Ulsterman, Empire Builder Hill overseeing the Catholic Irish peasantry who built his road and gandy danced and died in the blasting as he mined his way through mountains all that way across half a continent and more from St. Paul to Seattle. In marrying Louis Hill, A.D. married a fortune, but wasn't her own father an employee? A timekeeper of course, at least a bureaucrat, working in exactitude and science, safety and measurement. It was guys like my dad—Jim Millett started out in a logging camp—who must have felled his trees and cut his passes through the rock. Only fifty years earlier, my father, who escaped the lumber camp to be an engineer, would never have had that chance, been just one more Irish immigrant pair of shoulders to build Hill money higher. I used to imagine Grandfather John Millett killed on Jim Hill's railroad but Mother has sternly advised me he died in his thirties of a "natural" death from the 1918 influenza, leaving his wife to follow soon after and their six children orphaned. And then Dad build dirt highway beds as an apprentice and took care of his sisters, educating them at the university until one married the heir of the iron road, beautiful Louis Hill Junior. Then came the sunny days—if not forever, two decades of golden youth; treasure and place becoming at last an old woman dying alone. But what notions of honor did those orphaned children inherit or invent? And then what newer notions refine upon while being the golden people at the top of the heap? That they should throw dishonor in my teeth for nearly thirty years.

Now you are the shade across the table from me. Loved all these years, and loving you anyway, I wanted to like you as well. Because my soul always dreamed of and hungered for your companionship, ever since I was five and you treated me as a friend when we played together. Even when we spent time together and were serious, you did not treat me like a child, with that mortifying condescension which adults impose, which one is obliged to play up to and which makes being a child so tiresome, the falseness. You were my friend then. And I wanted to be friends always but especially when I grew up and was a peer or at least an adult too. And if I worked at it very hard, studied with monstrous diligence and achieved things, sculpted, painted, wrote, published—even after I knew it was over and there was no hope—I still kept at it. Unconsciously now, still plugging away for that recognition that I was indeed a person, although notoriety never led me to imagine I was smarter or better. So wondrous was your power over me, my awe, admiration, my infatuation, that it could go right on being a source of energy deep inside. Long after the surface self has said to hell with her, let the bunch of them be damned. I am maybe not a Millett, not one of them at all, a changeling since they reject me so entirely, exile me so abruptly, persist so perfectly in never forgiving me. Or else, screw 'em—I am a Millett indeed and they are a bunch of stuffy creeps and narrow-minded provincial bigots; I'll be the Millett and outdo them all, my dad's heir, the last of the line.

THERE WAS FURTHER and additional blame for what the media rather automatically presented as my father's character, a drunk who beat his children—wasn't he Irish? "Do you think I would really tell some nitwit from *Time* magazine that my father was a kid basher or something, Aunt Dorothy? Good God, do you?" Looking her straight in the eye, my eyes fighting right into hers for once in a lifetime—some things I will not put up with, some misconstructions. "Good God, you have subscribed to that rag for twenty years; do you really imagine they print the truth?" Her eyes wavered, gray today like Daddy's rather than green, not her own color, and then neutralized in a nearly certain relief. My father was dead only a few months now, probably with a little assistance from the magazines which had painted him a black Irish boozer and lout. "Listen, I once—off the record, to Nell Mcsomething or another in Washington—while talking about child abuse, because I thought she cared about the issue, I admitted I got beaten a few times as a kid—spankings if you like, though it's an asinine, idiotic, and hypocritical term—they hurt and I hated Dad for them. All I was trying to prove was that I knew whereof I spoke when saying it was a completely general phenomenon, smacking kids around. Yes, even in my sunny childhood, etc. I don't think she printed that, but if she did Lucy may have seen it." "She did and she called me. And saw to it that your Aunt Harriet had a copy too." "But this isn't where the rest of them got their notions 'cause every reporter who came to the studio began—the minute the little background question elicited that I was Irish—Millett's supposed to be French—right away, automatic reflex, they want to know if my father drank. Who doesn't drink? Matter of fact he did. Next did he beat his wife? I said he sure as hell didn't. But one word on the kid issue—and I always try to talk about it—I'm fourteen years doing a book on a kid who was put to death in a basement and the whole thing about hitting kids is crucial to me so I sound off and they have got my father down as a child basher and a. . . ."

"Your father was not. . . ." "Listen, I know it. I never saw my father drunk in the whole course of my life. Only heard him drunk once when I think he slipped on the first stair and did not even hurt himself." Worrying at the time: did he hit her, Mother, did he ever finally after all these years of not hitting her—though it took a divine self-control once she got going, needling this human being in despair and bankruptcy and failure, his hopes going out like the lights of the town he would so soon never see again. And did he hit her? No, thank God, he didn't; he merely fell quietly and then like a gentleman got up and went to bed. No reporter I have ever met would begin to understand the man who was my father. Let alone how much I loved him, adored him.

Instead I had to be their cheap bigot's false sociological case. Irish, father drank, beat wife and kids. Explains me—sour broad. Right psychological profile for pop psych: hates men 'cause hates father, married Jap, probably queer. One paper in Indiana even called Fumio a Jap in print. So did the *Village Voice*. Look for the queer angle. Look for the old man, the father angle. Only a few months later the flesh was cold on his big body.

And we dueled in her living room. But the tar was there. What sort of Millett was I? Had I no sense of the code, the sword, the clan, the collective honor in those old stag heads with spears and lances through them? A little thought and you begin to realize that they are supposed to represent something or there wouldn't be two such crests for the same name in the heraldry book, each very like the other; animal totems, not trophies, but symbols of identification with some tender victim who died. Not by the fine hunting arm of the seal ring's owner, but far otherwise; the wounded beasts are instead pictures of his or her own soul, which would never relent: death or dishonor. A seal worn thereafter by those sworn to the rescue of everything wounded, raped, and in pain.

How is a downtown artist who is also a scholar finally released from graduate school, living a merry bohemian life with a samurai sculptor and abruptly faced with a reporter, to understand, recollect, and marshall all such significance? Too late, that's for sure. Hadn't I fallen into their traps? Should I say my father lived on root beer? Must I swear he never raised a hand against me? I did make it plain, when they were gross enough to ask, that he never struck my mother: I think "wife-beater" was absent from most copy. "You said he abandoned you." "Prove that he didn't. I am Mother's child and that was Mother's version as she raised us; I knew no other."

Of course you dealt with the press all your life through the society columns which are rather kinder than the treatment meted out to radicals and women's libbers disturbing the peace, so you could be airy about newspapers and claim it never mattered what they said as long as they spelled the name right. With two t's. As a feminist I expected every improbable lie; as a radical I even understood their reasoning in the lies they chose. But it simply did not occur to me that the members of my family would be grist for anybody's mill. Or that my father would read a magazine some kindly or unkindly neighbor made sure reached his bedside following a serious heart attack and just upon returning from the Mayo Clinic, and die a few days later, perhaps also in grief at what he had read about himself.

Only months after he and I were reconciled. For we had been friends again after twenty-one years of silence and estrangement. Which Mother imposed but his sisters transcended, sending him east by airplane to see me and Mallory, knowing he was old and ill and near dying. Fumio knew it too and saw it in his eyes: "He is already a ghost but very beautiful." How good this reunion. May, the May before *Sexual Politics* was published in July. The newspapers, the television, the late summer and the fall. And then the attacks. In November, *Time* says I'm queer and therefore my book is suspect, its footnotes might even be inaccurate, my learning and my argument are fallacious because I have "confessed," "admitted" to being a homosexual. Actually I was busy flaunting it and gay liberation, but now am said to confess and admit and am canceled. *Time* had me on the cover in August but being ill my father missed it; being at the Mayo until Christmas he hadn't picked up on old publicity—a proud man, his daughter's book gave him great delight. She has done something; she is in the papers. *Time* had this version of my life: "A father who beat her and her sisters, then walked out on them when she was 14" (*Time* August 30, 1970, 18). An unsigned article "researched" by a reporter who haunted me for days, riding along in the next seat in airplanes, angling for missteps, statements out of context. They had boiled our existence to a tabloid brutality. My father is handed this absurd ugly false public identity just as he is about to die. He was home again with his second wife and children at Christmas but his voice was faint and hard to hear. A neighbor had loaned him all the magazines. "You must be careful how you read that stuff, Dad; they have all sorts of axes to grind when they write about us." "Sure, honey." Another week and he was gone. And now I stand here in A.D.' house on the lake and she tells me some lousy magazine article helped push him over the edge. No, damn it, no. I will not buy that nor be party to it either. I do not write that junk; it is written about me and I have no control whatsoever, cannot even sue since they are way too damn smart to get nailed at anything, have boxes full of lawyers to get them off the hook; it's a business—you don't "say," you "imply"; you say a person is "said to" be this or that, etc., rather than "is." "Listen, I loved my father; I would never have put those poison-pen sons of bitches on him; I hate what they say; it hurts me too. I have hated this; I have hated the whole damn thing."

In my entire life I have never raised my voice before her. She grows quiet and listens. Something of understanding forms in her eyes of what it has been, who I am. She almost trusts me; I am almost one of them. A warrior too, but one on the scrappy side at the front: real blood, not inherited money; public trouble, not divorces or quiet private bankruptcy. But finally I'm improbable.

Mother and sister Sally know something of where I stood: they know politics, they know feminism, they know the chances, the hopes for success, the dangers, the public infamy of lesbianism; they also shy away on behalf of the married lady in the suburbs who obsesses Sally, or the dilemma of the verdict of respectability versus humanity's final claim for its rights which worries Mother. Yet both would protect me and see me through despite disagreements in tactic, even in principle.

But with Dorothy there is only the tribe. The Milletts. Family. Their name and fame and fair honor. *Sexual Politics* was a treatise to be proven like a well-made tract; she once teased me that the footnotes were reliable because she had gone to the trouble to check them periodically through the book. I can see her chuckling her way through her library. "You win on your footnotes; you persuade by the weight of your references." As if it were merely a big crossword puzzle. My father was beautifully, movingly persuaded by what I said. My aunt being a woman of course knew all this stuff already and even having it said did not impress her; what interested and amused her was the manner of saying these things. But she could not admire entirely; she really had to tease erudition and pedantry.

In the first glow of its aftermath, before it became a newspaper nightmare, I could still crow over it to my aunt. Probably a little less pompous than when I came home chock-full of Brit scholarship from Oxford; thirty-five now, a bit less obvious, comical. "You see, I was trying for a combination of English critical writing—you know, relaxed, civilized, not your hard grinding American treatise on the number of commas in a Richardson novel—and then throw in a bit of direct American plain talk too. Outside the academy but not quite the Bowery," I said to her. Proud of myself and newly published, made much of: one leg crossed, a hand hugging my ankle, wearing slacks for the visit, fancying myself before her as I probably never had on any previous occasion. "Hmmm," she said, trying not to smile, smiling anyway.

And now only a few months later, my father's death coming into the depressing, unheated loft in January, I had not gone to stand at his grave beside the stranger he married, the strangers he fathered after me, Sally having persuading me it was not worth going for: she wasn't going to go. And when I changed my mind and called saying I really did want to go—she had changed her mind too gone already. And it was now too late to get a plane. Dorothy didn't go either; neither did Harriet or Lucy. When Dorothy died, neither of her sisters went to Minnesota. The Milletts do not go for death, only life.

But I had wanted to have gone for Dad, have wanted to have been there these fourteen years since I missed the chance to pay whatever straggler's respects and expiation were possible while still possible. If only not to have missed out on a rite, on tribal burial, on family bond. On claiming him. Even before those others whose presence had first frightened us away—that and the general futility of getting a dress and a ticket and crossing the country to stare at some hole in the soil in the presence of people you can only embarrass and annoy. Who have better claims than I anyway. Why go late to the feast and spoil it, even a funeral feast? "Jim Millett isn't going to know one way or another; he's dead, kid." "Yeah, yeah, yeah—but Sal, it's something we could do for him, don't you know?" "No, I don't. He won't know." "I guess not. But I would." "It's stupid—I'm not going." Meaning of course that as the eldest and head of the family if she doesn't go, there is surely no purpose in my going, merely the second child, his mascot but not his favorite; it would be somehow inappropriate if I went.

And I lacked imagination or conviction or wit or intelligence—surely I have paid for that omission dearly all these years—and I did not go. Did not get a ticket or reservation, did not go to the bank, did not find something suitable and just get there, didn't do a damn thing but cry and tell myself it was pointless to cry. I hadn't had a father since I was thirteen and I was thirty-five now. He went twenty-one years without bothering to see me, hadn't he left us, etc., etc. Mallory thought it was stupid to cry or drink whiskey about it either when Fumio and I showed up at her loft that night. Whiskey seemed to me the right way to deal with it—I even made sure it was Canadian Club. Bullshit, she said, always clear-headed. So I wavered and lost to irresolution. Of course there was no point in going, as Sally said. Then why did Sally go? For the same reason I would have. Being the first and favored one, her reasons were clearer or occurred in sufficient time to make plane connections. And being the second kid who worshipped from afar I couldn't get up the courage in time, so skulked in would-be and unsatisfied love through these years of regret, remorse, missed opportunity.

So why didn't I go to Wayzeta? 'Cause I just plain didn't want to. Was pissed at being represented in Ransom's stuffy way, was utterly uninterested in suppressing my obsession before your chums the matrons. And had another plan in mind anyway. Too jealous to share, too possessive to commune at the champagne brunch, I wanted you all to myself. Even in your absence—no, what I mean is—your still persistent lingering presence in absence.

SO I WENT ON MY OWN. The soft gray trip I gambled for. 'Cause it was a gamble, a maneuver, arrived at through negotiation. With Ransom. Better yet with Ransom through Sal, lawyer to lawyer: she set it up and took the trip first herself. Paving the way. It all began back with the photographs, with the hope of saving some remembrance through pictures. Of you. Then of the house. Your shrine. Your masterpiece. It began as early as the stoplight on Second Avenue as I headed toward the Bowery coming from my gallery the night Mother told me you were dead. Aunt Dorothy is dead. And at that stoplight, its red like Christmas reminding me I had just been home and hadn't even called; at that stoplight there was a moment of still time when I realized everything: my folly, my own coldness, my loss—and that there was not even a piece of paper recording A.D.'s existence, not even a series of tones and shades in gray and black and white that verified her ever having lived on the planet, this woman I had loved all my life, this being I had yearned for and now had lost irretrievably. Jesus, not even a photograph, I said to the steering wheel, my gut registering utter futility. And then the panic, the scratching of activity—I'll get one, I'll get one out of those damn lawyers, those saintly bureaucrats in charge, functionaries packing things up, her letters, her books, her little store of brown envelopes and old pictures of youth—that is the one thing I'm going to be brave about. I'll enlist Sal and put her up to it too. When Hank Ransom called I was brave enough, marching my teary voice along in a semblance of slow careful speech: "I wonder, Mr. Ransom, if it would be possible to have a photograph of my aunt; I have had only this charming old-fashioned silhouette all these years. But now . . . it would be so wonderful." "Well, of course there hasn't been time yet." "Yes, yes, I understand." "When we begin going through things." "Sure, you might just come across something like that." Of course there's the possibility she may have destroyed pictures of herself in the past. The inference of age, vanity—but it doesn't sound like her. Does he know her better than I? Of course he must, a neighbor many years, must have seen her once or twice a week for several decades.

How often have I seen her in the past twenty years? Too often and never, each awful little interview surging into mind, the mind numbed with grief, yet with the need for having one's wits about one while talking to this thoroughly intimidating attorney, this image of rectitude and St. Paul. Even if he is Minneapolis: at this moment he is home and place, the assembled frowning face of it, those who stayed there, owned it, claimed it, lived by its rules and now enjoy proprietorship. He is fifteen or twenty years my senior, rich, a member of the bar. I am an overaged adolescent trying to build a drawing rack in an inadequately heated loft in a New York slum. Wanting to bother his progress through the day by clamoring for photographs of a dead lady towards whom I harbor the most inappropriate sentiments: a bewildered hurt and resentment, and the remnants of a lifetime of an irregular infatuation. It would be absurd to explain: choked stupid phrases that I adored my aunt, am ravaged by her death—the mewling of an heir, the pieties of the survivors of the rich, searching for clauses. No wonder he dredges up this bequest and presents it like some kind of looked-for good news, expected, part of his job. "Fuck your bequest"—how difficult to shut up and not say that—tell him: listen man, to hell with bequests: I wanted her. I do not want her goddamn money. After all these years is it still going to be about that lousy money? I want her alive again, I want her friendship—I want her love, her talk, her companionship, I want to have lunch with her and laugh, I want to drink martinis with her and talk and agree with her finally.

Swallow and be still. The man is a thousand miles away and you had better keep this under your hat; you are already a suspicious character to him for sure. Is it sure? Did she ever mention me to him? Did she talk about that scapegrace niece who lived in New York, wrote books, and was always coming apart at the seams? Did she explain me in one petrified and onyx phrase such as "Kate has disappointed me bitterly," or dismiss me in one highball laugh: "The one we really did our best for was the one who went right off the track."

I must have imagined that deep kiss at Christmas; I must have imagined everything. It is clear when you hear Mr. Ransom describing her funeral or lack of it that my aunt was no more than my aunt, a woman of substance in Minneapolis who has left some thirteen million dollars to the symphony, the chamber orchestra, the Tyrone Guthrie Theater and the Minneapolis Institute of Fine Arts. She is not the beauty I spent nearly fifty years in love with, not that arch and wonderful goddess but an institution about to be divided into pieces to feed and be absorbed by other institutions. Who are too stupid and greedy even to save her house, the gift of art she gave them—but must turn it smack into cash. Never mind how dumb you sound, how real your disappointment and regret that the Guthrie will not be keeping the house for its staff and visitors. So that you might even sneak in once sometime by currying favor and finding pull—just to see those rooms again. That were her. Her essence, her achievement, her perfume, her mind, her eyes and taste and travels. The perfect rendering of her spirit into material form, its calm, its creative space and ornament, arrangement order and detail.

Damn 'em, the bastards. And you, Mr. Ransom, and your complacency at seeing all this wasted on whatever rich moron from Minneapolis will buy the place and "redecorate." "The zoning laws as I mentioned before," I hear him going on fussily, energetic suddenly, defensive. Fuck the zoning laws too, I think, how lame, how stupid. Surely the Guthrie could get Wayzeta—big shots like you urging the cause—to waive the bloody zoning laws—are artists unfit to live on Lake Minnetonka? Does the director drag race on a motorcycle, would the folks imported from New York turn out to be faggots, are European ballet dancers and opera singers going to bring down the tone of the neighborhood? I find I'm getting pretty hot under the collar listening to him.

Jesus, are they that silly back home that they would defend their suburb against the artists they so piously leave their bucks to and drag up on every occasion as their civic achievement, the accomplishment of the rich to bestow culture on their city, as if its general population gave a hoot over the "high" art these nabobs have converted into their own property and privilege? And yet will not permit into the neighborhood when push comes to living next door—it's the same old business—the aunt's line about artists not being the kind of people one invites to dinner. The same stuff, now from Ransom. She gave the theater her house, everything, lock, stock, and barrel, from what he says.

"Did she know it would be sold?" I actually ask him this right out loud, into the wire, right to his face as it were. "Of course, the zoning laws make it impossible for the theater to retain the house; the trust is to benefit from its sale. Actually they prefer that."

I get it: the bureaucrats who run the arts, the fundraisers and those types, they want cash. Not a house. Not a thing of beauty, but currency. Money at interest. Fools—they deserve to lose it. Did they ever even see it, I wonder? Sure, plenty of times I expect, out there toadying to get it. Looking it all over, looking ahead, figuring what it would fetch. The staff of the Minneapolis Institute of Fine Arts might relish the Han horse beforehand, but the monetary minds of the theater and the symphony must have looked around and assessed the whole setup. Hell, they were probably trustees anyway, rich folks and neighbors; who else gets up money for the established arts? Fellow patrons. Or simply those youths who go from college art history departments into curatorship and art management, pale children of wealth who perpetuate the same taste and control they inherit. Goddamn it, Ransom—madder and madder after I have hung up the phone—that they would all stand by and let this house be destroyed which was her gift to them.

"All of her personal possessions left unclaimed by the four beneficiaries of the trust, the symphony, chamber orchestra, theater, and fine arts associations, will be dispersed either through sale or distribution to friends and relative so that on the first of July the house will be taken over by its new owner." Who could buy it, I wonder? The price beyond price, a way of life gone now. And so far away. It did not occur to me to buy it, even in fantasy. But neither did it occur to me that the one who bought it would destroy it.

Literally. I do not mean by spoiling its rooms with his own litter and plastic American rubbish—I mean physically. For that was the next thing we heard. It would be knocked. Razed—bulldozed. So we better get going. It would not only be stripped of all that remained of our aunt by July 1, but it would no longer stand even for one to drive by and yearn for. Sally and I laid our plans. It would be the last look. The last chance. Of course there had been the last chance of the funeral or non-funeral or whatever, but I did not wish to cruise through those rooms like a supervised ghost in the presence of the wonderful personages who had been my aunt's good friends and cronies. Bless them for assembling to bless her, but I did not want to bring my grief before those strangers and spend the hours of the "party" and the champagne brunch and so forth lurking in the library hiding my tears and outlawed difference. I wanted my aunt alone. Not with her friends, but all to myself.

Even if she were not to be found in those rooms, I was sure to find her. The sorrowful absence there would be one for me alone, the presence direct and personal. I wanted my own trip. So did Sal. So we set it up. First Sally persuaded Ransom, lawyer to lawyer, with fine points about the great amount of personal property still on his hands and so little time left to dispose of it to friends and relatives as per the will. Whereupon Sally became very amiable about acquiring property for herself and for her four children. And for me and Mallory as well. Sal got me the boat sofa. But despite his predicament in having the entire furnishings of a mansion to get off his hands, with only a few months to do it, Ransom is tough: Sally may go and look and make a list—but it is only a "wish list." Walter's daughters have bespoken a bedroom or two, the bedrooms they too stayed in on visits. Good. Sally goes on making lists of what's left; Ransom still calls them wish lists, promising nothing. Sally spends days on inventories and appraiser's catalogs, lengthy as briefs in themselves, then more days on the phone negotiating from Nebraska. Her son Steven is right there on the spot. Steven, whose promise and charm as a law graduate enjoying his first clerkship for the chief justice of the Minnesota Supreme Court recommend him to Ransom from the beginning—and Steven, a splendid young man and most ingratiating, is delighted to take some furniture off Hank's hands.

Sally is a good lawyer and firm. She has a definite and personal interest in these effects, determined they will go to the family rather than to those she now calls the fiddle players. And since she cannot save Aunt Dorothy's house she will see it again, memorize it, love it one last time with eyes that have loved it for decades. And photograph it.

Flash gun expert and all. Sally is quick and relentless in argument and understands property. I am slow as a slug but I slide in behind. There will be no flash gun and no expert when I go there. Just myself alone in the house with a still camera, my own eyes needing and desiring the place far more than a lens ever might. That windfall chance to see it, to be in it, to live in these rooms one last time, time in them that will have to last me forever. What will they mean, what will they say, what of her presence, her spirit, its message, its enduring and distilled power, will enter me? Or fail to? Will I see and forget, drink my fill and come away empty, needing another draft, another time when it will be there no more?

And of course I could louse up the pictures. Lose the shoot. I who never go on shoots, who photograph my friends and when it doesn't work out, just forget it, doing almost everything important in the darkroom anyway. My exhibition prints are arrived at through alchemy and never originate in the perfect shot. But this is a shoot—it's fleeting—and it goes away like a parade or historical event—you either get it or you don't. 'Cause they are razing the house. You could never get in there anyway once someone bought it, but here they are buying it to destroy it—the news having reached us that a local plutocrat is buying the house just to tear it down and build another, paying three quarters of a million dollars just for a piece of lakefront property, a building site.

"And ruin all that beauty—Sal, you're kidding." "Nope." "Who is it?" "A Dayton." "Minneapolis." "Figures, doesn't it?" "Yup." Having another drink over the phone, words fail us and we sip in silence. "Anyway, I got it arranged. Ransom is letting me go in April." "Good, Sal; I'm going in May then." "Don't wait any longer than that." "I won't. . . . It's a big lake, Sal, you'd think with that whole lake. . . ." "You would, wouldn't you? They must have been looking at that spot for years." "But they were friends of hers." "Inside job." "Shit." "How early in May can you get there?" "Not very; I gotta plant at the farm." "Hurry it up." "There's a good rate after the 15th; I could go right after the East Coast Women's Festival in Atlanta, be on a plane for about three days, but still." "Get there, kid." "Better believe it." "If your snaps don't pan out, you've got mine." "Yeah, it's seeing it that I want, seeing it." "Get there, then." "I will."

And when I stand in the drive, seeing it, I am still afraid I will miss it. Indeed it seems I have, since no one is here to let me in. This whole thing was arranged with Scotch tape, too much on the fly, I realize now. Steven drew me a rough map this morning so I would not repeat my previous errors and in fact I am in time for once. Her house and she is not here. No false turns, none of the nightmare delays of the past. I drove as studiously as if I had an appointment with her. But it is with the gardener instead. Still I have knocked at the great front door, for form, from superstition, a lingering rush of mad hope that she would be there and open it herself. Not even the butler. But not even the gardener either, this guy Paul who Mr. Ransom said would be here and expecting me. Too chancy, too iffy, the whole thing. I should have called the gardener myself and made my own arrangements. No one answers the cottage door where Paul is to be living while he bridges the gap between my aunt and the new purchasers. Despite the coming invasion, the garden must be kept up at any rate. It seems the Daytons approve of and will keep the garden. How will they build then without spoiling it? Piles of earth everywhere, the bulldozed house.

Looking fine and quite unfit for destruction. It is maybe fifty years old, wood and stucco, large, boxlike, plenty of windows, generous in dimension, plain and old-fashioned country club and restful. Revealing little of the treasure within. It was Uncle Walter's house, or similar old Minneapolis money, not showy, serviceable, supremely comfortable, unpretentious—a big house on a lake was still a lake home in those days. Built to last, it is in perfect condition; there are perhaps some twelve inches of wooden wainscoting that could use paint, maybe ten more of stucco, both on a corner where the wind hit—the kind of thing she would have had attended to in the spring. If she had lived till spring.

And now in spring, late spring, early summer—the plentitude of the garden, a big garden, perhaps an acre of lilac and tulip, the last daffodils and jonquils, little walkways. It is bigger than it used to be, more elaborate. Once it was the trees she treasured most, but a big storm took many of them so she turned her energy into flowers, got a gardener, made a full-time thing of it. That visit when we talked about our trees, probably the only nearly successful interview in the last twenty-five years: her trees and my trees and how hers had died in the storm. I did not even take time to register that fact in my eagerness to display the farm, impress—what a nitwit. And what a garden, the number of plants; the care and time humbles one. This man Paul must have given her great happiness, a wonderful happiness in her last years. Already I like him, even love him for this.

BUT STILL I can't find him. Well, take that phone number and go down to the village and see if you have any luck—it may be the number for his own home phone or something. No reply there either. Stubbornly, I buy more film—if not today, then tomorrow. I have come all the way to Minnesota to go inside a house and find my aunt there in its rooms one last time and I'll be damned if this delay is going to stop me. I'll keep calling, and if that doesn't work out, go back to the house and wait. Ransom is out playing golf for the day. I sit in Mother's car in the driveway feeling silly: the intruder, the misfit, the sentimentalist. So photograph the garden, since that's all there is to see; do your outside shots; no one will stop you. On this quiet lane no cop to restrain you, no security man—he has been here already for the day. Each time he comes by he leaves his card and the time of his visit, comically obvious, since the cards have now piled up in the crack between the door and the jamb, proving that no one has opened the front door in nearly a week. Paul must use the back door; it's handy to the cottage.

No one will stop you unless the village policeman comes by and finds your car unfamiliar and suspicious. So probably you can look and even photograph with impunity. As if it were Virginia Avenue, which is a public street. Nights that Sally and I would go by there and stop, the obligatory cigarette, the deep confidences, the euphoria of a few drinks that made all clear—we could understand ourselves, our circumstances, ancestors, town, heritage, even our future in those moments out of time before the old house we had loved. But this is different: Minneapolis, Wayzeta, the fancy enclave, the humble yet so arrogant fence that screens this house from the road, the fact that you can have no commerce with the house unless you dare to enter its drive. We would never have dared. You don't sit outside this kind of place talking through the Irish understanding acquired in the Commodore Bar. And you do not enter this fence without permission.

Indeed it might even be illegal to be here. You could always try to persuade them you were the late Mrs. Lindeke's niece; Mr. Ransom would confirm—when he's home from his golf game. Little bit of a wait of course in the hands of the constable. I sure wish this man Paul would show up; I feel increasingly awkward and embarrassed. My precious time here is flying away, the light too.

Yet in an odd way I have the run of the place. Of course, not the promised run with the key and permission. Still locked out of the house and it was the house I had come to see. But just the fact that I have come here without her invitation and may look at her garden, respectfully and carefully and with great admiration—but without her leave. That she had to die for me ever to dare to be here without an invitation, to enter that drive—it comes up so quick you go right by it, so private it is, so easy to miss, just past the bridge—and then stand before her house and her door without being summoned. Only because I wanted to come. It makes my knees shake—this realization; for I have been here a thousand times in my mind where it is only an instant's distance from New York or England or Japan or even Provincetown. Yet this was the first time I have ever dared to be here on my own initiative.

I remind myself: You could have besieged her all these years, flown home, rented a car—forget the motel room business which could launch you from neutral ground so you would not be coming to her from your mother's house—just hop on Hertz or Avis and show up. Ah, but that's not how it's done, I argue back. Of course you never dared to try it either? Don't be preposterous; I could hardly just arrive and surprise her. Not if you'd swallowed her mandatory legislation that you telephone first for an appointment. Certainly not calling from New York either—remember her closing remarks last time you got impulsive—"Do not call me long distance anymore; it upsets me. Write—or wait until you are here and in your mother's house. It is time for my lunch now; goodbye."

She had to die before you could get here on your own steam. Were free enough. Were permitted. Were brave enough. How craven then all these years. No—it is her house, her privacy, her rules, her space in which to be her own woman. Besiege her and if her scathing command did not dislodge you, she would most certainly have called the police. You don't truck with this lady. So now when she's dead, you can hang around all afternoon waiting for the gardener to need some tool or another and show up to let you in. How peripheral you are then, after all, the long-faced most persistent mourner.

Hypocrite latecomer in May. Did she know you were home at Christmas, the last days she lived, the days following the holiday, her death a final sigh of loneliness three days after the New Year? What was the truth—that she had nothing at the end but a gardener and her money, kin and maybe even friends a bore, a disappointment? Or did she drive all away, the "favored version of things," the mean old woman, the figure dining alone as a just punishment for a life of bullying and cantankerous behavior? Caricatures, one thinks, looking at the flagstones, the walk up to the door, the knocker and the small pearl push button that when pressed gives out an empty chime within an empty house.

I had fancied I would open the front door with the key Paul would be here to give me, the act itself almost sacrilege and yet a final momentary inheritance. Of all those left I was one of those so privileged, a niece. The worst niece of all, but never mind; death itself would change that, heal, transform. My grief or pity would give me leave; my terrible love would have this last indulgence. But when Paul finally did arrive, a man with a good face and carriage, complicated, intelligent, an impressive man striding toward the house along the cottage walk, he did open the door for me—the back door. So that the first thing I saw was the kitchen. And the next day I did have that dubious thrill, the curious honor of arriving alone and finding the key where he had told me he hid it, under a hammer in the toolshed.

Initiated, I walked through the front door alone. Almost as if I were she. Or Uncle Walter. Who else would have such entry? It was a strangely shivering experience and I drew back from it at once; leaving the front door open I returned the key to its place and unlocked the back door as well, thereby keeping the house open the whole time I was in and out to photograph its rooms and lawns and gardens. So that the bar of a lock and the taboo of opening it or simply enduring those emotions and memories would not intrude again.

But it was good to see the house first from the kitchen. The hominess of Paul's house, the familiar milieu of Paul's Mrs. Lindeke. Wonderful how much he liked her, this cantankerous old lady, this gutsy drinker and cusser, this nonchalant tough old soldier, a big cut above the other rich critters he works for. For he knows them all, just as she did, and it is clear he admires her for withdrawing from them all at the end, even if it left her lonely. "You'll want to look around now; we can talk later." He withdraws tactfully, sensing my tumult.

The kitchen is yellow and full of sunshine. It is still really the cook's kitchen; my aunt is as foreign here as I, though she commanded this place. Its muslin dish towels, its painted table and old-fashioned "peanut butter" chairs as we used to call this kind of round-backed kitchen chair; Mother had the same kind at home. While we sat in them, our Celia dispensed cookies or we munched a concoction I took credit for, toast smothered in butter and peanut butter, the whole mess melted under the grill. This is a homey room, for all its oversized iceboxes and the profusion of silver, the luxury of glasses in the butler's pantry where drinks are made and stirred with a thousand sterling silver gadgets, silver ice buckets, and crystal. The serious business of drinks in a house serious about drink: Paul has begun to make me realize how serious.

My aunt was drunk nearly every night of her life in the four years he had known her. Falling down? I wonder and wait while he squints and licks his lip and looks past me at the kitchen table. Yup, he nods stoically. "You might say it was medicine, a kind of medicine; she wouldn't take any kind of pain reliever from a doctor. Drugs. Dope, that kind of thing. This was her own remedy; she'd lived by it, she knew it." I swallow and try to imagine her life those last years, here in her own kitchen. "She was wonderful, a wonderful woman," he says, with absolute conviction. "Such wit, such courage."

That wit, that courage now begin to accompany me through the house. The threshold where you enter the big dining room. If you were to leave the kitchen by the other door you would already be in the library, but it is too soon for that. On that side the sun cries out through the library windows onto the lake; look once and then away and do not go that route. Not yet. But I know the library is still there, past a little powder room that seems new to me. She had fallen in the one by the front door: the other bathrooms would mean negotiating the stairs. And she had not been able to climb stairs for four years, not since her legs were threatened with amputation, the great hospitalization I was never told about. Since then Paul has been here: since then she has been an invalid whose greatest pleasure was her garden.

"Did she ever go upstairs again?" "Yes, sometimes she'd be up there for months on end, then suddenly she'd want to be carried downstairs to see the garden." "And you carried her?" "She was nothing; she weighed ninety pounds at the end." I wince at the disappearance of the tall handsome woman I had known: five feet six, a hundred and twenty-five pounds, a horsewoman's strength, a skier's grace. All her adult life. And to become a wizened child figure carried in this man's strong arms? Thank God he was here for her. One is too grateful to envy him, too ashamed of one's absence to begrudge him her affection, their delight in each other or a certain kind of iris, a particular rose.

At the threshold of the dining room, just beginning the house, by its big fireplace, the diminutive chairs on each side strike me like an unexpected shock—God, I had forgotten them. They were of course our chairs when we were little enough for them and on every visit they would occur out of the corner of my eye like an old rebuke, like an unexpected splinter of remorse underlying the certainty of never again belonging. God knows where they are from, fashioned for dwarves but covered with brocade and large brass studs, the seat no more than a foot high, the back another ten inches and formal, the wood ancient and carefully carved. Today will be hard. The place will be full of things like this and she will no longer even be here: to mitigate with her anger, to take the stage and intimidate and exceed the objects. Which now carry the full burden alone.

THE KNOWLEDGE of losing her finally will be made perfect here, the grief brought to a head. Perhaps even assuaged. For the quarrel has ended, must end with her dying. For both of us. Forgive and see who she was in the things she had brought around her, her fortress, the expression of her soul in the manner she permitted it expression. And no other—at least to you. Probably her sisters, certainly her cronies, knew the full range of her warmth, her bitter and tender humor, her view of the world—a thousand times more mellow and humane than you ever imagined it to be, listening only to your mother and your sisters and the echoes of your broken childhoods. Other people knew her; you never did. You only imagined and invented. Out of the heaven of her beauty and the half-remembered kindness or crossness of long ago. So go on, pit all that is left—this house—against your every grudge, your artist's arrogance, your envy and lesbian desire. See the place now. Without her. Revealed and plain. These rooms: their stately grace is not merely a lot of high bourgeois living you could scarcely aspire to and find it easy to ridicule—they really are a life you only appreciate in books. Here and in books. For here was formed your own notion of aristocracy, your templates of behavior, your primary sources and examples, the cloth and paper patterns of what manners are. Even a certain kind of moral perception and the knowledge you have fallen short of it all, run away, chosen differently, gone bohemian, become a farmer, run to the ranks of the feminists, stood by the barricades of women's liberation, bent your elbow in gay bars, stayed out all night in Tokyo, watched the sea in Provincetown, found the rent on the Bowery, rebuilt barns, followed your star.

Walter's piano gleaming and silent, the French screen behind it, panels of a pastoral. And then the Han horse and the golden fan in the fireplace. The vast room otherwise entirely gray, the lovely grays of civilization. Decorum. Quiet old paintings by Uncle Jerome Hill. How good of her to hang his pictures all her life, her own brother-in-law, in and out of marriage. He was also a homosexual, a fact she must have overlooked. Or permitted in a gentleman. Did she imagine he was discreet? I have met men all over the world who knew and admired him. And praised his generosity, admired his work, but loved his character. Why was it all right in Jerome? Romie, we called him—he was not only a homosexual, he was an artist. Did being a millionaire excuse this? More likely it was his being of her own generation, her own age, beyond changing, a peer. Not a child to redirect or find incorrigible. What will they

Above: The boat sofa.

Opposite: A.D.'s living room and library.

do with Uncle Romie's pictures, I wonder: are there folks out here who will treasure them and make a collection?

The sofas are just so. White brocade over eiderdown. And a great Chinese silk sofa under a mirror which no one ever sat on that I recall. Too formal and intimidating even for this room. Here one sits on either side of the fire in the love seats, cigarettes in great green glass or sterling silver boxes, matches and ashtrays always to hand—in every part of the room—the hospitality of a smoker. Other or private conversations may be had in other parts of the room and at the far end near the round table down by all the windows—the lake present in them as though they were portholes.

The water so close, the dimensions and proportions of the windows somehow special and ingenious, nearly magical, for as large as they are, they have the quality of portholes onto the sea, the room itself relating by some trick of its design to the level of a ship's deck just above water, the water pouring in together with the light of the day, light intensified by water. And just as it reaches the edge of the room it is softened, grayed by the grays of the walls, the many grays and whites of the furnishings, the dark mahogany of the tables at the end of the room, the round one and the baize-covered one, so that one sees the intense light of the sunlight on water outside yet never experiences its glare inside, carefully filtered away by the time it enters the room, muted. So one looks from a soft light into a brighter one. It is difficult to take a camera reading here, so diffused is the light within compared to the glorious sheen without. How carefully she must have planned this effect of safe cool watery air. And what is too soft and low for a camera to register fully is sheer bliss to the eye, to all the senses, restful, protected. Light directed, yet transformed as well, the luminous euphoria of civilization, its refinement of life, a sense of masterful enhancement.

The camera bag is a kind of crutch here; it dulls the pain, busies one. When an object has too keen an edge, reminds too hard, recognition like a knife under the ribs—that vast silver egg cooker or whatever the hell it is, for example; how it fascinated me as a child, how I would recognize it anywhere in the world and it would symbolize a thousand things I had loved then learned to deny, disapprove of, despise, revile. And so forth. Now its sudden appearance under a mirror brings me to the hurt of tears.

Then the horse, finest of all, the Han horse—and I am conquered and cannot see the place, only feel it like waves of anguish sharp as a little heart attack. The self lost utterly to nostalgia and might-have-been. The wish that she were here now. And I could finally tell her. Really here, not some conjured presence. She is present everywhere around me, ineluctable as a scent, coming and going across the threshold to the dining room, to the front hall outside the little powder room where she fell once, a presence that exists only through absence: if she were merely upstairs these would be empty rooms, but now they are as full of her person as if there were music, the currents of being. Waves of personality emanate from every surface or object. She is there yet not there, wonderful and not enough and the spirit thirsts and is in pain with craving. Stronger as the hours go by.

Stronger the second day. When certain things take a firmer meaning. The little bed she slept in, for example. Coming upon it yesterday, it merely shocked and horrified me. This tiny wire frame. Antique something or another, lovely supposedly. But grotesque. She who always slept in great double beds, married or unmarried she had the space of a queen, here in this narrow confining little thing—Jesus—was this some nurse's idea of the appropriate? Of course not, she would have endured no choices but her own. Why this anchorite's discomfort, itself a statement of terrible import?

As for the nurse, she had a room of her own, furnished according to her taste in some awful British stuff I am amazed and delighted my aunt ever paid for, let alone permitted in the house, a whole suite of an impossibly heavy print that at first sight gave evidence of senility until something Paul hinted at made me realize it had been got up according to the nurse's own formula. Fine, the nurse has a suite to her liking. But who had arranged this sad back room to be A.D.'s sickroom with its dismal orange light, the immense light of the afternoon coming through its bamboo hangings like a science fiction sunset, like death?

And in the center of it that tiny procrustean bed, a child's, a shrunken old woman's bed, the bed of death. How dramatically it enshrined dying. Its shame, its terrible smallness, its discomfort, its hieratic and rigid formality. Almost Incan. And opposite this bed, the boat. Here finally was the boat. No longer in the library. Now I realize why that room looked odd. The boat was its trademark; the boat was where you read all afternoon when your aunt was out. Even sometimes if she was in, wonderful times you both sat in it together, one at each end with your feet up snuggling and reading and gossiping or telling jokes or quoting passages or making remarks out of nowhere about the people you knew or the places you were going to explore when you were grown up or like A.D. had already explored by being around the world a couple of times. So here, at last, was the boat. And the vicuña lap rug with fur on top that went with the boat and covered you up but also joined you together when you sat in it with another, and was as comfortable as it was outlandishly luxurious. Old now, a little tattered. And the boat reupholstered for the umpteenth time, its shape shining right through whatever fabric it wore so that it did not matter; it was still the great boat sofa.

The fur was indeed old now; probably it had not been worth the while to buy another: she was dying. Paul said she wore her clothes to tatters at the end. Yet there was a whole closet full of designer dresses by Hattie Carnegie and Schiaparelli: these were people she had known when she was young and she kept all their clothes. Now the Institute of Fine Arts is making a collection of them: there had been a special clause about it in the will. "We had them all dry-cleaned before sending them. Five hundred bucks—the estate paid for it, not the museum," Paul laughed. "Actually had to throw away the clothes she'd been wearing the last few years; they were shot." Like the luxury of the boat and its fur and vicuña rug in apposition to this dreadful little iron bed. As if in contrast to her past. Her present dark and puritan as the past had been voluptuous and indulged. Now this rigor, penury, this hard dying alone in a room like an altar to dying. Here with the nurse.

The bathrooms in this wing and the closets are empty and unused. For they are not on display. Her upstairs sitting room has been all too long unused, the private place of a lady who is long gone, stretched out alone down the hall in her difficult little bed waiting to die. While a nurse takes coffee in this room. For convenience—if she went back to her own rooms she might not hear the call for help. So she puts her coffee just there, disturbing nothing, taking no license. The books on the tables untouched for months even though they are dusted; one can almost estimate how many years have passed since they were moved.

And there by the door of this sitting room, just where Sally had warned me they would be, thinking to cheer me up—"She had your books—every damn one of them." "Which ones?" *"Flying."* "How did she ever get that? I couldn't have been crazy enough to send her one." "Maybe she was capable of calling the store." "No way—she just plain refused a whole pile of stuff I brought her once—*The Elegy* . . ." "She had one." "You're wrong—she couldn't have: it's practically a private book; there are only three hundred fifty signed copies and so forth." "I know, but she had it; I saw it there on the sitting room table when I went out." "How could she ever have gotten it—I tried to give her a copy that day—listen to what she said—'I hated Sita; I sure don't want another book about her.' Hated, Sal." Sally chuckles: the inference of jealousy amused us both. At the time I was sick with embarrassment and shame—my offering; what else could I offer but my books, my life's achievement up to that moment? And she said, keep 'em. But Sally was positive the *Elegy* was there in this room. "Couldn't be," I insisted.

But it is. I hadn't believed Sally, had argued with her. "Sal, she hadn't let me leave a copy with her that day—I'd inscribed one to present—but she was so damn sure she didn't want one. How would I ever have dared to leave it behind on a hall table for her to break down and look at once I'd left. No, no way, she showed me out herself, threw me out, you might say; it was real cold hospitality." "I know the kind." "You don't suppose she wrote to New York for it?" "You got me." "There's no other way—you can't buy it in a store, it's a private publisher, you'd have to have a copy in hand just to get their address." "I know, Mother sent away for a copy to give me as a birthday present," Sally laughs because this is the first time anyone in the family had to pay for a copy of one of my books.

Seeing this book on a table I feel the wave of a curious and recurrent fantasy: that my aunt watched over me somehow, knew when I was captured in Iran. Had sources, connections, information. Riddled as the family is with spies and CIA men, that wouldn't be hard. This is the sort of notion that would come to me when I was supposed to be crazy, that she had intelligence of where I was locked up, saw to it I was well-treated, or tried to. Poppycock. When I finally reached her from the Mayo psychiatric wing at the university she was utterly innocent of my recent insanity trial in St. Paul. Or pretended to be. But surely she would have thousands of sources of information into that very private affair, private only to the press or the populace, but hardly unknown within the circles of my own lawyers who were her oldest friends.

Could she then have gotten her bookstore people, who must have traced down many interesting and curious books for her over the years, to find her this one? Does it have an inscription? Take it up and see. My hands tremble to find that in has none—she bought it herself. It's proof, it's proof. All too late. Stop following this revelation, just revisit, find peace, go through the other rooms again, the bedrooms where you used to sleep while you stayed on nice long visits, so many of them, even that time after Oxford, the blue and white rooms, upholstered in her characteristic stripes of blue and white ticking—you made sculpture for years using this same ticking in your fantasy furniture—never even noticing you were trying to get something back.

The four-posters, the white organdy curtains that give onto the lake water and the light, full and bright up here, permitted, as it was filtered and turned to pearl in all the rooms downstairs. In these beds you were a happy child; stare at the old Irish woolen rugs, perfect in their way, the billow of light in the windows, the crisp lines of the blue and white chaise, the slipper chair. Never your way to live, never would be. Even if you could, you would not make rooms like this anywhere and live in them.

No more than you could have stayed at her side by this lake, a lifetime of caretaking and companioning, being told what to do, what to think, what to read, say, whom to know. How could you have stayed on as your aunt's niece after Oxford? A notion entertained over the years and returned to for a moment in hard times. In the same category as your starving artist fantasy of joining a nunnery or being incarcerated in the women's house of detention with all the paper you could use and three square meals a day. No distractions, no heartbreaks, celibacy in short. A kind of being buried alive that would permit you to sculpt or draw without interruption. Never mind that there would be nothing to sculpt or draw even if church and state were to permit it. In the loony bin you tried to order India ink and Japanese brushes by telephone, intent on doing up the walls.

Within your aunt's house over some thirty years, what on earth would you have done? Impersonated someone wealthy? Read books for eight hours a day and dissected them over dinner? It would be a snob's jail to have lived here; it would have been hell. In two weeks there would be a battle royal and if you lasted beyond that you would be a flower pressed under glass, a rose for Emily, a grotesque.

Why did you ever think of it; why do you remember it now? Because she is dead and it is now forever impossible even to spend a fortnight in disagreement or amity. What if you'd been a good one, with plenty of smart friends to visit in St. Paul, buddies at Marine on the St. Croix—your cousin Jamie's crowd—and you came home again now and then to play with them? Not just to visit your mother, confined by her little house and its filial piety, but to stretch out on these folks' houseboats and sun or go down the Apple River in inner tubes and live the endless Fitzgerald picnic life that St. Paul still has just as it had then? In fact this is its very essence, its distinctive and wisely unpublicized charm among all the cities of the world. So wholesome and of the River if not of the West. So urbane, hankering backward toward the East. Yet insulated, protected by its neat small-city wealth and comfort, uncomplicated by big commerce and greed, transatlantic snobbery. A little Buddenbrooks, this place; when you leave it you surrender things you will never have again. Because they will never seem as good. So you live without them. You go from this house to the Bowery with no sense of having stumbled.

You leave your class and your generation permanently. The people you went to the university with; you will never have personal acquaintance with their equivalent type again, wealthy young businessmen like Percy who can buy whole city blocks in order to restore them—you will be an artist but never know collectors. There will be no Percy Carroll in your circle, nor David Delaney who now presides over the bank. The only fellow spirit you will have is Washburn. And Terry, who lived on booze driving a cab in San Francisco because he wanted to write a novel, looking for F. Scott at the bottom of a bottle. You will never in the course of the next thirty years meet and befriend members of the middle class. You will drop utterly out of sight. You and Washburn.

We laughed over it once at Percy's house in that grand big old kitchen, as grand as the one in this house, also with an entire room set aside just for the mixing of drinks— "Imagine, you and Wash on the Bowery all these years," Percy's gesture contrasts this with his fifteen-room mansion, "and"—We all laugh. "But it's marvelous—you still did the better thing, you took all the chances, you had the adventures." I wonder, is it not some sort of adventure to live in this house, to live near the French governor's mansion and my Aunt Lucy's first apartment, the old golden stone of such buildings, the wide porches, the colonnades, the light in those big rooms? "Honey—let me tell you," and Percy is bitter now and jaded, as big as Oscar Wilde when stout and angry, Percy those years just before his own fall—"to live near the University Club is the biggest bore in the world." But you have everything, you have the rugs of a king, you run the Arts board, you buy and sell half the town. He reads my thoughts—"I started out nobody, from the wrong street, you might say." He will never say so but I always imagine that Percy Carroll is named for Carroll Avenue because my Uncle Harry, his mother's particular friend for many years, fathered him but gave him no name of his own. It is almost there between us in drink, in veiled allusion, in an extra affection and an extra archness and irony. A bite, for he is all bite now, a man profoundly dissatisfied with his wife and his two beautiful children and his big house. Another siren calls. You can see it. I wonder if Sheila does.

On the Bowery of course everything goes. The wealth of freedom we gained by running away is so incalculable that Washburn will not even return on visits. Regards my forays back home as foolhardy bravery. We know the clutch. The power of recall. The old attractions to those ways and places. So we have as a defense isolated it in an older generation, blocking it hardest in our own. When I go home, I slide by because I now know hardly anyone my own age and cannot face class reunions. Too sad, too distant. Percy and Sheila were later divorced and their house was sold. I never kept up with anyone else. Only Mother. Who grounds me. A week in her house and I needed to go back to New York. In order to write, even to think or be. It is her house, not mine. She has no interest in tying me down. For all the flurry of cooking in my honor, a visit is a visit. While I'm there I must tape my aging aunts, her sisters. "So that you know your roots. You must know your roots. And they're going fast—this is the only chance you will have." Knowing my roots I can leave—my life is elsewhere and she knows it. The Bowery, a milieu she has deplored for twenty-five years and regards as excessive and theatrical. And the farm, something else, something a farmer's daughter's must approve of even for a writer. "The farm is the best thing you ever did. Buying that place—still better paying for it—

the smartest thing you ever did, Katie Millett." Yes, Mom, I smile.

Mother was born in Farmington, Minnesota, and has lived in St. Paul for sixty years without even noticing anything glamorous about it. But St. Paul meant other things to Washburn and Percy and the rest of us though we already realized it was a glamour we had chosen or invented or inherited. Fitzgerald was not yet taught at the university so we read him on our own and fell for or reconstructed the myth or finally brought it home. And found one truth in those old houses, those tree-lined streets, the boulevards of elms on Summit. Here was the golden world of the bourgeoisie, here they arrived at a pinnacle of good living and amiability, sweet ways and admirable decency, values that made culture into civilization.

Naturally the first thing we had to do was to get the hell out. Run away, pile on to ships leaving Frisco for Japan, make for tough streets, docks and bars and Mexican hotels, drunks and bums and a romantic, perhaps Italianate, even operatic poverty. So that we would never be tempted to stay home. Nor ever come home again. If we did we would never be artists and artists was what we wanted to be because art was the one thing this very comfortable place didn't have, didn't like, or didn't approve of. A sign of its shallowness and our grandeur.

But all over the world we would remember St. Paul. Surprised, insulted before New York rudeness, Poughkeepsie's wire-necked mean-winded chill. Gratefully susceptible to the beautiful manners of a samurai in a gentle sculptor or a black painter's courtly Southern goodness further mellowed by the Paris art world. We would spy at and reject the memory too in chance glimpses of Connecticut. And long for it on Manhattan's Second Avenue. And thrive without it; its very absence made us strong. Because it was already inside us. But we could not go home.

It always puzzled me that though Fitzgerald never or rarely wrote of home, he often wrote at home. Had a lovely spot on Summit and did *Gatsby* there, finishing it off by finishing off the mirrors at the Commodore. At the bartender's suggestion he celebrated by breaking all the mirrors and paying for them the next morning. Or so they say at home. Those that remember and save up the stories and point out the places; knowing you're a writer, they would fill you with the nectar or the poison of myth. We didn't need Fitzgerald by the end, decided he wrote a shabby magazine-level prose. We had also either transcended or digested the lie of high living, once we noticed that Fitzgerald transposed it always into Eastern terms as a result of his tragic mistake in having attended Princeton. Thereby becoming a snob. Also forgetting he was Irish, something he can reconstruct only in *Gatsby,* a Jew in Long Island, though thank God he can remember it there, even after a lifetime of denying that he was a middlewesterner.

Easy enough to do. The snicker at the cocktail party, the customary jocular description of anyone ugly or stupid. We have borne this for a quarter of a century, sometimes even proudly—at times actually announcing ourselves, telling them, insisting on the fact that we are from St. Paul. Sitting back to watch them decide we mean Minneapolis. Lazily trying to outline the difference—sometimes. Usually there is no point. Ours is a hidden city, a hidden world. Why bother? "Who would want to advertise it?" Percy always laughed—"The New Orleans of the North. God, it would be awful; people might come here."

But we couldn't stay. The curtains and the lake and the chaste feminine loveliness of the blue and white stripes, the old golden walnut, the pearwood, the snug slipper chairs. A life of reading books. The light of sunset through crystal on ice and gin, a candle, a lemon wedge. No. The very inevitability of that now distracts me, saddens me far beyond the fact. If I were to bid goodbye to my mother's house, that refuge, home itself, just as she is—even her wallpaper—pray God it will never happen though it must—it will tear the very meat from my bones: it will be to lose my real connection with humanity. Because she is that.

Aunt Dorothy was something else: high culture, the lure and comfort of money, of style, of a class assurance that always made me deeply insecure, of an impossible love not only forbidden and without hope of realization but also finally, at bottom, immoral. In that in loving her you had to love so much that was intensely unlovable, was so hateful, snobbish, small-minded, narrow-hearted, contemptuous, proud, vain, ungenerous, and smug. Not only in her own self but in her world. Its perimeter and its possessions. Even art itself became suspicious under those terms.

Who made the Han horse that Louis Hill's money could buy? And when these hands formed it did they become a national treasure? How would the Minneapolis Institute of Fine Arts feel about giving this man or woman—it could have been a woman too, it has an edge of the folk in it, is not aristocratic only, is too good and strong for that—some more clay and a place to live? Would they or their ancient Chinese equivalent in official patronage purchase the thing directly from its maker? Or does art only acquire aesthetic as well as monetary value through its contact with the rich? Their purchase and sale and resale. Their jacked prices after auctions and deals and benefactions give it status, magic, its air of the sacred? Is that why its price is never reasonable like the price of other things, but fantastic, putative, assigned, projected?

And the rich then fall back on this as their reason to despise the sycophant in so many artists, the fool that will come to dinner and perform, will sell his soul, will swoon with gratitude when a hot patron buys for a big price, not because of the money but because the rich bastard is some "famous" collector—as if that were a distinction he could arrive at without money. The poor and the rich of it, the ugliness of this system, its humiliating perpetuation despite art education and the democratic possibilities of the art print and multiples. So of course the moneyed get an art that says what they want. And of course you turn your back not only on St. Paul but on uptown New York. More pernicious by far than these so-civilized rooms.

To say goodbye to these rooms is to say goodbye to a

life I never had and now no longer may even enter on a visit. There is a tinge of sadness. This is how I might have lived if I stayed home. This or something like it. As Percy did. His mother's house was small and pinched by comparison—the comparison we saw everywhere around us. Was not Fitzgerald's own house on Summit a boardinghouse while he was growing up? And the obvious destiny for us after the university, being bright and well-polished and bent on succeeding according to the formulae around us, was to earn through some cleverness or hard work all the things we had never inherited. What our college cronies had been born to we could attain if we made careful note of the style and improved on it. Good students, bookish and witty, superior achievers, we might work a miracle and come to rest surrounded by comfortable beauty—Percy did it. I didn't; I left.

And maybe the real reason I left was because my aunt had sent me off to study at Oxford. Whereby she showed me the world. I would never need St. Paul again because I found what I liked in it everywhere else. And I found a great deal else besides. If I'd stayed: graduate school at the university, some disastrous marriage where I would have hurt some man as I did several college beaus before Jaycee. Or perhaps Jaycee or another Jaycee right here in the Twin Cities? The idea makes one dizzy—in those days. Not in these. There are probably lesbian feminist comrades all over the university village of Dinkytown now, but not then. Would I have taught or had babies? Would I have made the good marriage my aunt saw as the natural path to follow even after an Oxford First? Dubious; somehow I never attracted the right kind of young man. If they were intellectuals they were also poor or unfashionable. And rich boys were always so smug, so empty, so boring, so superior in the smallest ways—fun in a crowd but too blank for intimacy.

So in watching the afternoon move through these rooms, I relinquish not only the phantom hope of being a spinster niece, a rich dilettante in my own right—I leave off my last connections with money. A lifetime of being the niece of a great fortune, of having a pearl hidden, richer than all other tribes. "New money," Wash used to tease me, her family having pretensions to greater antiquity, old St. Paul and so forth. "Big money, baby, and hands off A.D. Whatever's wrong with her, whatever makes her so stubborn sometimes or such a bitch, she's got more lady and better smarts than any of those flakes on Crocus Hill who think they're Brahmin class." "Just trying to shake your wagon a little."

Wagon is not a bad word: in being Dorothy Millett Hill's and then Dorothy Lindeke's niece I had by birth and relationship tied my wagon to a star. No literary notable ever approached the power she seemed to wield here, had wielded all through my lifetime. And over me as well. The combination of love and money. So glamorous in childhood, so irritating in adolescence, so infuriating after graduation, so alien and poisonous as I began to be an artist, my back turned even on the graduate erudition planned for me. Their well-groomed scholar had sunk to the folly of clay and plaster in an unheated derelict loft on the Bowery. The cold of those years, the deprivation, the uncertainty: but you knew enough by now not to ask her for money if you didn't have the sixteen dollars for a coal delivery to feed the ancient potbelly stove. She wouldn't give you a dime and you knew it. She would also be completely uninterested, even nasty, about your little entry in the juried show, your new style or whatever. Mother supported the whole madness—even with money. Forty bucks a month and she earned it herself selling life insurance. I actually existed on that the first year and a half.

But you were dead to your Aunt Dorothy. There'd been Jaycee and the lesbian thing. Finally, it didn't matter whether you were straight or gay: you were an artist; that was bad enough. When you went through St. Paul on your way to Japan, with nine hundred dollars which was supposed to last you for two years, she was just as uninterested, just as devoid of encouragement or curiosity. You couldn't give away your bad early paintings to the Milletts. Aunt Lucy kept her example in the garage and when pressed about hanging it, frankly declared that it belonged in the garage. Mother hung hers in the basement. But she still has it. And every poster from every show you ever did. Each time I see them I am moved and astonished. She never liked or understood what I did, but I had done it.

Mothers are one way, aunts are another. But it is this aunt who made me an artist. Mother made me a writer. Worked at it steadily and carefully ever since I was a small child being recited to. Aunt Dorothy made me a painter and sculptor. Despite herself. Nowhere else did I see pictures, growing up. Indeed there was no place to see them. No galleries. No picture books. But Aunt Dorothy's house was full of paintings, some even famous. And the Han horse a sculpture of such perfection it taught you a great deal about sculpture all by itself. All those art books. You could go through them all day with your Aunt Dorothy and she would tell you about them. What was good, what was important. After a while she said nothing at all but asked you what was good and what was important. That was scary. Finally you just said what came into your eye—since there was clearly no right way to figure this out, unlike math or even literature questions—this guesswork often amused her and since you remembered pictures and had favorite ones and reasons, she did not condescend. In fact she was a brilliant teacher, a gifted teacher. Who nevertheless worked far too much on love and could dreadfully abuse her power. But charm is still a great incentive in learning and the very manner of my leaving her tutelage was some guarantee that one could overcome her prejudices, examine and reverse such of her values as were dangerous. Then became an artist in spite of her. "Giotto drew on the rocks when he was eight," Aunt Lucy moaned when she learned of my terrible new resolution. "Don't expect anything of me," Dorothy said. I didn't.

Indeed I seem to have sinned more in becoming an artist than in becoming a lesbian. The latter might be undone for a while; the former never. I married a man several years later but my aunt was unimpressed. When after ten happy bohemian years we separated, Fumio and I never even formally divided our property. Except for the farm, we owned nothing anyway. The farm was mine; I had bought it and paid for it and Fumio was far too much a sculptor to even want a farm. I still have it, though it's a funny thing for an artist to have. Odder still to pursue my plan of making it a women's art colony, self-sufficient, a working tree farm, women's art surviving on Christmas trees—absurd, but there you are.

If I have my way, my aunt's library will be one of its best resources. Not that I dared to mention this to Ransom or to my aunts, though I did say the books would go to the farm and not to the Bowery studio—they probably have no idea of the colony and might very well disapprove if they did. Sophie thought so; I thought not and wanted to put this down as a philanthropic reason: hadn't my aunt left her money to cultural institutions? "Not like this one, silly. You had better keep it out of this." So I did, though I have no idea if the books will ever be mine. Ransom is to come by today and perhaps provide an answer, yet he has been so abrupt on the telephone the time or two I dared to mention the books, I am afraid to ask him again.

EACH TIME I enter this room I see the books chosen by the Institute of Fine Arts who had first pick. The library is plucked, disfigured with their tickets. As many as two hundred leather volumes, little cards inserted in them proclaiming them valuable enough. Of course they will get the cream of things. They got *Tristram Shandy*. I'll get your regular old just-plain-reading books. Fair enough. The less impressive they are the better they feed my affection for my aunt, my gratitude to her as my teacher of books, a final sense of the rightness of the plain things, books for their own sakes. But they have missed plenty of leather volumes and a number of plums, the professionals. They passed over a first edition of Joyce, and a great many of Edna St. Vincent Millay. Some books here are just lovely for their own sake, their bindings and papers. Some are delectable things you could leaf through on the spot if it were not for the anguish of being here under these conditions, the lady dead whose books I have not browsed in these twenty-five years.

Recent visits, those tense little occasions, I was rarely permitted to sit in either the living room or the library. Only that little alcove off the dining room, comfortable and sunny and probably convenient for her lameness, the mysterious ailment she refused to discuss, but clearly a spot only to light in, one quick drink and you're off. I would look out through the door into the library, longing for a fire, for the warmth of a room with books, for proximity with the great Chinese portrait painting over the mantel, for the fun of the African violets and the last afternoon light, remembering the high jinks of her poodles Cupid and Psyche, their propensity for jumping on the white brocade chairs or joining us in the boat sofa. The poodles themselves long dead and never replaced; she couldn't trouble now, it was perhaps too dangerous to love. Walter had died. I had turned out a disappointment, Claire lived in Hong Kong, Sally's and Mallory's children didn't interest her, the winter afternoon lengthened. I was sent away. The visit ended. And only then was William summoned to light the fire in the library.

The strategy of keeping me out of the library was most effective. She knew it was my favorite room, this rug my favorite rug, its portrait scroll, and its glory of books so that you carried on conversations about books while walking among them, titles reminding you of topics. You capped allusions here, did reviews in a sentence, even a phrase. Checked quotations for bets and to settle disputes simple enough so that you didn't have to call the Hill Reference Library which even at eight or ten in the evening would gladly give you the answer to a dinner party's quandary. There was always William Rose Benét, the "know-it-all book" if you couldn't remember or agree in which of Dickens's novels a character belonged, the date of Swift's *Modest Proposal,* the real lowdown on Falstaff, whether you're right or I'm right 'cause Keats was already dead by then so it must have been Shelley.

The strange rigorous quality of this room, however; probably because she had to teach herself the whole thing, had to make up for graduate school alone, had to piece it all together and tie in European study between Louis's business and hunting trips, had to know more and more exactly than any dilettante, had to aspire to virtuosity, the four major versions of the Bible, and so forth. Paul said she was importing great tomes in German right up to the end. Good for her. No rewards, no grades, no publications, no reputation really either. Her companions ran companies or owned baseball teams. Who in her circle of matron socialites and do-gooders, the "Busy Bees," would have been able to stumble through one of the passages she analyzed in language nearly as abstruse as Mr. Casaubon's in *Middlemarch?*

The library here, where we had our school, where for some ten years I was her favorite pupil. How bitter that she is dead and not here to have my thanks, humble and without protest, knowing finally all she gave me, past quarreling, defending, quibbling, or even apologizing. You taught me, gave to me, made me love it all; without you I might never have been a writer, even with all of Mother's input. She was the basics and the drive to record, you were the thrill of literature and tradition, the nuance, the touchstone of judgment, good sense, and discernment. Of course I would disagree once I was out of school. It was to be expected that youthful projects like my study of Henry Miller for Waseda University would necessarily strike you as vulgar, even opportunistic and sensational, since there was nothing in such a man that would ever claim your respect. Perhaps I was deliberately showing off my resignation from orthodox scholarship in favor of the rakish fine arts. But I learned a great deal from him of how the autobiographer conveys experience, shamelessness best of all, and a vivid sense of American color, language, and action. A good writer for a printer-sculptor type to read. And for an American with too much Eng. Lit.

Yet there was a time that I was your idea of prudish—your richly illustrated text of *The Beggar's Opera* struck my high-school eyes as indecency itself: such bosoms, such bottoms. And you were amused, so I felt doubly disgraced. A book Mother would disapprove of; I could imagine how the nuns, presently hounding me for my conspicuous friendship with a classmate, would respond to pictures like these. And in one evening you introduced me to caricature and the pleasures of the nude, a kind of hedonism new and wonderful, perhaps part of that larger world of sin, sensuality, and outlawry that already beckoned. An easy civilized appreciation of the sensual and even the comic, the breasts of Jenny Diver, the lavish and lovely shoulders of Polly Peacham, a highwayman's tale making fun of lords and ladies, official manners and morals. "Aren't the songs splendid?" you called out, playing my favorite again: "Before the barn door crowing, the cock by hens attended." It reminded me delightfully of Chaucer's "Nun's Priest's Tale" which I was already reading quietly during study hour at convent school. The librarian, Sister Joseph, was pleased with my ambition, presumably unaware how the Reeve and Miller and the rest of them, the forbidden tales, were also part of my curiosity.

And suddenly it was all right. The world opened up for me that evening. Because of you. Without you I would never have arrived at this understanding at thirteen, only many years after, perhaps never. That happened in the house on Virginia Avenue. Lost. And now this house about to be lost too. There are only a few more hours left to me here. The house itself has only a few more weeks.

AS IF in answer to a question, Mr. Ransom appears. "Hank Ransom here," his presence exuding the poignant well-tailored and -exercised youth of a man in his sixties, perhaps even seventies. A man who has just finished playing golf and takes extraordinary care with his clothes. A light blue shirt and a tan suit, a ruddy and remarkably handsome face above them. I am confused by his appearance. I had been crying when he suddenly materialized and must put away my tears; they would seem inappropriate, too real, explicitly antisocial in proximity to Mr. Ransom's hearty and simultaneously distant presence. We sit in the living room. I notice that for the first time I use the ashtray before me on a table rather than the one from the kitchen which I carry about with me so I will dirty none that have been laid out for use—what if I forgot to clean it and it were noticed? This house like an object wrapped in cellophane, on display for friends, my own visit a part of the plan, permitted; but you shouldn't push it. And now I notice I sit in a chair, cross a leg as if Ransom's arrival granted permission, authorized my presence, freed me to behave as a guest. He uses an ashtray and when he leaves he does not take care to clean it—others are paid to do that.

With Ransom I become not only a guest but someone who lives in the present, an adult—discussing affairs, the terms of the will, the moment when the house will be destroyed. He now confirms the rumor. The Daytons have bought it. He calls them Ken and Dottie or something and beams his approval: "Everyone's delighted they're coming into the neighborhood." "But surely they wouldn't consider wrecking a house they have just bought?" "That's why they bought it; they want the site." I glare. "It's the plumbing, you see." "No, I don't. There's nothing wrong with the plumbing." "Take a fortune to bring it up to date." "I know a little bit about plumbing and I'm sure that to re-plumb this entire house would cost very little—compared with the cost of demolition—let alone rebuilding."

"They want to do something modern. I'm sure it will come out very nicely." "But, Mr. Ransom, this is a beautiful house. Look around you—these rooms." Surely this man identifies enough with wealth and treasure to admire these rooms—"They could never be replaced; they're magnificent." "Time moves on, you know, can't stop progress." I have heard this idiotic sort of talk cover a host of crimes against architecture and I grit my teeth. He can't be serious. "Will they salvage anything?" "No idea. Up to them, entirely. But you might ask Paul; he's presiding over the transition—for the garden you know. They'll want that garden." "How will they demolish the house without destroying the garden as well?" "No idea; sure they'll figure it out though."

The Daytons' "garden design engineer" has already telephoned and left a message with me for Paul that the two of them are to "coordinate" the changeover, set up "conferences" and so forth—Paul was amused by the gravity of it all. "Engineer, huh," he grunted and stubbed out a cigarette. The Daytons appear to have carried all before them with the power of money, the weight of their name, the sheer force of owning and then despoiling. Paul is helpless. Ransom seems complicit but somehow unashamed; one imagines even a certain brazen quality to his frivolity in destroying what one would have thought it was his trust and responsibility to preserve. "Did my aunt imagine her house would be knocked after it was sold?" I ask him pointblank. "Of course she knew it would be sold and the proceeds go to the trust of cultural organizations." "You've said that—but that it would also be demolished—this perfectly sound and solid and beautiful place." "Well, it's old, you know." "No, I don't. In St. Paul we wouldn't regard this as old at all." " 'Course Minneapolis is a bit more up to date." "There is something wrong in doing this; it's wasteful, vandalous." "How things are nowadays. All settled anyway. They bought it; they can do anything they like."

One could labor the point forever with him: did they make their intentions clear before buying it? Couldn't preservation have been a stipulation? But before this obtuseness I am finally speechless with embarrassment, quiet with shame and anger. I begin to feel he knew and must have connived in this monstrous sacrilege, rape, betrayal. "About the books, now." Here is my fate. What will he have done here I wonder? "The Institute of Fine Arts of course have gone over them; they had their scholarly research team out here." I hold my breath and blink away the vision of the scholarly research team during Ransom's long and remarkably earnest lecture on their methods and procedure, their benefit to society, the rich stores of their preserved collection, its invaluable uses for learned persons. Humbled before all this rigmarole I wait to hear the verdict.

It seems that in addition to these high priests, one or two others have bethought themselves of a book. "Dodie Pillsbury for example wants some novel. She lives in Paris most of the time, but she wanted to drop in and see if she could pick it out." We are in the library now and my heart hovers near my throat. "Just the ones that people don't want, Mr. Ransom; I thought I'd like to have just what's left." There are a great many books and I see this fact finally dawning on him. Only two weeks remain before the Daytons' arrival.

Ransom is so easy, so assured, yet you feel his nerves vibrating under their tailored composure with a distant comprehension that there is so little time left, an understanding just now beginning to break over him. For a moment I am rather sorry for this man, who for all his great office and his powerful firm, will now have to stoop to acknowledge the reality of sofas and tables, rugs and glasses, kitchen chairs and bureaus and make them disappear somehow. He will need Sally's wish list soon. "Your sister listed some things that you might like from the house; have you thought of anything else since you've been here?" It is a moment, a rather long one. "No, I really cannot think of anything just now. No." I am acutely embarrassed even to have asked for the books but I did it by mail and before I came here. Standing now in this house, her house, so wonderfully outrageously her house still, her presence like a fragrance vibrant in every room, a perfume remembered beyond death—when the boat sofa and the vicuña rug arrived at the farm a month later out of a truck, her scent, Schiaparelli's "Shocking," was still in the fur and lasted there for three or four days, the first whiff was a knife that only time could turn into a caress, that loss becoming another possession, for now I can read in the boat all the rest of my days, sit and think and even summon her—but within these rooms that are so full of her, so possessed and controlled by her spirit that they are her work and very creation, I cannot tell this lawyer man, yes, thank you, I would like this lamp and that chair. I cannot say anything at all.

And then a curious thought comes into my mind: everything here has been exhaustively cataloged and counted, toted up, listed, appraised, desired, valued—but has anyone thought of the ashtrays? "It may seem a little thing, I don't know, but if no one wanted the ashtrays I'd sure be happy to have them." His very blue eyes examine me. "You see, I love tobacco. She did too." I begin to fear tears and talk over them. "I've loved her ashtrays all my life; they're big and sensible and this way I could think of her every time I smoked a cigarette—sounds silly, I suppose, but I loved her so much that an everyday thing like an ashtray would be a delight." "Sure, sure. Go right ahead. Where are they?" I lead him to where they are kept on their shelves right off the library, a little cupboard room matched on the opposite side by the gun rack, the fishing rods. "Hmm, sure—take 'em with you."

Even though this is an order and even though Mr. Ransom will probably—I fear inevitably—forget this request in what will come to be his flurry of shipping and directing several hundred items to distant destinations in six or seven states, I know I will not take these ashtrays with me. It would be like stealing from someone not in the room. Or perhaps right in the room. For when he leaves, my aunt's presence is restored to me again, the time growing short. I think over his offer; is there anything else I would want? It was good of him, having all, he can now bestow. It was even sensible. Given that the house is so full of things, many yet unclaimed by friends and relatives. How to dispose of it all is clearly a problem for him. "She didn't want a sale, you know." I tensed at the word, the idea. "She always said she didn't want strangers coming through here and gawking." "Yes." It need hardly be said that she would feel that way.

But I'm afraid I must trust Sal's wish list, because I cannot ask for anything. Kick myself afterwards maybe, but not here. Standing in your house, I cannot ask for anything at all. In New York or in years to come I may regret this, but at the moment I am silent and know I cannot commit what is so clearly an affront. You are not dead to me here. When I return to the farm you will be, but not here, not with your spirit in every room, gliding ahead through an arch or around a corner, lingering by those soft chairs in the alcove off the dining room where we had our impossible last meetings. Or, since the exchange of flesh for air in the spirit world, you mellow, kindly pointing out the little chairs by the hearth as I go into the kitchen, reminding me in blinding tears of how I sat in them as a child, your adored niece, your petted darling, your substitute kid—my God, is there anything to drink in this house, I wonder?

Paul has some beer in the fridge which he invited me to drink earlier. Maybe I will. Fortunately he comes up along the drive and then through the door, relieving me of the awkwardness of helping myself. But first he told me about the tulips, how he had forced bulbs for her and brought her flowers at unlikely times. Carried them upstairs for her the months she was confined to her room. There were always special things for winter. And once he had coaxed a great pot of yellow tulips and brought them to her in bed, presented them to her astonishment and delight. Incredulity. It was January, a day or so before she died. I begin to weep and can't stop it. Remorse. Even envy. The bitterest regret. Mixed with admiration. Happiness at their happiness. Gratitude, even awe for the man.

It was not that long a beer, but he helped me to let go. Made it plain that no, she would never have forgiven, had her principles, limitations, set notions. "And you had your books," he says, politely ignoring, talking right through my sobs. "So what?" "So you helped other people, people here too. What you said fought prejudice; that's something." I have to look up at him then, his blond, almost impatient, certainty. Such words in Minneapolis; this man is straight. Here is my final reward, balance sheet. He closes the ledger on each way of life. I remember the young amazons on his crew. This strange confirmation here at home. He puts down his glass. "You got to change things and she got to stay the way she was.

PART SIX

Three days of grieving over the farm. A bad year, or it seemed a bad year. Sitting around in Provincetown: dudgeon, dejection, and regret. Not writing. "Like a work camp," the women at the farm said, sitting about the table the last night of the season, "like a goddamn work camp." Okay, let's cut the day down to five hours; work in the morning and we'll do our own art the rest of the time—Sophie's idea. And I've bought it, sat up here in the mist and the sea and the furor of living it over and opted for doing it right. So the pioneer phase is over. Changing, the wrench of changing. Done now.

Nights in the fog-bound cabin of Number Eleven at Poor Richard's Landing drawing up schemes—how to get the farming done, how to paint the whole blue barn in a summer, in six weeks, extend the eaves, rent scaffolding—and bring it all in for only five hours' work per day. The rest of the day for ourselves. Time to run the place at last, time to rest, time for silkscreening—every afternoon will be my own too. Yes. And the next summer we'll work on the lavender barn, its decks, its coop, maybe even its greenhouse. Then the following summer, we might even do the attic at last. And the last year before harvest, the summer of '89, we can build some new housing for ourselves and even put the tractors under cover. Yes. Yes.

In three perfectly idle days I have planned my next three summers: planted, harvested, and replanted the tree crop on paper, designed and made the infernal lists that will henceforth govern my life. But I have not written a word. And this whole ten-day vacation was to write. To you. To resume the argument. Connoisseurship, I'd thought. I'd spend these ten days arguing with you about the meaning of art—making it versus buying, owning, and possessing it. Doing the thing rather than knowing and appraising it. Instead I spent an artist's time figuring out how to re-side a barn; since the blue barn is our studio I must prevent the weather from wrecking its fine old hand-hewn oak beams. Works of art themselves of a kind. The kind that holds up enormous weight and mass and has done so ninety-seven years now. The barn is actually signed on one high beam

"J. C. Hadden 1889." Unusual for a barn builder to sign his work but how right that he should. Like my father the engineer, the road and bridge builder, your wonderful Jamie—this man has made a structure bigger than any sculpture I'll ever do. And it even serves a purpose, keeps off the rain, gives shelter, and is a thing of beauty. I know that it's old and swayback on the southern side, and nearly impossible to side again with the novelty siding which decorum—perhaps even art—would require.

So what is art? J. C. Hadden's nearly anonymous barn-building or your Minneapolis symphony or my "small clothes" silkscreens which I have just shown to someone not interested in buying one? Nor, alas, even interested in bartering for one though she owns an art supply store. And dropped by to give me a generous gift certificate of twenty-five dollars worth of merchandise to thank me for the "gift" of two large art photographs I had exhibited here last fall. Actually, as we talked we discovered that they were delivered to her in error and were really intended for *Womantide,* an arts magazine up here which had requested copies in order to publish them. Somehow the post office delivered them to her shop instead. She kept them. Loves them. Intends to keep them. How can I tell her that she has made off with over two hundred dollars' worth of photographs, one of them my last good twenty-by-twenty-four-inch print. Somehow she regards them still as a gift, though she doesn't mind lending them to *Womantide.* However, one of them is presently hanging over her bed in Boston and it is not convenient for her to fetch it any time soon—she has no intention of surrendering either one.

And I, because she likes them, because I am flattered, take her little gift certificate, worth a tenth of the value of what she's gotten off me, and smile. Realizing she received the photographs in utter innocence and treasures them, is not prepared to pay for them, never bargained for that. She refuses to understand that she should return them, but was nevertheless good enough to offer something in exchange. Which I am still glad to have. Then haven't the nerve to suggest bartering a silkscreen for a little further art supply. We talk of the weather and she leaves: needing to get back to her store, needing to get out of my little cabin, needing to flee the hungry artist.

'Cause I must sell these silkscreens in order to repair that barn, to fix the tractors, to keep a women's art colony going. Nickel-and-dime philanthropist, devious and scheming foundress building with her bare hands. As a patron of the arts you were certainly a greater success than I. But then you had coupons and not just pictures to float things with. Coupons: sitting on the deck here before Number Eleven at Poor Richard's the other night, my friend Karen Katzel explained coupons to me. Like Richard, who is among other things an architect, Karen is my senior here—both of them scolding me for not being sure we'd put down fifteen-pound felt paper under the cedar shingles when we did the farmhouse roof this summer. Karen is also wise in the ways of the financial world. She knows what a coupon is. Has even seen them. "What you do is tear them out; you don't even cut them." "No scissors?" "Not necessary; they're at the edge of a page that's sent to you. You have only to tear them up and then across, pop them in an envelope and your dividend check will be sent to you. Otherwise it remains at interest."

I had been trying to tell her about that dreary book of your investments which Ransom conscientiously sent out, eighty thoroughly unreadable pages of American this and National that, a thousand shares at thirty-three dollars, two thousand shares at forty-six dollars, forty-five thousand parts of one inscrutable product, a hundred and seventeen thousand parts of another—trying to imagine it as a life. A life's work. Work at all. I keep trying to tell this to Karen: "Imagine. Even to begin a page puts me to sleep. So abstract, so tedious." So ephemeral and immaterial that it would be more interesting to work at Woolworth's, I think to myself as Karen goes on explaining. But it's not being alive, I want to say. It's money, she might tell me, having a healthy curiosity for wordly things and a vital respect for money. Things I imagine I too have in my way. Though I seem never to have evolved further than a child playing store, a painter looking to sell something to some delighted hedonist for the price of a few dinners. Mercantile, pre-capitalist.

I have my triumphs with money, little private moments of happiness, victories of survival. A writer must feel secure when the rent for the next two months is covered even when that sum is all there is left in the world. Two months is sixty days; something will happen. Something will come up as I always tell myself, not even needing to say it aloud or *sotto voce;* the voice in the mind says it by rote. Remembers Fumio's old chuckle which is part of my subconscious now—"Be aright"—the wink, the sublimely sophisticated nod of a little boy who has mastered reality, actually mastered it, through an adroit blend of optimism and fantasy which now enables him to work. Freed him with the gift of time so that he could make paper kites as big as rooms, wooden bicycles, wooden typewriters, and wooden French horns. So much more substantial than Con Edison bills. Only food and wine matched them in importance—everything else in life was free: laughter, sex, friendship. Something would happen and the wooden bicycle would turn into food or the exact sum of the rent money just the day before it was due. And it did.

This is a long way from coupons. Not that near to connoisseurship either. The differences remain. Driving back to Mother's after his first audience with my terrible aunt, Fumio remarked that she did not deserve her furniture. His way to deal with being snubbed, treated like a Japanese beetle, treated like a small adolescent boy, an interloper among your silk sofas, your Chippendale chairs. He recognized every object in the room, as familiar to him as a theme in a Haydn sonata, or the "tune," I would have called it, of a Bach oratorio. He had spent his life studying these things, was in fact a connoisseur at thirty-seven, steeped in the arts, eastern and western. You looked at him as if he were an undergrown insect, or so it seemed to me, trying to bridge the gap, home from Tokyo, bringing along my "best friend from there" a guest in my aunt's great house.

As always I was frantically eager to display A.D. and her milieu, my pride and joy, what made me different and apart—my mentor in her aura of perfection, my first love. Perhaps that was the problem. Mother adored Fumio; he got up early to help her make the orange juice and to "visit" with her in his peculiar but very charming English; he massaged her feet in the evening, all the offices of a son who dearly loved his own mother. That he was my lover, even that he was foreign and of a different race seemed never to trouble Mother or her people: racist cousins stopped saying Jap and invited him ice-fishing, plied him with bourbon, took him under their big wings. But when he appeared at Aunt Dorothy's—in his best suit, the one tailored after the English fashion, a somewhat antiquated fashion, the legs too thick, the coat wrong—how suddenly vulnerable he became, this young man who had conquered everywhere with his very goodness. Of little help to him here on the rack of the Chinese silk sofa, the formula talk, the ritual sparring, the suspicion. She knew at once who he was. The interloper. A man, not to be cried down with a word—lesbian. And delightful—how she must have detested his charm, his modesty. Foreign, exotic; the cosmopolitan in her never hesitated to employ all the contempt of one race for another.

I was in pain for him, for myself—even for her—this terrible aunt annihilating him. As he tried to annihilate or at least dismiss her on the way home. One well-placed word—snob. "She is a snob." Of course he is absolutely right; it has just been mathematically demonstrated for me. But you do not annihilate my aunt, nor do you dismiss her. Never mind what I've always known somewhere, feared everywhere else—that my idol can also be a bitch, a selfish horrid old woman, the arrogant and mean-spirited rich, the collector, the enemy of art, even of the humanity of the artist. Still she was that aunt, the great love and influence of my childhood, still vivid if transformed today to shame, ambivalence, embarrassment. Never mind; there is no choosing between them. I will live with this man henceforward, marry him even. Yet never renounce her; however far apart we move, I will go on harboring her through the rest of my life.

EVEN DEAD. Two years dead now and I spend a perfect day in Provincetown scrambling my woe into an old portable typewriter which transposes my persistent if divided emotions into still further incoherence. Why? In order to elevate real persons with their quirks and inconsistencies into abstractions, ideas, representative intellectual pinballs, principles? And then attack them all over again. Yes, your aunt was a snob and heartily disliked your Japanese beau, the young man you were passing off initially as your best friend during a stay abroad—that kind of hokum was simply transparent to her and probably in bad taste. In snubbing him she revealed his own self-satisfaction, further revealed in his very smug definition of her as a snob.

Though witty and adroit, his was a snob's reaction to declare her unworthy of her furniture. Mother couldn't help but approve since she detested the snob in Dorothy and adored Fumio's simplicity and kindness.

A few days ago Fumio divorced me in an official paper after some fifteen years of separation; we are still great friends. In fact this afternoon I am supposed to be reworking the text of a little book we are planning to publish together, his brush drawings and my retelling of several Japanese folk tales. We put it together for fun one rainy winter seventeen years ago to amuse Mallory's little daughter Kristen. When Mother had surgery for cancer a while back Fumio telephoned her hospital room with a characteristic beautifully mannered devotion. My aunt is still my aunt and Fumio still himself; Mother, thank God, is alive. Each of us in our place since that afternoon by the lake when Dorothy saw her rival and lost.

What did she have after all to compete with: her provincial city, her palatial home, her damn money and her age? We were young and in love and on our way to New York. He was Prince Genji. Even in the wrong suit. I could imagine him in any suit in the world, even the silk of a samurai—for he was one. And we were on our way to the Bowery to be artists and starve in freedom and joy. You can't beat that kind of thing. Her elaborate discourtesy, the disapproving glance, the deliberate exclusion of this man from an idle and unedifying conversation, the attempt to despise, the obvious slights—all just a loser's tricks. A.D. was ungracious, but gracious nonetheless even to pretend hospitality that afternoon, meaning it so little, something undertaken for my sake. Because I was so glad to see her again, still so enamored and unconscious. And backed up by Mother—you don't invite Mother to lunch and then beg off with headache—the eye of one's own generation demanding the forms.

I was always so engaged by the glitter of what was said on the way home—the unthinkable denunciation, the ingenuity of denying my aunt her own furnishings and defining her in one short English word: snob. Mother said it all the time but somehow it had no force until it came from a man from halfway around the world who even recognized each type and example in what were to me just a bunch of chairs, wonderful only because they were hers. So that it has never occurred to me until this moment to imagine what A.D. felt after we left. How were things among those rooms, those peaceful beautiful rooms? Did she dismiss us as I have always imagined she dismissed every irritation: some Schubert and some scotch? As if the beauty of the rooms forbade passion, prevented it? How stupid. Does the perfection of this seascape through the open door ward off remorse, chagrin, tedium, frustration? A room full of pretty things can become a further irritant at certain times. But you have to have one to understand that.

I just had a loft. In itself a calamity of leaks and without heating or plumbing, its very hopelessness rather funny when we got there and tried to live in it. Fumio declared it uninhabitable after a short look around so I got busy and painted every inch of it, found a plumber to invent a shower, install a sink and hot water—Fumio was beginning to weaken and help out by now. And we were off and running. You were stuck by your lake, the Minnesota cold in winter, a fashionable beauty in summer, flowers, a garden, finally a gardener. Paul. Bringing you tulips in January: as welcome, as sustaining as Fumio had been rubbing Mother's feet. A tall man bearing an old woman yellow flowers out of season. I feel a gratitude to him far past my envy.

All this is fudging the "issue," adulterating the aesthetic and moral question with mere sentiment, mere individuals. I came up here to slug it out with you. Fumio is meant to beat you hands down: as an artist, a foreigner, a penniless young lover. Now when I realize that he did, I relent and see your side of it for the first time. Before it had only been my side, torn between the two I loved, leaving the one behind for her coldness, her remoteness in age and geography and sympathy—what does she care about art or artists—just a collector. On the word of a real connoisseur she isn't worthy of her booty. But my aunt, my beloved aunt. Gone, all gone in her cold attitude, her bored presence, her distant look. Two years later when I was married she sent me a check for six hundred dollars. When Sally married she got eight thousand—it gave me a notion of where I stood. But then Sally had married a white man, an aviator of German American descent, a local boy. The eight thousand was in Minnesota Mining stock which has doubled three times since. We spent our six hundred on the wedding itself and had a wonderful time, a party that lasted for days. Everyone came except Aunt Dorothy.

What could one expect? A pair of artists getting hitched as the direct result of a deportation order. Certainly not a ceremony worthy of her, I figured, and did not permit myself to think past that. Just the hurt of it. Still more reason to party. Our way. I had danced at cousin Claire's wedding, also in New York but with Peter Duchin at the Plaza, the aunts in full attendance, Dorothy herself there. In fact I rather overdid it in a slinky black dress, sexy and flirtatious and showing off, trying, I suppose, to prove I was not that lesbian after all. And now a few years later I shall be married in a white dress on Lexington and Eightieth, inappropriately uptown, but the only church in Manhattan who would unite a lapsed Catholic to a Buddhist with a little casual Methodism several generations back. Ritually dressed by my sisters and my mother—having slept with Fumio the night before in the ramshackle loft where we live. I got up and put on a smart coatdress and went to be prepared by my women while Fumio stayed for his best man to put him into "the funny clothes" of a stroller and striped pants. They got to the church twenty minutes late. It was all funny—though there was a moment waiting to walk down the aisle and he was late and everyone else was hung over when it was not that funny.

The wedding party a wonderful mix of downtown artists and Middlewestern relatives all united by alcohol and song and a fierce love of the celebrants, even of the celebration. Black, gold, and white, painters, sculptors, scalawags, each astounded by the ritual, the perfectly serious mockery of it, the sentiment, the songs, the toasts, the thousand toasts—a happening. And I was the center of it. Because he was there, late but still perfect. As he had been the night before, perfect in the family kimono we each wore for the bridal dinner he gave in my honor. All the happy inebriated faces in those photographs toasting, traipsing home with our kimonos fairly well undone and getting dusty, laughing and discussing each friend as we fell asleep, stroking them, the thought of them.

Always the one element missing, A.D. But did I miss it that much? Just the hurt, the sense of being let loose, cast away. And in a funny way, my father, your brother made up for it by sending us a check that was a lot for him, and his blessing as well; one Millett didn't give a damn what name or nationality I loved. Aunt Lucy sent a sugar bowl I still use. Aunt Harriet sent a magnificent eighteenth-century candelabra which a thief made off with the very next time the loft was robbed. But she and Uncle La Rue met Fumio and liked him very well; if they hadn't been cruising around the world they might even have come to the wedding.

There was only Aunt Dorothy to miss, but as the years wore on one thought of her less and less, tried less often at Christmas to shower her with presents to get a response. I wrote letters, unanswered letters, less often as time went by. But remembered her every time I ever took a drink, which was pretty often. Her name, some reference to her, some explanation to a puzzled stranger tripping me up with a question, some quest dragging me into long-winded explanations I could never quite explain away. "Yes, I see, you had an aunt. Hmmm. Disowned, well that's a pity, isn't it." "But you don't understand; she was that beautiful." "Ah." "That intelligent, I adored her." "Well." "I mean I was in love with her as a child. . . ." "Yes, do you have a little more ice?"

So that finally everyone knows about this aunt. And Fumio explains how hopeless she is; my pal Washburn describes her as *nouveau riche;* one of my sisters passing through town regales us with further tales of the ice palace and a folklore is erected upon which I can communicate telepathically across half the distance of the continent, wordlessly, a figure on the battlements waving. In the era of the telephone and the post office. Too afraid for the former, spurned through the latter. Talking, talking to persons who will never see her and cannot intercede. Once I even thought I had a live wire in my friend Buffie Johnson who turned out to know someone I took to be one of A.D.'s intimates. For weeks I poured out my heart only to discover after tardy recourse to genealogy that it is Louis Hill's sister she knows. And on her latest visit west Buffie met Louis Hill, Uncle Louis. Whom she found very tedious indeed. "How could you ever find these people interesting?" Buffie demanded. "I am not in love with my Uncle Louis but with my aunt." "Mystifies me," she sighed.

Mystified everyone. Carrying the torch for an old

woman who's driven you off. Pointless. Have you thought of therapy? It might help you unravel all these threads. They seem to be holding you back. If she's so obdurate, so fed up with you, why are you wasting your time? And from what you say of her she's really not a very attractive personality either. Old, stubborn, rich, cold, heartless. A little chant, a little series of curses, a magical formula set up to still the yearning. Meant to be particularly effective when we sisters repeat them together. In practice, the opposite is true: we only stimulate each other, egg each other on. Were the phone to ring and her voice purr at the other end—"Hello darling, this is your Aunt Dorothy"—ah, we know it never will be—are just that sure of it. . . .

THE QUESTIONS OF ART, of money, of love—riding with the little sailboats moored in the water a few feet from the door, for it is high tide. Solzhenitsyn divides literature into four categories by social status, either the writer's or his subject's: the upper class writing about each other, those below writing about those above them, those above writing about those below them, kind-hearted but without experience. And finally a proletarian literature yet to come. I suspect that this would belong to the second category of those below describing those above—and toward this genre he directs the following strictures: "looking upward from below" he perceives to have the same faults of inexperience as those above have when looking down—but there is also, and even worse, a quality of being "poisoned by envy and hate—sterile feelings which do not create art." Troubling. The danger is that one falls into "the same mistakes revolutionaries always make: ascribing the vices of the upper class to the class itself and not to humanity as a whole, while failing to imagine how notably they themselves inherit these vices." It hits home.

Or else, on the other hand, work of this kind "has always been spoiled with servile fawning." Dryden's *Prefaces*. Spenser's tributes to the Faerie Queene, his Gloriana, Elizabeth the iron virgin, etc. Less of that. But some. Her beauty and her money got awfully mixed up for me with her charm. And her chill. Why not realize this was maybe just someone you could never make love you? Someone you could never have. For excellent reasons if insufficient to restrain your obsession. Why do you dream of her still and awake happy because in one dream you saw Fumio and a lady lute player you adored to no purpose twenty years ago and the lute player, Elizabeth, the very image of joy, hedonism, and the *vita nuova* you once aspired to, holds a wooden sculpture she has made in emulation of Fumio and cries out delightedly, "Aunt Dorothy, Aunt Dorothy," as if she were a herald announcing a new age? Then you come to on a Bowery morning in February, all of these treasured beings absent from your life in any intimate sense from now to the grave. And wonder again what it was about A.D.

And did you convey her at all? Did you even understand it yourself? Are your pages about her only the diatribe Solzhenitsyn warned against? Or servile praise of lucre? Or a love story of some complexity and nuance, circumstance and relationship, time and blood and custom, rebellion and desire? Never satisfied. And that craving a cause in itself, a stimulus, a quest, an incentive, a long puzzling hurt that drives one to resignation and then further to more dangerous inquiry. Then despair. Then a hope of understanding, of figuring it out merely by portraying, conveying, taking the being who so puzzles and attracts, distilling that essence onto matter with words on paper and holding it in the hand, outstretched. See—here it is. Here is why. Here is who. I loved her. Of course a reader needn't. In fact a reader may even dislike or disapprove. Or prefer her to me. Fine. Take her part and see her point. But if I make you see her or why I loved her, why this kind of being is lovable, full of power and energy—for reasons right or wrong, then would I have succeeded?

Not really—and I am still trying to find her myself. For A.D. is a being within me. Invented. Inherited. Fantasized or remembered. But—you forget, you cheat—others knew her. And she had this force and vitality for your sisters as well. Some version of it even for her friends. They knew her; you make her up. Do I know more than last year? here at the end of the world before an ocean where I come each year for ten days around my birthday to tot things up, add and subtract myself annually. This morning I sat in the loft bed under the eaves of this cabin and listed the year past, my fiftieth: finished one book *(The Loony Bin)* and nearly another (Aunt Dorothy's), painted the loft on the fifth floor of the Bowery, two quick trips to Paris on invitation, facelifted the farmhouse, finished reclaiming the fields in a good farming season, and ended with eight hundred dollars in the bank to last me the rest of my life. Never mind that A.D.'s bequest is also in the bank—it's not to be touched even to prevent starvation; it's the down payment to buy my loft. Otherwise I'm pretty close to broke.

I go on hoping that a grant will come through from Germany to live on this year and beyond that I'm itching to gamble three hundred bucks plus freight on arrival to buy a silkscreen rack. If I had a rack I could print alone. Without an assistant, without anybody helping me at all, at any time of year. Completely independent. Something that empowering is worth building yourself even if it were a fussy job and took forever 'cause they won't charge it to Visa. Listen, you just charged a pair of sandals to Visa and may have to charge your stay here at Poor Richard's as well.

This creates small debts, but apart from Visa I have no debts in the world, owe nothing anywhere. Wait a minute, you were three hundred dollars short on the school tax, even after throwing in every cent of picture money, the first silkscreen sales as they came off the press. Here in Provincetown I hoped to pass off a few more pictures, polish off that deficit, my eye still on that rack. A sickening awareness in the back of my mind that there will be several thousands dollars of tractor repairs to be done this off-season. But no one comes to look at the new prints; even friends must be reminded, keep postponing their glimpse, must finally be asked outright. Of course with friends, you don't sell them, you give them away—not that sure they really want one either.

Art. Money. Living. The new manuscript, *The Loony Bin Trip* book, was handed in around the beginning of March. It is now September and it has not been gobbled up, is presently being nibbled at. Just to be published now is all I can hope for, forget being paid. Or try to forget it. Or that an advance could buy the land for sale across the road. Or go a little less mad and fix the red tractor whose clutch is gone, maybe the transmission too; Big Wayne at Reardon Briggs said it needed a total engine overhaul two years ago, was only working on one and a half cylinder even back then—now it won't mow at all.

And you must mow at once when you return to the farm, the whole place, every field. To hold the advantage over the brush you won this summer, running the little guy of a tractor right into the ground, because it had to keep going. Now it's time to get it fixed—urgent. Of course they will take forever to do it because they are busy and backed up and you know right now they will not release the machine repaired until every cent of the bill is paid. If you had an advance you could pay it—either that or hurl what might have been your grocery money over the winter right into the gearbox, the great maw of mechanical necessity. Cars get fixed for hundreds, tractors for thousands.

And books don't sell. Nor pictures. Art. Money. Surviving. When you think too much about money it has a bad effect on art; you do arithmetic instead of drawings, do numbers instead of the figure. You huddle in bed, figuring, refiguring—budgeting to entertain the tribe at the farm for the coming family reunion. Then if you had another four hundred bucks you could buy that old VW from the kid who lives near the farm, a twin to your "yellow peril"—that car has no clutch, mine still has—combine, cannibalize. I might come up with one usable chassis and assorted parts and get through the winter—might come out with a heater too for crossing Bear Mountain on cold winter nights coming up from town. Hope begins like an engine catching on a chill morning.

Who wants a picture? Try not to be absurd. If Stephen would show them—but he has a show on now, and he gave you a show up here last year. But if he would even come and look, maybe like them . . . desperation mounts and the little sailboat rides smoothly at anchor, the sun shines. And the night comes down on you alone eating another little piece of meat you can't quite finish, the Pernod at sunset and then the wine, the wine making you sleepy, ready to read yourself to sleep in the little loft, saying again that this is your vacation, such a lazy time you don't even write the first three days—a most uncharacteristic leisure, just read a book and lie in the sun. As if that were it, all there was to it.

Not age nor fear, the old elastic growing saggy, a potbellied lethargy, unglamorous and lonely, undermined somewhere by defections and betrayals, lovers gone or driven away, Sophie the latest, announcing this summer was her last there at the farm. Even with her new lover installed along with her, the colony fell beneath her expectations, bored her, failed its objective. It is made clear that all of this is my fault. Five times a day up here I am asked by some innocent, sometimes for the second or third time—where is Sophie—she didn't come up this year? Nor last year either; but they have already forgotten that. I spent the winter without her, living alone on the Bowery and liking it, to my surprise. Finishing *The Loony Bin,* a book she loathed at first, a book which could not have been finished any other way. But when summer came she was with me again. She has built the farm as she says, founded the colony with me, is its mainstay, mechanical genius, chief contractor and builder. All given in gratitude. And the lover she brought with her a wonderful person I genuinely like. Why is it then that her sarcasm, her rage at me, her hurtful words can still spoil a summer there, poison me with such toxin that I cannot really be present to the others there, abstracted, wounded internally to such an extent I am worthless. Better for the colony that she stayed—only Sophie can keep the mowing machines going—better for me that she goes. That the wound heals, is not torn open four times a day by the same old harsh denunciations, the unmasking of my vulnerability, inefficiency, my injured preoccupation before the others. That dead shell I become under her assault.

Yet how much better after all if we could have maintained the dream together, continued to create a paradise for those we brought into it; how much better if we could have succeeded. Gone on being friends. Bookie too. You see, the three of us were the musketeers. We could found the farm together; we were the farm—for several seasons now. The three spoons, I called us, all friends and lovers. I had been Bookie's lover once, years ago, was Sophie's for seven years. Then over last winter Bookie became Sophie's lover. Alas, Sophie toyed with Bookie's saintly celibacy and dropped her after a season. Just before that I had great erotic expectations for the three of us, including myself, when Bookie took me as her lover again, all too briefly. But it did give rise to utopian schemes which fell on their noses. Bookie and Sophie fell apart. Or rather Bookie held on passionately and even made herself endure part of the summer with Sophie's new lover on the scene—then just quit one day. Left the farm. Understandably, though I felt I was the one she was letting down. Sophie had announced her resignation even before this.

So I have everything and nothing to look forward to next year, running it alone. Even success would be stale and alien without them. And I bring all this to Provincetown and sit on it for three days. Then insist on writing, presumably about my aunt and so forth, related topics of art, money, etc.—and come up with the bitterness of the summer, the hopelessness I feel at farm's end. Three spoons. How silly—but it was deliberately silly, because the undertaking was so grand and heroic, an earthly paradise for artists—that we could minimize, make childish its instruments, more pacific and less important than knives and forks. Mere spoons: the gravy spoons, the wooden spoon, the tea spoon, a foolish coat of arms, but judiciously balanced, unpretentious, amusing. For it would all be fun, an adventure.

YOU SEE, dear aunt, I have not been a raging success as foundress, philanthropist, engenderer of artistic institutions. What are my recalcitrant buddies and their dead-end affairs and my broken tractors compared with the utter simplicity of leaving your millions to the symphony? With meticulous instructions that result in some carefully chosen composer being commissioned to write an operatic evening culled from the personal correspondence of Elizabeth Barrett Browning, including her sketch of her Irish maid? The whole thing performed first at the Kennedy Institute in Washington and then Carnegie Hall in New York. I didn't go. In fact I didn't even remember it was going to be on at Carnegie until I saw a review the next day. Although your lawyer had informed me in time for this triumph of patronage, this munificence toward some fortunate musician, this is his second commission with the symphony—whose agents courted you and other fancy folk, arranged the committees and the receptions and the dinners which precede and determine such bequests and beneficences. Did you at least get what you wanted?

On the other hand, if you'd given your eleven millions to twenty-two or forty-four or eighty-eight artists, you'd be sure of getting someone's baby clothed, maybe even a couple good pictures or a book done. If you'd set up your own grant with those bucks you'd have maybe done the best thing of all. But they have to be administered by smarter-than-ordinary persons. Who all have to be paid: an institution, investments, officers, administrators, etc.—all rigmarole. You just handed it over to the folks with the rigmarole already in place and a good track record. Your own symphony where you'd been guarantor for decades. And our own theater in Minneapolis. Throw in the St. Paul Chamber Orchestra for good measure, and the local museum. After it's absorbed into running expenses, salaries, it's unlikely to filter into a painter's pocket via purchase.

Not me; I go right to the heart of things: tractor transmission, leaky roofs, we sew quilts for the very mattresses our artists sleep on. Turn a barn into a studio, raise trees for a crop and be self-sufficient. No government funds, no patrons—not a damn penny from the rich and so forth. Sweat in the fields and make our own bucks, paint the house and rent it over the winter and pay our taxes. All without a mortgage—the place is free and clear. And then have no idea how to pass it on, incorporate, perpetuate. Even to retain it is a yearly struggle. Of course it's beautiful but there is so much still to fix.

Now my friends are gone. How could they have cared as much, loved it as much, wanted it as much? I still owned it, they didn't. Why should they? But why should I? How could it be publicly owned, or unowned—trustees? My trustees are gone too. So, like the little red hen I must go on: I'll do it myself, she said. And she did. Me too. It's just not much fun. At least not yet. May never be; nothing but an obligation taken on that cannot be got rid of. You see, other women, the volunteers over these six years, gave their time and strength and hope and that cannot now be gone back on. So I have to keep at it. What lies ahead seems bleak but obligatory.

You didn't get yourself snarled up in this junk, A.D. You were never so daft about the arts as to stoop to growing Christmas trees. Of all things. How wild-eyed I must have seemed coming from my land into your living room even during the one satisfactory discussion we ever had during the last twenty-five years of our relationship—that afternoon we talked of trees. The Minnesota evening ripened from one martini to another while we solemnly paraded from elm to oak and over to the conifers. Your trees had been wrecked by a storm; for once I could be knowledgeable and correctly sympathetic. Even then I was probably bragging about how many trees I had—thousands, I can hear myself, at capacity we'll be thirty thousand—etc.—who wants to hear about thirty thousand Christmas trees when three one-hundred-year-old elms have fallen? Each as real to you as the supernal elm behind the pond, our very emblem at the farm.

But it was still some ground for discussion. Like two weathered Norman baronesses stately in phrase, solidly landed, our silk chairs riding over the terrain even as we spoke. The gesture of an arm, a cigarette lit or put out, the drink raised or set down, the voices calm, full of weight and proprietorship.

Because today is my fifty-first birthday, I began it solemnly. By making a list. Nicely ensconced within the cabin's loft with the window open, a skylight trap window open on to the sea and the perfect morning; that light, that Provincetown light and the line of blue across the horizon like hope—hangover or not. The morning after a nice session in the Landmark Bar drinking something silly with Erna, a painter crony here, saying even sillier things; art brags, curses on the market, the public, the state of things, happily getting it all off my chest. The summer, the frustrations of having made five hundred silkscreen pictures to support the colony and being unable to sell even one. Even some pie in the sky, trying to talk Erna into dealing me since she manages Harvey Dodd's place and has been selling his pictures like hotcakes in the little shop down the lane. The two of us going on about how utterly blessed it was—though they are neither her pictures nor mine—to see anybody's pictures buy food. "A bottle of wine"—I keep saying—"that a picture could convert itself into a bottle of wine." You get the drift.

So of course this morning I am alive fairly early, unable to sleep, curious to discover if I actually have a headache. Not really. Because today is my fifty-first birthday and I am as earnest about it as a child. With a Virgo's list of what to achieve in the coming year. Yesterday I ticked off what I'd done since fifty, then reduced it all to finishing a book, which seemed a sufficient if lonely task. But next year, the research against torture, the next book. You must also draw every day. And plan sculptures for a show the following year—last night Erna actually recalled the cage sculptures I made ten years ago. Flattery and gratitude astonished me. So that's on the list even if prematurely. Underline that you've got to draw every single day. Use the darkroom too. Further down the list are grander, increasingly crazy schemes: renovate the blue barn next summer, re-side it, save the beams, sheathe them again safe—forever—it will be perfect, rain-tight. Further flights into tractor repair, the fantasy purchase of a brand new, actually virgin, machine, not our usual twenty-year-old cripples. Narrow, lithe, pretty new paint, a slender wheel-base so as not to kill trees. On and on in this vein. Then the Bowery: move the kitchen, install another Franklin stove—after all, this is just a list—cross out one stove and put down two. Never mind getting the six hundred pounds up the stairs, the expense, the nuisance plumbing the gas pipes.

Make everything snug so you can study all day, never leave the place, steep yourself in the literature of political prisoners, the corruption of South American dictatorships, the collusion and manipulation of North American government and business. You have four years ahead of you to absorb and reflect the sufferings of interrogation, state terrorization, the locked door, the cell. I want to do a sculpture of a group of people sitting calmly on folding chairs inside a cage, I told Erna last night. And outside the cage are another group sitting calmly on folding chairs watching them, facing them. She put her arm around me and we laughed out loud. That said it.

But saying it in print is different, longer, harder: the

profusion of details, factual and emotional, symbolic and actual, metaphorical and metaphysical. Quixotic stab: to try just by writing about it, thinking about it, feeling it, to make others feel it, care, get mad, be ashamed, make waves, refuse to put up with it—torture. Climbing the funny ladder Richard has made out of two-by-fours which brings one, however perilously, up to the loft bed while balancing the second cup of coffee, I realize I'm scared to death of this job ahead of me, find it hard to discuss with myself even in private, avoid thinking about it sometimes. Of course it's a big intimidating project—but until this moment I did not realize just how frightened I was. Having realized that, perhaps now I can start; knowing I'm scared is always my beginning.

BUT ON MY BIRTHDAY, drinking coffee in the still perfectly acceptable early part of the morning, the time you can fritter and call it thinking, putter and imagine it's planning, even contemplation—my particular delight is to resolve, finally after twelve years of living in my studio, to put doors on the closet. They will be red, japanned like the fantasy furniture sculptures that still live with me. And with pictures on them—silkscreens—some of this years prints—or should I paint in *sumi* ink on magnificent sheets of heavy rice paper, lacquered and protected forever—have some more coffee and ponder these choices. See them both; go through the steps. With doors on the closet you will never have to look at clothes again and I loathe looking at clothes—the closet at the farm for example—no, forget it. That will never get done and this is your birthday. Feel the sun. The light, this fabulous light. And the line of the sea. Be aware of being alive, come back to life out of your recent depression, bitterness—forget the damn farm, play with your loft. Imagine your cat Bread installed upon the comforter before the fire, picture her in the luxury of the Bowery while you read. Table after table for reading, notetaking, catalogs, three-by-five cards—God, not those again—graduate school. Ah, but this is study; you have not studied in years. The rigor, yes, but the sheer voluptuousness of it. To read and not to write yet, only to prepare, only to inform, consider, weigh, figure out, learn. Without yet having to teach or regurgitate or persuade. Who would dare do this book? Sartre, de Beauvoir; invite his shade, her spirit. Like the perfect elder couple; let them come to dinner nights you dine alone. Bigger than life, like royalty. Unfamiliar, yet not entirely: Uncle Bob prepared me for Sartre a little, the best in all my aunts makes me revere Simone.

In fact—you, the Milletts—all of you, but you most, A.D., the chief of them and the favorite, were my preparation for all the world I found later after leaving you. Left you to find in fact. Yet without you I might never have seen it. Beauvoir and Mother would get along beautifully; Mother would love and respect Simone, Simone would inquire after Mother for years to come with all kindness. Whereas Dorothy and Simone would probably not hit it off, each on their mettle. Yet for some twisted reason I expect I would never have known de Beauvoir if it had not been for A.D. The savant. The singular figure in my childhood, an ambitious intellectual, rigorous to tedium, to cruelty, to irony, to an angered obsession with study and emulation. A tough teacher, mean even at times, or unnecessarily, but a driver.

Then too, how else could I be a downtown artist—the underfinanced foundress of an art colony bent on surviving through Christmas trees with the aid of broken-down tractors housed behind boards I have nailed together myself, stubborn as a hammer, a weatherbeaten aging broad with long hair going gray, an eight-year-old's brown eyes figuring out one more goddamn time how the tree house is going to hold together—how if it had not finally been for you? Of course your example—for contrast. It was easy being different: throw out the silk sofa and substitute the Bowery. Chuck the stocks and bonds and buy a do-it-yourself book on plumbing and carpentry. Forget the lady business and get street tough; learn how to saw a straight line as your seamstresses knew how to sew one. You designed your dress and furnishings; I'm gonna design everything in my whole world including the eaves and electrical layout. You commanded all; I'm just doing it all. All that you learned in a lifetime of study was ordered and achieved through the prowess of money and the agency of persons following instructions for hire so that the achievement was still yours. That house. Your milieu. Your collection.

Wait a moment—you didn't paint the pictures, you just bought them. Not content with making pictures I have jumped right into making houses, a community, a little province even, eighty acres of land. I feel like a kindergartener showing off, bragging to you. That I have done the things you loved, the things you taught me to love. Making beauty, living an aesthetic. *A la paysanne,* Tolstoy—I've turned your aristocracy upside down, democratized it and gone on being a hard-shelled aesthete, insufficiently redeemed by communal pretensions or intentions. The damage is in being exclusive, removed from reality, humanity—the struggle: "La Lutte" one hears everywhere in Europe. Whereas if an American installs a flush toilet he imagines he has fought and won a revolution, joined and then transcended the proletariat, saved money on union plumbers and invented the device only to be bilked of his patent.

Plenty of days my utopia is just a messy toolshed I should stay out of, leave to craftsmen, write books or make pictures or do something that shows less obviously when it's been botched. The farm's no big deal. Not Yaddo or MacDowell. Just nickel and dime. No crop yet either, no proof it could work yet. Like being halfway through graduate school and still without a thesis topic.

Why did I think of a farm anyway? East Bushka at North Oaks? Your farm. Or Louis's. I was just a kid and it seemed like paradise, people and horses, talk in the country. Resting like a germ against the bigger reality of the farms in Mother's family—real farms, big and sad and unkept after Grandfather died. Finally only property for lots, Uncle Bill still hanging on trying to farm, a widower going to bed in dirty clothes, the untended house, the go down end of farming whose broken pieces I picked up here again at what had been the Cramers' farm. Fourteen years fallow. The barn roof going, not likely to last the winter, demanding it be rebuilt fast by the first fast-talker I found, so fast he neglected even to give me eaves on the back side of the new roof. The side I hadn't noticed. So now that whole wall is in danger, soon the structure itself. Summer after summer we rescue it. And the house, sound enough from the beginning but unlovely, was uninhabited for three or four years by anyone but the ne'er-do-well son of the realtor and his girl friend and two poodle dogs she never bothered to housebreak. Pick up the dog shit, take off the wallpaper, paint it, get going. Now it gleams. The front porch just got rebuilt with brand new five-quarter fir and even has spar varnish. It was simply too beautiful to paint. And fine shingles, the best cedar roofing; the clapboard glistens with new white and the nine million shutters are a perfect indigo.

The farmhouse restored, the lavender barn converted to housing and the blue barn transformed into studios—does it make sense to you that all that was just as satisfying and rather more difficult to do than books and pictures? Physically more strenuous, intellectually as demanding—even more so since it involved learning a great many new things. Also that it was sculpture, that it was done with these two hands and with all my friends, Sophie, Bookie, the women who have been volunteers: Keats, Nina Newington, Janey Winter, Barbara George, Sara Keaveny,

Katie Dumont, Lee Parker, Stephanie Schroeder and something like fifty more of them—over six years. That we could hardly go to bed at night sometimes for needing to smoke another cigarette and just admire the damn thing, or make one more try at figuring out how to build the right scaffold or hit on the perfect insulator, how to join, how to strengthen, how to keep out the rain or cold or prevent fire; what timber, what fastener, what magical color or sealer or stain or fabric; the perfect skylight, the best casement design, or flooring. And how to do it all for damn near free. Except for the extravagant gift of our labor, the loving splurge of our time. For weren't we building for ever? For the future. For the women who would come after.

Why do I imagine you encouraged me in all this madness? When you couldn't, on the surface, be further from this sort of thing? Why is it something of a legacy? Like stashing your bequest in the bank to be the down payment on my loft if the city will agree to sell to the artists instead of the speculators—making you the one who makes me a New York artist with a piece of the rock somewhat more secure than eleven years on a thirty day lease. There are days I wonder if this is filial impiety—you never wanted me to be an artist. You even said so, came as near to forbidding it as you could. Made it real clear I'd better not get any notions that you were going to support this kind of nonsense.

After you had so generously give me a literary education my turning to sculpture must have struck you as an indecency. To be buying my studio for me? For me to be using this money to buy a studio and write my name among the fellowship in brick and mortar in a town where you are an artist only if you have a studio. And the day you lose it, you are not only not a New York artist, you are neither a New Yorker nor an artist—I learned the hard way when I lost the old place. But if I buy that loft with my neighbors I am safe for the rest of my life. After two decades of threats, evictions, urban renewal projects, when every mail could bring the hated xeroxed document that ends my life then and there.

So I have used your generosity to nail it down. I even think you would approve. The new improved up-to-date you whom I have invented, rearranged, intuited, and counterfeited—just plain forged since your death. Because there were always two messages. Who could be more scathing about the Wayzeta rich?—Paul mentioned that over and over, a damn-them-all iconoclasm. Who saw through symphony politics but still heard the music; loved a picture, famous or not—hung it in a certain place and kept it there decade after decade, seeing it when passing, fondling it with the mind and the eyes and the heart all day, feeding off it in the years of solitude? Somehow you made me know that pictures mattered. Something no one else in St. Paul, the family or the town, ever did for me. Without you, no pictures. Still less sculpture, rarest and hardest of arts. To begin life with a Han horse is really starting out at the top.

Somehow even the farm comes from you. Trees. Art. A bunch of unruly artists, of course; I grant you that's troublesome. But the place, the perfection of the place, the care and excellence, the reach for the exquisite—all in such another vein than yours, granted. But you're in there. Your urge to make things happen in art, your urge to give and see results—to share, though not your civic-duty way of seeing it—is in my roughshod tough painter-lady *bon vivant* style, dirt or ink or whatever under the fingernails but still holding the good glass of red wine come all the way from France before candlelight or a kerosene lantern, still a romantic, still living a Fitzgerald life.

THE INFLUENCE here is not the late aunt of the stock report booklet and the empty gray rooms of a winter evening—but the young aunt, the beauty, the bonny one, the friend of all the lights and talkers, the wit with the magnificent green eyes and the mind of a rapier, as spring, as sharp, as eager; the Jamesian lady for whom civilization was invented and before whom the centuries had labored to lay it at her feet as she stepped forward in freedom, the A.D. who sent her long-ago Isabel Archer niece to Oxford. And the niece came home and did these things. Remembering always an idea. Not what she was told, but what she saw. Not what was lectured to her to keep down her puppy-like enthusiasm (Aunt Dorothy, I think I'd like to be a poet. Like Wordsworth). . . . A.D. sitting through this sort of confession in her car, just as she is about to deliver me to Mother's door, and I blurt it out like someone trying to steal a kiss or saying I love you. Which is really all I meant.

Loving her, I wanted to be a poet, a painter, a sculptor, a writer. Mother wanted a writer, and only a writer. Though a writer of rather more correct books than I have encompassed yet. But Aunt Dorothy made you want to be everything. Theater, the world as theater, as a golden Fitzgerald novel in which she starred as heroine and actress, savant and lady, collector and cut-up, wit, vital energy itself.

And of those late years alone, the gray of evening, age and loneliness, the bitterness of solitude—perhaps they wait for me too. Fifty-one and so may know that sorrow to some measure and in the foreseeable future—give me the guts you had. And may I be spared your sorrow, the luck to hug enough souls near me against the cold of age, infirmity, and death. Forgive me for not being there, for not trying harder to get through the line, for not being the young man with the tulips. And bless him that he was there. I see him again as he told me of it, his yellow hair, the back of his head which for some inexcusable reason I want terribly to kiss. Imagining him that New Year's morning ascending the stairs with the unearthly yellow flowers, seeing him from the back, then seeing him as he approaches that terrible little iron bed, ornate and antique, but what a model of discomfort and sorrow.

And then you smile at him, the flowers. I see only the back of his head. And your face. Still so beautiful, God, so beautiful, the smile, the crinkly hair, the eyes, those cheekbones. There is an urge to intervene, to interfere as the pot of tulips advances toward your frail hand. Contraptions for walking, the little elevator, wheelchairs all around, that ghastly light in the room, western, very strong but filtered through orange fabric and bamboo to an unearthly color, luminous as death, Zen in its radiant finality—the tulips are nearly there. Your hand reaches toward them in rapture, Hepburn's smile. I strain, wanting to cheat, to kiss that hand, to replace or supplant a tulip. And then I know I can't. Mustn't. It is his glory, not mine. It was he who brought her what she wanted. I had loved her a whole lifetime. But never well enough to give the pleasure this man has troubled to take even as a professional gardener, the very ingenuity of forced—no, in January you don't really force tulips—your create them. Out of whole cloth like God the Father. A miracle.

And that miracle is his, but I have seen it. It took a good many hours of concentration and much pain, tears even that are like a hymen breaking or the birth of something resembling peace. In order to know your death. The hours alone in that house I have known for years in several depressions. But until I could resolve the end I could not go back to the beginning and fashion you into my companion from here on in, my fellow spirit, "guardian angel" as we used to say. Ageless, you can be all ages now, my age or even younger. Imagine, I can be older now than your younger self. As easily as we both can be twenty-four-year-old know-it-alls. My joyous aunt. Now finally my constant one. With a bit of each era. The irreverent young beauty who still whispers outrageous things to me in public places amid pomp and stuffiness. The wisdom of the woman of the world, the traveler, scholar, private student of how many obscure books and historical ruminations, the judge of real and fictional characters, the expert on phonies even when she was being phony, the enemy of snobs even in her snobbery. The creator of moods and milieu, rooms and costumes and parties and arrangements of this with that, a flower or a scarf, a chair or a table, a piece of music or a dish of food.

Someone who made you feel that life was a very big thing, really worth the trouble to live well and thoughtfully, whether it was lovely or hateful at a certain moment, season, or year. It was serious in the most beguiling way, whimsical in the most terrifying way, dull in the most fascinating way, exciting and yet also slow or lilting, able to open up with a single bar of music whole experiences never had, like going to Baghdad, whole memories crushed and buried, lifetimes that were someone else's life, not yours, but yours through a paragraph of prose, a certain shade of gray caught in a mirror, a photo of a street in a city you have never visited and now feel in the marrow of your bones. Like you feel color and light, like you know poetry, like you will hear Yeats all your life, including the instant you die, like an echo, like race consciousness. Like the sins of the fathers and the slavery of the mothers, the warmth or spite of the sisters, the callow arrogance of the brothers, the rudeness of shopkeepers, the kiss of a good lover, the curse of a bad one. Full, full, full to overflowing. As miraculous as yellow tulips in January in the hands of a yellow-haired man who was never part of the story. All surprises, all miracles. Let go.